Advance Praise for *Beat the Bots*

"Brilliant! I was blown away! Jane Cleland has written a how-to book that is both a practical guide to novel writing and a celebration of creativity. Every writer needs this incredibly valuable, and timely, resource. Yes, Jane clearly sets out steps that will propel ideas into a book, but she also explores our humanity, our ability to empathize, the fact that, unlike bots, we are not derivative, we are original. We have imagination. The thought she put into this book! Not only as a practical application, but as a reflection of how far technology can go versus the human imagination. Jane makes the complex clear. Amazing! Brava, Jane!"

—Louise Penny, *New York Times* #1 Bestselling Author

"In this comprehensive and reassuring writing guide, Jane K. Cleland emphatically demonstrates why the creativity of writers will always *Beat the Bots*. Through the depth of her knowledge, generosity of her instruction, and plentiful exercises, writers can't help but be inspired to sit down and create. This is a must-have for every writer's shelf in the age of A.I."

—Amy Jones, editor-in-chief, *Writer's Digest*

"This book is terrific! A writing guide tailored to our times, Jane Cleland's *Beat the Bots* is packed with smart, insightful, utterly practical storytelling advice paired with an entrée to a supportive community of like-minded writers."

—Hallie Ephron, *New York Times* Bestselling Author

"With humor, insight, and a generous spirit, Jane Cleland provides the tools to navigate a changing creative landscape in this fresh, entertaining guide."

—Daniel Stashower, *New York Times* Bestselling Author

"I loved this book! *Beat the Bots* is the essential, hands-on guide to bulletproofing your writing career in the age of AI. Truly, this is a great book. I'm recommending it to every writer I know."

—Paula Munier, *USA Today* Bestselling Author

"*Beat the Bots* is a masterpiece. A year ago, I thought AI couldn't pierce the arts. Now I believe it might decimate opportunities for creatives— unless you follow Jane K. Cleland's lead. *Beat the Bots* provides an infallible roadmap to succeed as a writer in today's world."

—Joe Klemczewski, PhD, *The Diet Doc*, Health and Social Science Writer

"This book could not come at a better time. With the advent of AI and murmurings in the writing community about whether we writers will be out of a job, Jane Cleland offers a measured, sensible alternative. In an age when writers might worry about becoming obsolete, *Beat the Bots* shows exactly how we can make ourselves indispensable and craft stories in a way that no artificial intelligence ever could. This book pairs clear explanations of the craft with in-depth examples and practical exercises. After reading *Beat the Bots*, writers will not only have a better grasp of writing techniques, but they will also know how to put those techniques into action."

—Gabriela Pereira, Founder of DIY MFA
and Author of *DIY MFA: Write with Focus,
Read with Purpose, Build Your Community*

"I consider books about the craft of writing a success if I get one of two good ideas from them. *Beat the Bots* hit that mark in the first chapter!"

—Donna Andrews, Award-Winning
Author of the *Meg Langslow* series

"*Beat the Bots* is spectacular! Are you worried about AI—or tempted to use it in your writing? Stop immediately and read Jane Cleland's new book, *Beat the Bots*. 'No matter how sophisticated AI becomes,' Cleland says, 'it can't tell your unique stories in your distinctive voice.' So true. But encouragement and inspiration are only the beginning as Cleland provides practical tips and tools you can use right now, writing prompts to help you focus on the emotional truth driving your story, and exercises in every chapter that enable you to plumb the well of creativity we all possess. With chapters on voice, point of view, plotting, dialogue, handling backstory, and ramping up the conflict, *Beat the Bots* is the most practical and usable book I've read in a long time. If I had a highlighter, I'd be highlighting whole pages. If you buy only one book on craft, this is the one."

—Connie Berry, *USA Today* Bestselling Author of the *Kate Hamilton Mysteries*

BEAT THE
BOTS

BEAT THE BOTS

A WRITER'S GUIDE TO SURVIVING AND THRIVING IN THE AGE OF AI

JANE K. CLELAND

A REGALO PRESS BOOK
ISBN: 979-8-88845-495-4
ISBN (eBook): 979-8-88845-496-1

Beat the Bots:
A Writer's Guide to Surviving and Thriving in the Age of AI
© 2025 by Jane K. Cleland
All Rights Reserved

Cover Design by Cody Corcoran

Publishing Team:
Founder and Publisher – Gretchen Young
Editorial Assistant – Caitlyn Limbaugh
Managing Editor – Aleigha Koss
Production Manager – Alana Mills
Production Editor – Rachel Paul
Associate Production Manager – Kate Harris

As part of the mission of Regalo Press, a donation is being made to Reef Renewal Foundation Bonaire, as chosen by the author. Find out more about this organization at: https://www.reefrenewalbonaire.org/.

This book, as well as any other Regalo Press publications, may be purchased in bulk quantities at a special discounted rate. Contact orders@regalopress.com for more information.

This is a work of nonfiction. All people, locations, events, and situations are portrayed to the best of the author's memory.

No part of this book may be reproduced, stored in a retrieval system, or transmitted by any means without the written permission of the author and publisher.

Regalo Press
New York • Nashville
regalopress.com

Published in the United States of America
1 2 3 4 5 6 7 8 9 10

This is for the scores of writers with whom I've worked whose dedication to their craft inspired me to write this book.
And, of course, for Joe.

"Writing is a struggle against silence."
Carlos Fuentes

AUTHOR'S NOTE

As I write this Author's Note, TikTok's future in the United States is in question. If you can't access TikTok by the time you read this, I'd love it if you'd join me on Facebook and/or Instagram Reels instead. You can find my pages at www.janecleland.com/facebook and www.janecleland.com/instagram/. Don't forget to use the hashtags specified in this book for each post so the rest of the community can find your responses. I can't wait to see your creativity in action!

CONTENTS

Introduction xv

PART ONE: FIND YOUR INNER MUSE

Chapter One: Creativity Tactic #1 3
　Idea Fishing: Find Viable Ideas
Chapter Two: Creativity Tactic #2 30
　Forks in the Road: Track Character Motivation
　with Jane's Character Transformation Roadmap
Chapter Three: Creativity Tactic #3 53
　Mind Wandering: Plot with Jane's Plotting Roadmap
Chapter Four: Creativity Tactic #4 83
　Conceptual Blending: Choose Settings That
　Inspire Reader Curiosity

PART TWO: YOUR STORY, YOUR VOICE

Chapter Five: Creativity Tactic #5 125
　Divergent Thinking: Determine Your Point of View
Chapter Six: Creativity Tactic #6 151
　The Sensory Connective: Reveal Backstory Artfully
Chapter Seven: Creativity Tactic #7 174
　Conflict Generator: Write Dialogue that Does
　Something, Not Simply Says Something

Chapter Eight: Creativity Tactic #8 213
  Random Access: Writing Thematically

PART THREE: POLISH TO PERFECTION

Chapter Nine: Creativity Tactic #9 253
  Mindset Structures: Raise the Stakes on Your
  Protagonist—and Yourself
Chapter Ten: Creativity Tactic #10 284
  Creative Analysis: Revise Your Own Work
Chapter Eleven: Creativity Tactic #11 318
  Journey Mapping: Get Organized
Chapter Twelve: Creativity Tactic #12 344
  Failsafe: Create a Customized Action Plan

Afterword 365
Appendix One: Jane's Character Transformation
  Roadmap 371
Appendix Two: Jane's Plotting Roadmap 372
Appendix Three: Jane's Timing Grid.....................................373
Appendix Four: Scrivener in Use 374
Appendix Five: The Continuous Improvement..................375
  Writing Process
Index 377
Acknowledgments..395

INTRODUCTION

"I love the writing process. I love it."
Dana Perino

BRING YOUR HUMANITY
TO YOUR WRITING

Many authors fear becoming obsolete, outwitted by an algorithm. Fear not! Artificial intelligence is more artificial than intelligent. Just ask Steven A. Schwartz, the New York City lawyer who relied on it to prepare a legal brief. Not only did the chatbot provide fake judicial opinions and legal citations (falsehoods known as "hallucinations" in the AI industry), when challenged, the bot defended them, insisting they were accurate. Ask a chatbot if the text it's providing for a novel is copyright free, and it may well say yes, even when it's not true. Chatbots lie and poach! Further, text generated by AI is likely to be riddled with clichés, trite allusions, and stilted dialogue. When the literary luminary, Salman Rushdie, read a paragraph written by a chatbot, supposedly in his style, he called it "rubbish," adding, "Anyone who has ever read three hundred words of my own writing would immediately recognize that this couldn't possibly be mine." No matter how sophisticated

AI becomes, it can't tell your unique stories in your distinctive voice.

Even though artificial intelligence is based on a technology called "machine learning," computers can't learn to be creative—but you can, and this book will show you the way. AI is, by definition, derivative, not creative. It's also not sentient, so it can't empathize. Further, it can't bring rational judgment to determine the quality or value of its work. When you bring that trio of capabilities to your writing, your stories will touch readers' hearts and minds—and those are the stories readers crave.

Just as real food is better for us than processed food and actual social interactions are more meaningful than social media, when it comes to writing your story, artificial intelligence can't replicate your individual human intelligence, imagination, and sensibility. Technical wizardry can't tell *your* story. Only you can do that. Your uniqueness is what separates you from a chatbot, and explains why you can't be replaced by an algorithm. You'll succeed *because* you're human, not in spite of it.

Yes, artificial intelligence does the easy stuff better than people can, so inevitably, chatbots will pick off the low-hanging fruit, the easy-to-replicate work, the formulaic stories. To succeed, you need to bring ingenuity to your projects in ways AI can't. That's where this book comes in. *Beat the Bots* offers science-based creativity techniques to:

1. Guide you through the writing process
2. Unlock your imagination
3. Create compelling stories that resonate with emotional truth

NAVIGATE AN EXCITING NEW LANDSCAPE

Beat the Bots is divided into three parts. Each part includes four chapters, and each chapter features a creativity tactic designed to ensure your stories are innovative, powerful, and astute—an accomplishment that requires you, a human, to take the helm. Through engaging FAQs, invaluable Pro Tips, and AI Weighs In revelations, you'll be able to apply the writing lessons and creativity tactics to all aspects of storytelling, bringing your distinctive vision and voice to your projects in ways AI simply can't. Thought-provoking guided exercises challenge you to apply each chapter's lessons to your own writing. Four original and engaging prompts per chapter, designed with TikTok in mind, invite you to experiment with key ideas, tailoring them to your projects and sharing them with the supportive *Beat the Bots* community.

Pro Tip: TikTok's BookTok and AuthorTok

As you may know, BookTok is a powerful engine engaging readers (and writers) through book reviews and book-themed content. AuthorTok is a growing community of writers eager to learn the basics and nuance of craft and to receive constructive feedback from an enthusiastic community of like-minded writers. *Beat the Bots* is part of that community, and you're invited to join in!

Each chapter in this book includes original writing prompts, all of which are designed to encourage

---

you to focus on the emotional truth driving the elements of story. The evidence is clear—the more you reveal honest emotions, the more readers relate, and the more readers relate, the more books are sold. In her *New York Times* article, "How Crying on TikTok Sells Books," Elizabeth A. Harris highlights the effect of readers' "displays of raw emotion" on reader engagement, reporting that booksellers, including Barnes & Noble, say they've "never seen anything like it." An analysis of reader comments on Goodreads reinforces this finding—books that are laden with emotional candor receive the highest acclaim. To help you capitalize on this phenomenon, you'll find brief videos about each creativity tactic at

- BookTok: https://www.tiktok.com/ @beatthebotsbook
- AuthorTok: https://www.tiktok.com/ @janekclelandauthor

In addition, each writing prompt comes with easy-to-follow instructions on how to participate in the *Beat the Bots* TikTok community.

I'm excited to watch your videos and celebrate your success! Please know that you're more than welcomed to my writing community—you're valued.

Here's what I know about you: you're committed to your craft and eager to become a stronger writer. You wouldn't be reading this book if you weren't! In these pages, you'll find an affirming and supportive environment as you work to manage the duality of the writing process: innovation and assessment. Two caveats before we jump in:

- Customize your approach. All of the creativity tactics discussed in this book may work for you, or you may find that one isn't a good fit. That's okay! Experiment. Play around with the techniques. Combine them. Tweak them. They're intended as a guide, not a straitjacket.
- Separate the creative process from the evaluation process. Quieting your internal critic and welcoming your internal editor ensures you'll be able to use the tactics and processes discussed in this book to best advantage.

Your story. Your ingenuity. Your humanity. Your judgment. You're irreplaceable in the world of storytelling. Ready? Let's get started!

Reflection on Creativity

"There is no doubt that creativity is the most important human resource of all. Without creativity, there would be no progress, and we would be forever repeating the same patterns."
Edward De Bono

PART ONE
FIND YOUR INNER MUSE

"The most difficult and complicated part of
the writing process is the beginning."
A. B. Yehoshu

CHAPTER ONE

CREATIVITY TACTIC #1
IDEA FISHING: FIND VIABLE IDEAS

"Before you can write a novel, you have to have a number
of ideas that come together. One idea is not enough."
Joyce Carol Oates

EMBRACE YOUR HUMANITY

With all the talk about AI wizardry, it's easy to assume you're
about to be replaced, but I take a different view. Because AI is,
by definition, merely derivative, those writers who bring true
innovation to their work will always be in demand. Chatbots
don't have their own stories to tell or inner lives to share, and
no matter how many stories and emotional truths they study,
they never will. Chatbots can write only what they've been pro-
grammed to produce, approximating the human experience,
not reflecting or revealing it. The answer isn't to surrender to

the doom-and-gloom predictions. On the contrary, it's time to lean into our humanity, to do what artificial intelligence can't. AI can't possibly understand what you want to express. If you bring your creativity, your individuality, and your judgment to your work, you'll outwrite a chatbot all day long. Compelling, viable ideas are everywhere, and this chapter will help you find them and identify the winners.

The most effective ideas come from the sentient experience, which means that creative writing is an inimitably human endeavor. Chatbots don't have rich inner lives, so they can't have stories to share. And even if they did, we couldn't follow them. As Austrian philosopher Ludwig Wittgenstein said, "If a lion could speak, we would not understand him."

FAQ

Q: I was at a book event and a famous author was asked where she got her ideas. She laughed and said she didn't have a clue. That's so discouraging. How can I hope to find an effective writing process if there's no reliable method for coming up with ideas?

A: Many authors rely on their subconscious to come up with ideas, and that may be what that famous author was referring to.

I have discovered, for instance, that if I pose a question just before I drift off to sleep, be it about how to unravel a plot tangle or enhance a character's motivation, invariably I wake up with the answer. The old adage to

> "sleep on it" works for me. Another example of subconscious creativity is Lawrence Block's reliance on serendipity. He puts it this way: "Look for something, find something else, and realize that what you've found is more suited to your needs than what you thought you were looking for."
>
> The trick is to experiment with different techniques, to try different strategies until you find the one that works best for you. Maybe subconscious creativity isn't a good fit for the way you think or work. That's okay! The Idea Fishing creativity tactic discussed in this chapter uses a methodical approach to the task, and I'm confident you'll find it easy and effective.

ADOPT A FLEXIBLE MINDSET

One of the greatest limitations we put on ourselves as writers is thinking of ideas as good or bad. Instead, we need to assess whether they're effective or ineffective, how appropriate or inappropriate they are. Shifting your mindset from one of judgment to one of assessment changes everything. Let's think about this: judgment versus assessment. Judgment is critical. Assessment is encouraging. Judgment tells you what's wrong. Assessment guides you forward. Judgment is demoralizing. Assessment is affirming. We'll talk about this distinction at more length in Chapter Nine when we look at raising the stakes on ourselves as authors—and why we shy away from doing so—and again in Chapter Twelve, as we work to develop a viable action plan. For now, be alert for any inclination you notice in yourself to avoid taking risks when trying to come up with new ideas. Remember, all the creativity tactics detailed in this book are private, just between you and you, until you're ready to share your ideas with the world.

Prompt #1: Building Blocks of Life

It's important to think about your journey to becoming a writer. NASA is studying an asteroid sample that contains carbon and water, which may explain how these vital elements, what they call the "building blocks of life" reached Earth. What were the building blocks that led you to this place at this tune? When I asked myself this question, I remembered my dad's cigar boxes. I haven't thought about them in years. When I was a kid, we couldn't afford to buy blocks, so my inventive and loving dad haunted smoke shops, carting away their empty cigar boxes. He covered them in brightly colored and boldly patterned contact paper, and voilà! I had a supply of building blocks. I spent hours up in the attic building towers and bridges and castles. My favorite accomplishment was tossing an old sheet over four towers to create a cozy tent. I brought in a battery-operated hurricane lamp and read for hours at a time. Those building blocks represented far more than simply materials to create structures. They represented my father's love and support. If not for his nurturing, I wonder if I'd have found my way to become a writer.

BEAT THE BOTS

Now it's your turn! Complete this sentence: When I consider the "building blocks" of life, I think of _____.

To participate in the *Beat the Bots* TikTok community:

- Record a video of your answer and post it, including the hashtag #beatthebots and tag me at @beatthebotsbook
- You can also tag #authortok and #booktok to connect with other writer and reader communities!
- Watch other writers' videos by visiting the TikTok hashtag #beatthebots

Join the conversation!

If you're in a creativity slump, constrained by embarrassment, shame, anxiety, or fear, acknowledge it and move on. While you feel as you feel, you don't have to act based on those emotions. The goal isn't to try to change your feelings—the goal is to change your reaction to those feelings, to not let negativity inhibit your ability to fire up your creative engine. Consider the definition of "creativity": According to Dictionary. com, creativity means, "the ability to transcend traditional ideas, rules, patterns, relationships, or the like, and to create meaningful new ideas, forms, methods, interpretations, etc.; originality, progressiveness, or imagination." Inherent in the definition of creativity is the word "transcend." You need to transcend those emotions that hold you back. Give yourself

7

permission to try new things. If an idea you come up with isn't effective, so what? Move on to the next one!

Part of the trick, of course, is keeping track of your ideas. We don't want a fleeting thought containing a gem of an idea to disappear. It's easy to lose track since ideas often come to us when we're doing something else. The legendary novelist, Agatha Christie, said the best time to plot was while washing dishes. For you, it may be mowing the lawn. Or making your kids lunch. Or brushing your teeth. Because you're busy engaging in a hands-on activity, it's painfully easy to forget the idea if you don't memorialize it in some way. Keep a notebook handy at all times (or have your phone readily available for recording), and be sure to include enough detail so you remember the substance. George Bernard Shaw, the great playwright, reportedly felt exasperated with himself because he kept waking up with faint tendrils of memory alerting him that he'd come up with a great idea for a new play, but by the time he was fully awake, the idea had evaporated. Determined to prevent losing a good idea again, he placed a pad of paper and a pen on his nightstand. Sure enough, the next morning, he woke up with that same sense of having had an interesting idea. He eagerly reached for the paper, relieved and happy—until he saw his note: "Write play." Learn from Shaw's experience and don't let your ideas disappear into the ether.

GENERATE FRESH IDEAS

A reliable approach to coming up with novel-worthy ideas is to mine external and internal sources. Ideas can come from anywhere and everywhere, from news reports, overheard conversations, and observed incidents to those unspoken desires that fuel ambition, the unanswered questions that linger in your mind, and the unresolved issues that drive your actions.

The Idea Fishing creativity tactic helps you link disparate ideas to come up with new ones. Here's how it works.

1. Choose something to think about. It could be tangible (a person, place, or thing) or intangible (an emotion, concept, or memory).
2. Fish for ideas using "what if" and "so what" questions and follow the trail of answers until you can't go further.

For example, in 2005, I read an article reporting that the movie star, Elizabeth Taylor, had won a lawsuit involving a painting she'd put up for sale, a Van Gogh. She'd been sued by a woman who'd alleged that she, not Taylor, was the rightful owner of the painting, that it had been stolen from her family in 1939 by the Nazis. The court found that the painting had been sold fair and square, but the seed had been planted. All I could think of was the horror of government-sanctioned art theft. The ignominy of it. I found myself asking questions to probe the consequences, the implications, the danger. Note my questions started with "what if."

- What if a Nazi official kept some of the stolen paintings instead of turning them over to the government— where would they be now? Did the official feel proud of himself? Did he feel guilty? Did he think he'd been clever? Did he justify his actions with a craven, "It's no big deal. Everyone does it"?
- What if the grandson of the thief is now in America? Without clear title, he can't sell the paintings for top

dollar. Would he display them? Keep them hidden? Turn them over to the FBI or some other law enforcement agency? Would he feel ashamed of his grandfather? Embarrassed? Proud?

Over the course of a few hours, the basic story arc of *Consigned to Death*, the first Josie Prescott Antiques Mystery, came to me. Not the full plot or all the characters, of course, but the overarching story. That one question—what if a Nazi official kept some of the stolen paintings—opened up story possibilities I hadn't even known existed.

Prompt #2: An Important Decision

What's your best writing decision? Why?

New York Times bestselling author Louise Penny says, "After suffering five years of writer's block, I realized I was trying to write a book to impress everyone. For validation. Finally I realized I needed to simply write a book I would read. And that's what I did, and am still doing."

What's your best writing decision? Why?

_____

_____

_____

_____

_____

_____

_____

> To participate in the *Beat the Bots* TikTok community:
>
> - Record a video of your answer, and post it, including the hashtag #beatthebots and tag me at @beatthebotsbook
> - You can also tag #authortok and #booktok to connect with other writer and reader communities!
> - Watch other writers' videos by visiting the TikTok hashtag #beatthebots
>
> Join the conversation!

Note that I concentrated on the underlying emotional truth of the situation—not the facts. This is an important point. Those of us who love research tend to feel bound by the facts. I often remind myself to step away from the truth. When you're writing fiction, aim for plausible, not actual. You need accurate details to add verisimilitude, but you don't need to limit your imagination. Think of your job as using facts to write fiction, and remember, readers' favorite books are those that resonate with emotional truth, not factual accuracy.

Pro Tip: Step Away from the Truth

News reports and other fact-based sources can be a useful tool for jump-starting the idea generation process. Authors have been using this technique for as long as novels have been written, and not only historical novels.

Here are a few examples to help you envision the potential:

- Rosemary Harris got the idea for *Pushing Up Daisies* after reading an article about an infant's skeleton that had been dug up in a suburban backyard in Connecticut.
- Yomi Adegoke's skepticism of #metoo spreadsheets that anonymously outed men alleged to be sexual abusers or predators led to *The List*.
- Rachel Beanland turned a family tragedy (Beanland's own great-aunt Florence's death) into a gripping novel in *Florence Adler Swims Forever*. Florence's mother kept the news of Florence's drowning from her other daughter, Fannie, who was in precarious health.
- A documentary about the Taliban reporting they'd banned kite flying led to Khaled Hosseini's *The Kite Runner*.

When you take this approach, remember that you're not writing nonfiction, so give yourself permission to veer off the literal truth, to take a thread of the story and weave it into a tapestry of your own creation. Only you, an actual person, can determine which threads to keep and which to discard. Likewise, asking "what if" and "so what" questions to hone your ideas is a singularly human endeavor, and a proven tactic to help you come up with new ideas, a surefire way to beat the bots.

FIND IDEAS FROM INSIDE YOURSELF

Asking "what if" and "so what" questions also works with intangible or abstract concepts. Elaine Viets did this in her *Dead End Jobs* mystery series. What if—there's that question again—what if a woman who was being abused by her husband couldn't escape? He'd always be able to track her down because he was a cop. To stay safe, she'd need to stay under the radar, only taking work where they paid her in cash. Those positions were, inevitably, dead end jobs.

New York Times columnist Thomas Friedman wrote a book called *Thank You for Being Late*. He realized that he didn't mind a whit if his breakfast guest was late. It gave him time to eavesdrop ("fascinating") and people watch ("outrageous"), and most significantly, it gave him time to think. He wrote, "...I connected a couple of ideas I'd been struggling with for days."

Have you overheard any conversations lately? Observed any interactions that piqued your interest? Witnessed anything, no matter how fleeting, that inspired curiosity? These happenstance interludes are ripe with possibility, but only if we pay attention. Dr. Samuel Johnson, the eighteenth-century British man of letters, wrote, "The true art of memory is the art of attention."

Prompt #3: Pride in Your Writing

Think of a writing accomplishment you're proud of. It could be something big and public, a story or book sale, or it also could be something small and private. For me it's nailing a sentence—I love it when I write unambiguously, where there's only one way to understand what I'm trying to express. I find that level of clarity thrilling!

How about you? What's a writing accomplishment you're proud of?

_____

_____

_____

_____

_____

_____

_____

To participate in the *Beat the Bots* TikTok community:

- Record a video of your answer, and post it, including the hashtag #beatthebots and tag me at @beatthebotsbook
- You can also tag #authortok and #booktok to connect with other writer and reader communities!
- Watch other writers' videos by visiting the TikTok hashtag #beatthebots

Join the conversation!

BEAT THE BOTS

Let's put the Idea Fisher creativity tactic to work. Remember that your goal is to come up with as many ideas as possible. Later, we'll assess their merit, but for now, separate out the idea-generation phase from the idea-assessment phase of the creative process.

Exercise Part One

Idea Fishing: Finding Ideas

In Part One of this exercise, we'll work to generate ideas, the more the merrier. Part Two (see below) offers a metric for evaluating their usefulness. Note that this exercise uses a news article as a prompt. You can adapt it to other source material, such as interactions you witness, conversations you overhear, your own unresolved conflicts, and so on. The process is the same, regardless of the source.

1. Scan today's news headlines from a national or local source. Find an article that arouses your interest. The article: _____

   _____

2. To help you home in on what captured your attention, write a one- to two-sentence summary that completes this sentence: The most interesting aspect of this article is

   _____.

3. Ask yourself the following questions, jotting notes about your answers.

15

- What if this event took place a hundred years ago?
- What if this event took place a hundred years from now?
- So what if it doesn't work out?
- So what if it's backward?

4. Ask yourself how this process makes you feel right now: _____.

5. Write down a premise for a novel based on your observations and notes:

_____.

Here's an example to help you see how the process works. After I develop this idea, I'd go back to the article I'm using as a prompt and ask more "What if" and "So what" questions to help me generate additional ideas.

1. *Scan today's news headlines from a national or local source. Find an article that piques your interest.* The article: "At NY Dog and Cat Film Festivals, Love, Licks and Looniness" (*New York Times*).

2. *To help you home in on what captured your attention, write a one- to two-sentence summary that completes this sentence:* The most interesting aspect of this article is that there's an audience for short films about dogs and cats.

3. *Ask yourself the following questions, jotting notes about your answers.*

- *What if this event took place a hundred years ago?* There would be a lot of sepia tones. Maybe the stories would be told using stereographs. Or—and this is funny—via a silent movie.
- *What if this event took place a hundred years from now?* Cats might run the world, with dogs as the worker class. Cats might become fluent in English. Dogs would still have limited vocabularies, expressed by barking and growling. Cats and dogs might form a cooperative government.
- *So what if it doesn't work out?* Cats will still have staff. Dogs will still have owners.
- *So what if it's backward?* It makes me wonder about the role of perception in assigning roles.

4. *Ask yourself how this process makes you feel right now.* Amused. I kind of love the idea of assigning human qualities to cats and dogs. I've always enjoyed allegory.

5. *Write down a premise for a novel based on your observations and notes:* I could create a world where cats and dogs are at each other's throats, each determined to become the supreme leader. By the end, they establish a power-sharing relationship, with cats stealthily working behind the scenes and dogs working the crowds, the public face of the government.

Now it's your turn! Pick your article or other prompt, go through the Idea Fishing steps, and see how many ideas you discover. Remember, during this phase of the process, go for quantity! Don't worry about quality. When you're done, I'd love to hear about your experience!

Complete this sentence: I tried Jane's Idea Fishing creativity tactic to coming up with ideas and

_____ .

To participate in the *Beat the Bots* TikTok community:

- Record a video of your answer and post it, including the hashtag #beatthebots and tag me at @beatthebotsbook
- You can also tag #authortok and #booktok to connect with other writer and reader communities!
- Watch other writers' videos by visiting the TikTok hashtag #beatthebots

Join the conversation!

CONSIDER GENRE EXPECTATIONS

Now that you've come up with a bunch of ideas, it's time to assess their viability. Doing so requires an understanding of reader expectations within your genre. For instance, romance readers expect happy endings. Readers of noir do not. Think of it this way: publishers tend to be risk averse, which explains why they want to acquire manuscripts that are simultaneously fresh and familiar. This duality sounds like an oxymoron, but it's not. If your story isn't fresh, it will read as derivative, and who wants to publish that? But if it's not familiar, publishers will worry they won't know how to market it effectively. If publishers can't identify the book's genre (and maybe its subgenre), how can they help a bookseller know where to shelve it? How can they identify appropriate keywords for online searches? To satisfy these imperatives, you need to know the parameters of your chosen genre and understand where your manuscript fits.

A sensible place to start is to compare the two broad categories of fiction, literary and genre. This chart highlights some of the key differences between them.

Literary	Genre
• Character-driven	• Plot-driven
• Focuses on a transformational event or important passage of life (e.g., coming of age, surviving a tragedy)	• Satisfies reader expectations by following genre conventions (e.g., in fantasy, world-building is crucial)
• Readers expect elegant, evocative prose	• Readers expect solid storytelling

Pay attention to subgenre, too. Analyze half a dozen or more exemplars—enduring favorites or current bestsellers. For instance, traditional mysteries and thrillers are both subgenres of crime fiction, but they differ in important ways. Traditional mysteries include limited onstage violence or sex and the solution to the murder depends on the deductive abilities of the sleuth, not forensics. Thrillers typically include graphic violence, onstage sex, and the solution derives from brawn as much as brains. Now consider how sub-subgenres further affect your decision-making. For instance, under the broad category of traditional mysteries, you'll find the subgenre of cozies. While some traditional mysteries include a working detective (like Hercule Poirot, for example), readers of cozies expect an amateur sleuth. Cozy readers also expect a quaint small-town setting and an overall wholesome feel. Likewise, there are subgenres of thrillers, from legal and medical to domestic and political, among others. Whatever genre you're working in, assessing your ideas through that particular lens will help you choose winners.

Prompt #4: Favorite Aspects

While I read widely, and enjoy both literary and genre fiction, one of my favorite genres is espionage, a subgenre of crime fiction. I like the righteousness of protecting your nation's secrets. I like the high stakes. I like the intrigue.

How about you? What's one of your favorite genres—why?

BEAT THE BOTS

To participate in the *Beat the Bots* TikTok community:

- Record a video of your answer and post it, including the hashtag #beatthebots and tag me at @beatthebotsbook
- You can also tag #authortok and #booktok to connect with other writer and reader communities!
- Watch other writers' videos by visiting the TikTok hashtag #beatthebots

Join the conversation!

When considering your genre, here are some factors to assess:

- What is the central conflict? What does the protagonist long for, and what will the antagonist do to stop them from getting it?
- What is the pace? Is there a slow build to the inciting incident or is the reader catapulted into action? How often do you find unexpected twists and turns?
- How do the characters change over the course of the story? Is there a major transformation or is order restored after chaos has ensued?
- Where and when does the story take place? Is it urban? Rural? Is there a single setting or globe-trotting? How does the protagonist feel about the setting(s)?
- What is the overall feeling? Is it dark and gritty? Safe and friendly?

21

- What unifies the story or gives it deeper meaning? How does this theme weave through the plot? Does the author include symbols or allegory?
- How long is the story? Do the chapters tend to be short?

Now that you have an understanding of what you're trying to achieve, it's time to evaluate your own ideas using this information as a framework.

NIA: A TRIFECTA OF SUCCESS

Before proceeding, it's important to evaluate your ideas using the following three-step NIA decision-making model: We're going to look at the idea's Novelty, Impact, and Alignment. When an idea satisfies all three parameters, you can be confident you're onto something. Note that the NIA process requires human judgment—no algorithm can replace this complex, multifaceted decision-making imperative. Only you can determine whether your plans are innovative, meaningful, and appropriate for your genre.

AI Weighs In

I asked a chatbot: Can you give me a new idea for a novel about a divorcing couple?

AI said: *Certainly! How about a novel where a couple decides to get a divorce but must continue living together due to financial constraints? Here's a brief synopsis:*

BEAT THE BOTS

Title: "Uncommon Grounds"

Synopsis: Sheila and Max have reached a crossroads in their marriage. After years of growing apart, they decide that divorce is the only way to find happiness again. However, there's a significant twist to their story—they simply cannot afford to move out or maintain separate households in their expensive city.

With an impending mortgage, shared debt, and the high cost of living, they are trapped in their co-owned home, forced to navigate the emotional minefield of divorce while still sharing a life under the same roof. As they embark on this unconventional journey, they each discover a new sense of independence, rekindle lost passions, and form unexpected friendships.

"Uncommon Grounds" explores the complexities of modern relationships, financial struggles, and the quest for personal growth and happiness amid adversity. As they face the challenges of cohabitating during a divorce, Sheila and Max find themselves confronting their past mistakes, reevaluating their priorities, and perhaps, rediscovering the love that initially brought them together.

This novel could delve into themes of resilience, personal growth, and the unexpected opportunities that arise from difficult circumstances, providing a fresh take on the classic divorce narrative.

> Say what? This isn't a new idea. It may be a good one, but it's not new. *New York Magazine* published an article titled "Live-in Divorce" in 1990. The author, Francine Russo, referenced Warren Adler's novel (later made into a movie), *The War of the Roses*, a story of a divorcing couple. Neither person is willing to leave the family home due to financial and emotional constraints, so they have to live together. She described it an "absurdist take on a modern reality." Adler wrote *The War of the Roses* in 1981. How can AI's idea be "new" if someone else wrote a novel based on the premise decades earlier?
>
> We need to come up with truly new ideas, and that's a singular human activity.

As you think about your ideas, use these factors to help you take an objective, 360-degree view.

1. Novelty

    Is the idea new? Are you taking a new spin on a familiar idea? If so, is your take innovative enough to surprise people?

2. Impact

    Is your idea big enough? Does it address thematically significant issues such as good versus evil, life or death, or belonging versus feeling like an outcast? Does your protagonist have a personal reason to act?

BEAT THE BOTS

3. Alignment
   Does my idea match my target readers' expectations? Is it appropriate for my genre and subgenre?

Note that to proceed with confidence, your ideas must satisfy the parameters of all three factors. Let's say I come up with a way to update Agatha Christie's Miss Marple mysteries. Instead of an elderly spinster who lives in a small English village (an amateur sleuth), I might create an elderly bachelor who lives in a city (an amateur sleuth). While it's not a wholly new approach, it's a fresh take on a much-loved concept, and appropriate for a traditional mystery. I think it's a novel slant. The murder will involve sex trafficking, clearly a big idea, impactful to the detective, the women and children being trafficked, and the reader. So far, so good. But here's the problem: readers of traditional mysteries don't want to read about sex trafficking. That's a topic appropriate for literary fiction, or if I want to stay within genre fiction, it might work in certain subgenres of crime fiction, such as thrillers, police procedurals, or noir. It might also work in romantic suspense, fantasy, or horror, depending on how I position the topic. But it's out of alignment for readers of traditional mysteries.

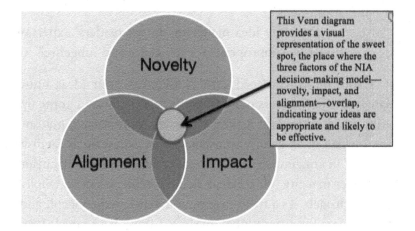

This Venn diagram provides a visual representation of the sweet spot, the place where the three factors of the NIA decision-making model—novelty, impact, and alignment—overlap, indicating your ideas are appropriate and likely to be effective.

Exercise Part Two

Idea Fishing: Evaluating Ideas with NIA

You'll recall that my article-based idea centered on a power-sharing arrangement between cats and dogs (see Part One above). I got to that premise by answering five questions. The sixth question will help me determine its likely effectiveness.

6. *Does the premise meet the parameters of NIA? Is it novel, impactful, and aligned with my reader expectations?*

    It's not totally innovative. George Orwell's *Animal Farm*, is, on one level, a fable where farm animals run a society that divides into factions.

On another level, however, the book tells the story of the Russian Revolution and expresses Orwell's rebuke of Stalinism. It also reveals the power of propaganda, showing how a gifted orator can spin even the most damning facts to his advantage. The phrase, "Four legs good, two legs bad," for instance, becomes a mantra designed to fire up antihuman sentiment, a metaphor for Orwell's underlying theme that in the wrong hands, language can be used to oppress people. This makes me realize I need to add thematic heft to my allegory about cats and dogs to differentiate it from what might seem to be nothing more than a silly fairy tale.

Yes, I think it's impactful, dealing as it does with issues of cooperation among foes, goodness, and identifying your strengths.

I think a literary novel using cats' and dogs' innate antipathy toward one another can show how even the most determined enemies can work together for the greater good.

This might be worth pursuing. That it's not a completely new idea isn't a knock-out factor since so much of the story is, in fact, innovative and timely.

Now it's your turn! For each idea you came up with in Part One that you might want to pursue, answer this sixth question:

- *Does the premise meet the parameters of NIA? Is it novel, impactful, and aligned with my reader expectations?*

What did you learn about evaluating ideas using the NIA model? Here's how I might reply: I learned that new spins on old ideas can, in fact, be transformative. I also learned that if you can get people laughing, you can slip in serious observations without coming across as sanctimonious or pedantic.

How about you? I'd love to hear about your experience!

Complete this sentence: I tried evaluating ideas using the NIA model and _____.

To participate in the *Beat the Bots* TikTok community:

- Record a video of your answer and post it, including the hashtag #beatthebots and tag me at @beatthebotsbook
- You can also tag #authortok and #booktok to connect with other writer and reader communities!
- Watch other writers' videos by visiting the TikTok hashtag #beatthebots
- Join the conversation!

BEAT THE BOTS

The NIA assessment process helps you sift through the ideas you've come up with, and, using your wise judgment, decide which ones to pursue. *Your* discernment, based on your knowledge, your experience, and your understanding of your genre (and thus your reader expectations) can't be replaced by a chatbot.

Now that you have identified worthy ideas, it's time to transform an idea into a story. In the next chapter, we'll look at how to ensure your characters are acting in ways that align with your plot by delving into what makes them tick. Jane's Character Transformation Roadmap will help you do just that. Your story will resonate with real-life readers because you're satisfying their longings—and these are the stories publishers want and readers adore.

Reflection on Creativity

"Let your creative and imaginative mind run freely; it will take you places you never dreamed of and provide breakthroughs that others once thought were impossible."
Idowu Koyenikan

CHAPTER TWO

CREATIVITY TACTIC #2
FORKS IN THE ROAD: TRACK CHARACTER MOTIVATION WITH JANE'S CHARACTER TRANSFORMATION ROADMAP

"People are complicated. People have secrets."
David Zayas

POPULATE YOUR STORIES WITH PEOPLE, NOT CHARACTERS

Now that you have selected viable ideas, it's time to populate your story with living, breathing people. Storytelling success requires creating relatable flesh-and-blood characters, people readers can relate to. AI can't write about people—it can only search through legions of source material to generate familiar composites, an effort certain to fail since these recommendations are, by definition, derivative. Further, your characters need to evolve over the course of your story, and this transformation needs to derive from the things that happen to them (external factors) and the decisions they make for themselves (internal factors). Only you, the author, can determine how they act and react. Jane's Character Transformation Roadmap (below and in Appendix One) will help guide this decision-making process by helping you ensure character motivation aligns with your plot.

An important note: broadly, there are two ways to prepare to write your story. You can come up with your characters, then give them logical things to do, or you can delineate your plot, then figure out what kinds of people would do those things. So long as your character motivations align with your incidents, it doesn't matter which approach you take. As Henry James wrote, "What is character but the determination of incident? What is incident but the illustration of character?" There is no one right strategy. If you prefer to start by thinking about your characters first, get ready to jump in. If you prefer to plot first, turn to Chapter Three, "Mind Wandering: Plot with Jane's Plotting Roadmap," then return here to work on your character transformations.

IMBUE YOUR CHARACTERS WITH HUMANITY

People differ from one another in both superficial and deep-seated ways. I know this probably isn't news to you, but fully assimilating this fact is key to developing believable characters. For example, the tasteless joke that offends one person won't bother someone else at all. A third person finds it funny, and a fourth is angry. You need to know, with needle-like precision, how *your* people will react to whatever happens to them. If you don't, their conversations, actions, and thoughts will feel false or fall flat. If you do, these things will resonant with emotional truth and propel your story forward.

FAQ

Q: What kind of character transformations are most effective?

A: Generally speaking, you want your protagonist to experience a major shift in perception, belief, or attitude over the course of your novel. Here are two examples:

- A man is cynical, certain that everyone has an angle. By the end of the novel, he's become a believer in the goodness of humankind.
- A con artist is caught and ends up assisting the police in identifying scams.

Sometimes the transformation is organized around a disruption. The transformation results in the character ending up right back where he began. For instance:

- A man lives an orderly, comfortable life. When his teenage son is arrested for murder, he works feverishly to prove his son's innocence. At the end, he's back living his orderly, comfortable life.

> - A group of upper middle–class college friends decides to use their tech savvy to start an extortion business, thinking its easy money. All is proceeding according to plan until they target the wrong person, a member of the mob, who sets out to kill them. At the end, they realize they're not cut out for gunfights in alleys and disperse, returning to their safe, middle-class lives.
>
> There are other approaches, of course, and no one transformation is best. When the transformation is grounded in emotional truth, it will be effective and engaging.

As you work with this concept, it's crucial to avoid assuming you can gauge other people's feelings with any degree of accuracy. We have to work to separate ourselves from our characters, which is easier said than done. To do this, it's important that we adopt an attitude of healthy skepticism.

If you're like most people, when you believe something, you assume it's true. It rarely occurs to us that we might be wrong, just as it rarely occurs to us that other people, as fair-minded and principled as we are, might look at the same events or facts and reach different conclusions. Yet it happens all the time. Given that we need to be able to write characters who aren't like us with empathy and understanding, we must be alert for signs that our preconceptions are creeping into our characterizations. As the Buddhist monk Thubten Chodron put it, "Don't believe everything you think."

Prompt #5: Three Adjectives

To help you get to know your character on a deep level, choose three adjectives that sum up their personality, appearance, and style. For example, one of the most engaging characters I know is Travis McGee, the protagonist in John D. MacDonald's long-running mystery series. He's a man all men want to be and all women want to be with. When asked what he does for a living, he says he's a salvage expert. He'll work to recover whatever you've lost, and if he succeeds, he keeps half. He lives on a houseboat, the *Busted Flush*, that he won in a poker game. He is tall and strong, and a real romantic, falling for dozens of women over the course of the series, and always treating them with respect. His best friend is a depressed economist named Meyer.

Here are my three adjectives. Travis McGee is honorable, tough, and charming.

Now it's your turn! Explain a little bit about your character and list three adjectives that sum them up.

To participate in the *Beat the Bots* TikTok community:

- Record a video of your answer and post it, including the hashtag #beatthebots and tag me at @beatthebotsbook

- You can also tag #authortok and #book-tok to connect with other writer and reader communities!
- Watch other writers' videos by visiting the Tik-Tok hashtag #beatthebots

Join the conversation!

ADD DYNAMIC ENERGY

To add to the complexity, we must keep in mind that people change, and tracking that change over the course of your novel ensures these emotionally significant shifts, whether gradual or abrupt, ring true. A change might come from external factors like a traumatic brain injury, or from an accomplishment, such as mastering a skill or overcoming an obstacle. We've all heard about a former addict, for instance, who conquered his addiction and spends the rest of life helping other addicts. Sometimes people change because of a singular experience like reading a life-changing book, traveling, or learning a new hobby. In fact, it's not uncommon for what some would deem a small incident to change a life.

We need our characters to be transformed. Otherwise, we're reading about unconnected incidents that have no effect on them, and where's the fun or entertainment or illumination in that?

Prompt #6: A Life-Changing Event

Describe an experience that led to a major change in your personality, attitude, or ambitions.

Here's my example: When I was in high school, I went to a friend's house and her mom made kielbasa, the Polish sausage, served in a sweet-and-sour sauce. I'd never tasted anything like it. Every nerve ending in my body twitched with delight. I couldn't stop eating. I ate and I ate, the glorious tangy sauce running down my face. I was totally blissed out. When I got home, I asked my mother, "Why have you been withholding this incredible food from me?" The lesson, of course, is not that I discovered a new food—it was that I discovered there were countless flavors in the world to discover. At that point, my knowledge base was concave—I was so ignorant, I didn't even know what I didn't know. My big takeaway was that if I wanted to discover new things, I would need to spread my wings. Tasting kielbasa for the first time led to a seismic shift in my attitude toward experimentation. It's not hyperbole to say kielbasa changed my life. Its effect was so profound that when asked for my future plans by my high school's yearbook committee, I listed travel as my aspiration.

Now it's your turn! Describe an experience that led to a major change in your personality, attitude, or ambitions.

To participate in the *Beat the Bots* TikTok community:

- Record a video of your answer and post it, including the hashtag #beatthebots and tag me at @beatthebotsbook
- You can also tag #authortok and #booktok to connect with other writer and reader communities!
- Watch other writers' videos by visiting the TikTok hashtag #beatthebots

Join the conversation!

Our lives are defined by the choices we make. So are our characters'. Some decisions are big. Others small. All are consequential. Even not making a decision is, effectively, making a decision. As you think about revealing your characters, keep in mind that we get to know people through their actions, through their reflections, and through other characters' observations about them.

To ensure your characters develop a story arc all their own, use Jane's Character Transformation Roadmap to guide your writing. This roadmap offers a graphic representation of the forks in the road we all face day in and day out—and how our choices impact us.

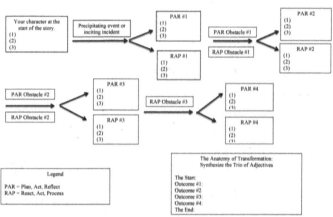

Here's how it works: Notice the first box (in the upper left) asks you to describe your character at the start of the story by listing three adjectives (note: we experimented with this task in Prompt #5).

Identify your precipitating event or inciting incident, then assess how your character will react. Broadly, there are two ways someone can respond to any incident: Plan, Act, Reflect (PAR) or React, Act, Process (RAP). Some people are methodical, others impulsive. Of course, there are plenty of shades of gray when assessing human behavior. Regardless of style, people are going to do *something* (or nothing, which is still an action). Based on that reaction, what will your character do next? Well, of course, it depends on how they feel, what they think, and what happens to them. It's important to note that as you work with Jane's Character Transformation Roadmap, there will certainly be more than four incidents. Depending on the scope of your story, there might be scores of incidents.

BEAT THE BOTS

At the start of Liane Moriarty's *Big Little Lies*, for example, one of the three main characters, Jane, who is twenty-four and a single mom, is fearful, reserved, and wounded. The precipitating event is Jane's move to a new town. Shortly after the school year starts, Jane's son, Ziggy, is accused of bullying a little girl on the playground. Jane is certain Ziggy couldn't be the thug that hurt the little girl, then realizes there's actually no way to know for sure, which terrifies her. "Did anyone really know their child?" By the end of the book, Jane is transformed. She's now more confident, more relaxed, and more comfortable in her own skin. No miracles, but a realistic, and thus touching, transformation.

Pro Tip: Demographics and Psychographics

To write relatable and credible characters, you need to know them—your people—inside and out. Two terms that can help guide your thinking are demographics and psychographics. Demographics are the facts about people—their age, income, marital status, and the like—a fact-based profile. Psychographics refer to lifestyle factors, how people spend their time and money—what they value. As a writer, you need to marry both aspects to develop believable characters. It's not enough to simply track observable facts. You also need to get inside your characters' heads, to learn what they believe and how those beliefs affect their behavior.

For example, let's say you have two characters, both women, who are office managers for different departments

---

39

within the same company. They're each forty-one years old. They earn the same amount of money. They drive the same make and model of car. They live in identical apartments in the same apartment building. They've each been married once, for twenty-one years, and they each have one child, a son. As you can see, I've described demographically identical people. Now let me change one fact and you'll see how everything changes: one of those women's son is about to graduate from college. The other boy is about to turn one. In all likelihood, these women have very little in common. Their attitudes toward spending money, expectations of their husbands, time management, vacation plans, and the like are certain to differ.

Psychographics relates to Maslow's Hierarchy of Needs, a model created in the 1940s by Dr. Abraham Maslow, an American psychologist, to illustrate innate human needs and values. He found that until your basic physical needs (clean water, fresh air, and so on) are satisfied, you can't think of anything else. Once your physiological needs are fulfilled, however, you can move on to other things. According to Dr. Maslow, after your physical needs are met, and you're confident you're in a stable and secure situation, you seek belonging, esteem, and self-actualization in that order.

Dr. Brené Brown, a research professor at the University of Houston and the author of numerous books on courage, vulnerability, shame, and empathy, says that one of the primary tasks associated with becoming an adult is figuring out where you truly belong. She makes

BEAT THE BOTS

the point that if you adhere to the mores of any group, usually they'll welcome you with open arms because you fit in. But, Dr. Brown explains, that has nothing to do with figuring out where you truly belong.

Scientists tell us that we humans crave belonging to communities that value us for who we are. This imperative has driven countless characters to act, including those we find in Gail Honeyman's *Eleanor Oliphant Is Completely Fine*, Lisa Moore Ramée's *A Good Kind of Trouble*, Jason Reynolds's *Long Way Down*, and Colette Fellous's *This Tilting World*.

While Jane's transformation in *Big Little Lies* evolved slowly, one PAR at a time, some transformations are dramatic. At the start of Irwin Shaw's novel, *Nightwork*, for instance, Douglas, the protagonist, is depressed, despondent, desperate. He's an ex-pilot, now reduced to working as the overnight front desk clerk at a seedy hotel because of bad eyes he can't afford to get fixed. On a dreary winter night, he finds a dead body. That isn't all he finds—in a tube next to the corpse, he discovers $100,000 (more than $600,000 in today's dollars). Can you imagine? So Douglas does what any depressed, despondent, desperate man would do—he takes the money and runs. After getting his eyes fixed, he flits around Europe, meeting people who expose him to new, life-changing experiences. Meanwhile, the gangsters close in, determined to find their missing money. Douglas is all about the RAP. The character transformation process provides a study in big moves leading to big changes. At the end,

> Douglas has reinvented himself. He's confident, urbane, and ready for whatever comes next.

EMPHASIZE EMOTIONAL TRUTH

To be believable, character transformations must be based on sentient experience, grounded in emotional truth. They can't be created by an algorithm because they're unique to each person—to your character's open and secret desires, ambitions, and needs.

The nature of truth, emotional and otherwise, has been debated since the beginning of time in myriad contexts, including philosophy, education, law, journalism, and religion. The word *truth* itself has a dozen or more definitions. It's used to indicate bringing forth from concealment, factual accuracy, actuality, sincerity, and more. A good starting place is to ask yourself what your characters long for and what they're willing to do to get it.

Prompt #7: Your Character's Longing

Name a longing that drives your character's actions.

The Last Thing He Told Me, by Laura Dave, tells the story of Hannah Hall, whose husband, Owen Michaels, disappears. Hannah longs for her husband, for answers, for clarity.

Now it's your turn! Name a longing that drives your character's actions.

To participate in the *Beat the Bots* TikTok community:

- Record a video of your answer and post it, including the hashtag #beatthebots, and tag me at @beatthebotsbook
- You can also tag #authortok and #booktok to connect with other writer and reader communities!
- Watch other writers' videos by visiting the TikTok hashtag #beatthebots

Join the conversation!

Life is a vacillating combination of physical, mental, emotional, and spiritual tests and dilemmas, so your stories should embrace this real-world flux. It was the ancient Greek philosopher Heraclitus who said, "Change is the only constant in life." When you imbue your people with genuine longings and individual perceptions that shift with their changing circumstances, your characters will resonate with emotional truth. Assuming, of course, they're telling the truth. Sometimes what we see is exactly what we think we see. Other times, it's feigned. People wear "masks" to appear normal when they really aren't, or to fit in when they really don't. Needless to say, this applies to unreliable narrators, but it also applies to people who have other reasons to shield their true selves.

> ## Prompt #8: The Lies My Character Tells
>
> Complete this sentence: My character lies about
>
> _____.
>
> To participate in the *Beat the Bots* TikTok community:
>
> - Record a video of your answer and post it, including the hashtag #beatthebots and tag me at @beatthebotsbook
> - You can also tag #authortok and #booktok to connect with other writer and reader communities!
> - Watch other writers' videos by visiting the TikTok hashtag #beatthebots
>
> Join the conversation!

Masking who you really are is a type of lie, or at the least, it's hiding the authentic you. Why would a character do such a thing? Researchers tell us that everyone lies—in fact, Seth Stephens-Davidowitz wrote a book about it: *Everybody Lies: Big Data, New Data, and What the Internet Can Tell Us about Who We Really Are.* He reports that people lie for reasons large and small. People lie to protect other people's feelings or to make themselves look better. People lie to please people they admire or fear. Sometimes people have fun pulling the wool over someone else's eyes. Some people go through life in a haze of pretense—they may not even know they're lying.

BEAT THE BOTS

Other people lie because they're ashamed of something they did, feel, or want. Sometimes they lie to protect their livelihood—it's rare for someone to bite the hand that feeds them. Why do *your* characters lie? Only by understanding what truly motivates people to act as they do can you hope to write the believable situations that underlie credible transformations.

AI Weighs In

I asked a chatbot: How should I align character motivations with my plot?

AI said: *By aligning your plot with your character's motivations, you create a story that feels cohesive and emotionally resonant. The character's journey becomes the driving force behind the narrative, and readers are more likely to become invested in the outcome.* Yes, but this addresses the *why*, not the *how*. AI offered additional suggestions, but they were generic. For instance, the chatbot recommended these steps to start: establish clear motivation and character-driven goals. Both of those suggestions make sense, but they're obvious, and no specific instructions were provided.

It's up to you, the writer, to get to know your characters, their needs, their longings, their fears, and then create a plot that provides them with opportunities to satisfy those needs, longings, and fears.

45

INTENSIFY MEANING THROUGH DETAILS

Adding details that change as the character changes can be a smart way to show (not tell) their transformations. For example, a character known for her terrible diet—she's strictly a burger, fries, and soda kind of gal—falls for a man who's an all-organic all the time kind of guy. He's a nurturer and over time, as their relationship deepens, she gravitates toward his healthier options. Her character transformation is emotionally valid and runs deep; the change in her eating habits illustrates the emotional truth. Novelist Brian Thiem wants to know his characters' habits surrounding coffee, believing that someone who drinks five cups of black before noon is a very different person than someone who has one fancy, frothy cinnamon-flavored cup a day. Likewise, characters' clothes, cars, and homes can signal how they want to be perceived, and can reflect their transformations. Tracking this information on Jane's Character Transformation Roadmap will ensure the internal changes correlate with the external manifestations of the changes to deliver a cohesive message.

LET CHARACTERS TRANSFORM OVER THE COURSE OF A SERIES (OR DON'T)

Many authors want to include character transformations in their series, although each book doesn't necessarily require a sea change of personality like we saw with Jane in *Big Little Lies* or Douglas in *Nightwork*. In my first Josie Prescott Antiques Mystery, *Consigned to Death*, the book starts with my amateur sleuth, Josie, sad, scared, and grieving. At end of *Jane Austen's Lost Letters*, the fourteenth in the series, Josie is excited, reflective, and nervous (in a good way). Here's how I'd express Josie's transformation in one sentence: at the beginning, Josie was a mess, depressed, fearful, and heartbroken; by the end, she was energized, eager for new adventures, and brave.

Of course, there are exceptions to the rule of integrating character transformations. Lee Child says that Jack Reacher, his protagonist, never changes. The setting changes. The other characters change. But not Reacher. In Rex Stout's Nero Wolfe series, neither Mr. Wolfe nor Archie Goodwin, Wolfe's assistant detective and the first-person narrator, change either. However, Archie's character sometimes experiences a disruption (described above in this chapter's FAQ). For example, in *Some Buried Caesar*, Archie meets Lily Rowan, the woman who becomes his girlfriend. During the course of the story, Archie's self-esteem takes a real hit and he loses confidence in his abilities. We witness him struggle to help Mr. Wolfe solve a murder, and celebrate with him when it's clear his efforts were central to their success. The character transformation takes Archie from self-assurance to self-doubt, embarrassment, and shame, and back to his usual confident self. That the transformation resulted from his own efforts, with the support of Lily and Mr. Wolfe, added credibility to the process.

To maintain reader engagement, it's often wise to integrate character transformations for each story within a series, and over the course of the series, but only you, the author, can decide what's best in your series.

UNDERSTAND THE WHY

By leaning into your ability to empathize, you'll develop characters that approach each fork in the road with real-world reactions. One important consideration is that while someone's behavior might seem odd or crazy to you, to that particular character, it's normal. I asked Major George F. Stanko, the director of law enforcement at the Cecil County (Maryland) Sheriff's Office, how law enforcement could investigate a serial killer when there was no motive. He said, "There's always a motive." Chilling. As writers, we need to move beyond the what to assess the why. As an example of the power of understanding *why* people do what they do, let's look at Dr. Donald R. Cressey's Fraud Triangle. He formulated this model to help explain why people commit fraud. He demonstrated that if someone had a strong enough *need* for the money, a good enough *opportunity* to commit the fraud, and the ability to *rationalize* their actions, they were extremely likely to steal the money. The graphic below illustrates this three-pronged analysis.

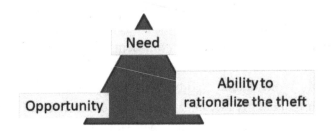

Let's say a bank employee creates false accounts and illegally transfers funds, then withdraws fifty thousand dollars. She's caught. When questioned, she explains that she's an immigrant and her beloved father, still living in her native country, needs an expensive operation or he'll die. She understands that what she did was wrong, but she can't believe that anyone would argue the ethics of her decision. To her bank, fifty thousand dollars is nothing. To her, it's everything. Are people really suggesting she should have let her father die? Using the fraud triangle as a guide, we can see that there was an inevitability to her decision. She had a pressing *need*, the *opportunity* to manipulate the accounts, and was able to *rationalize* her actions.

Delving deeply into what motivates your characters to choose the left fork over the right fork (or vice versa, of course) equips you to optimize the power of emotional truth, and that's how you'll connect with readers on a human level, something artificial intelligence can't match.

Exercise

Jane's Character Transformation Roadmap: Track a Favorite Character's Transformation

To understand how characters evolve over time, choose a favorite book, one you wish you'd written, and track the incidents that lead to character transformations. Analyze them by answering these questions:

1. What about the incident resulted in a transformation?
2. Did the transformation come from an external event or an internal reflection?
3. What about the character's personality, attitudes, beliefs, or feelings made the transformation credible?

4. Using the terminology discussed in this chapter, was the character's reaction to the incident a PAR or a RAP?

5. How did the transformation manifest itself?

In Chuck Hogan's *Prince of Thieves*, for instance, the protagonist, Doug, is a young man who's certain he'll end up in prison or die young, as do so many of the men in his life. Then he meets Claire, and for the first time, he perceives the possibility of salvation. The story revolves around Doug's struggle to become worthy of Claire while resisting his outlaw friends' efforts to pull him back into a life of crime. A pivotal moment in the book is when Doug is shot.

1. *What about the incident resulted in a transformation?* Doug knows he's going to die and is desperate to understand how it came to this.

2. *Did the transformation come from an external event or an internal reflection?* A combination. That he was shot is, of course, external, but if not for his need for mental clarity, he would not have dragged himself to Claire's apartment.

3. *What about the character's personality, attitudes, beliefs, or feelings made the transformation credible?* Doug had struggled since the beginning of the book with an existential decision—to keep along his criminal path or clean up his act.

BEAT THE BOTS

4. *Using the terminology discussed in this chapter, was the character's reaction to the incident a PAR or a RAP?* Definitely a RAP. He reacts, then acts, and only after acting does he process what just happened.

5. *How did the transformation manifest itself?* Doug manages to drag himself to Claire's door. He wants to know why she never asked him to stop robbing banks, explaining he would've done *anything* for her. Claire looks at him like he's crazy. Hogan writes: "And there in her bewilderment, he recognized his grave mistake.... When you give someone the power to save you, you give them the power to destroy you as well." Until that moment, Doug thought they were a couple, not understanding that to Claire, he was just a guy she'd dated a few times. Doug also grasps the deeper meaning—Claire hadn't failed him; he'd failed himself. This shift in perspective makes for a gripping, character-based epiphany—a genuine transformation.

Note that I examined one transformation. To understand the full character transformations process, start at the beginning of the book and track them all. That way, you'll see how the character evolved over the course of the story.

Now it's your turn! I'd love to hear about your experience! Complete this sentence: I used Jane's Character Transformation Roadmap to track [name the character]'s transformation in [name the author and the book], and I learned:

_____.

To participate in the *Beat the Bots* TikTok community:

- Record a video of your answer and post it, including the hashtag #beatthebots and tag me at @beatthebotsbook
- You can also tag #authortok and #booktok to connect with other writer and reader communities!
- Watch other writers' videos by visiting the TikTok hashtag #beatthebots

Join the conversation!

In this chapter, we looked at ways to ensure your characters' actions are grounded in emotional truth and result in credible transformations. In Chapter Three, we'll look at through-line plotting, with an eye to ensuring these two key elements of storytelling (character motivation and plotting) align.

Reflection on Creativity

"When writing a novel a writer should create living people; people, not characters. A character is a caricature."
Ernest Hemingway

CHAPTER THREE

CREATIVITY TACTIC #3
MIND WANDERING: PLOT WITH JANE'S PLOTTING ROADMAP

"A story to me means a plot where there is some surprise.
Because that is how life is—full of surprises."
Isaac Bashevis Singer

PLOT WITH ORIGINALITY

Now that you've decided on which ideas you want to include in your story and determined how your characters will evolve, it's time to plot. (If you have decided to plot first, then work on character transformation, that's just fine!) In this chapter, we'll review a powerful neuroscience technique called "Mind Wandering," also known as "spontaneous task-independent thinking." Your stories will captivate readers with I-can't-wait-to-see-what-happens-next unpredictability. This tactic equips you to adapt Jane's Plotting Roadmap (below and in Appendix Two) to your story by determining what is unexpected to *your* target readers, based on *your* characters, *your* genre, and the story *you* want to tell, not based on ChatGPT's generic suggestions.

Just as typing isn't writing, generative plotting isn't storytelling. Your plot, a series of incidents that, taken together, tells your story, needs to be filled with unexpected, curiosity-inspiring moments, the stuff of page-turners—and the antithesis of predictive plotting, the only method AI can use.

In this chapter, we'll talk about launching your throughline plot, integrating plenty of twists and turns, and creating satisfying endings.

START WITH A COMPELLING NARRATIVE QUESTION

Determining where your story starts is one of the most important and difficult decisions you'll face as a writer. According to the Pew Research Center article, "The General Reading Habits of Americans," you have five to seven seconds, not more, to capture your readers' attention. (I'm not talking about your most loyal fans...I'm talking about a random reader flipping to the beginning of your book in a bookstore or reading the sneak peek available at most online shops.) Let's do the math: People read, on average, 250 words a minute. Call it 240 words for a round number, divided by sixty seconds...people read, on average, four words a second. That means you have somewhere between twenty and twenty-eight words to capture their interest. That's a sentence or two. I'm not telling you to write to a mathematical formula. I'm telling you that your opening

BEAT THE BOTS

matters. The strongest openings present what I call a narrative question. The narrative question represents a promise to your readers—that whatever situation is introduced at the beginning will be resolved by the end. When your ending satisfies the implied promise set out in your narrative question, you create a through-line plot.

So long as your narrative question reveals an emotional truth, it can be delivered with a punch or woven gently into description or dialogue. Make your decision based on your voice, writing style, genre, and reader expectations. This kind of multifaceted analysis on linking your character's emotional truth to qualitative metrics requires human judgment. Artificial intelligence can't compete with your unwavering focus on those emotional truths that will touch your particular readers' hearts.

Your narrative question serves multiple purposes. It must:

1. Engage readers' interest
2. Create a mood
3. Inspire curiosity
4. Get people thinking
5. Introduce people and a situation that includes an implied question—a conflict, a problem, an opportunity, or a dilemma
6. Offer an implied promise that by the end the conflict, problem, opportunity, or dilemma will be addressed or resolved

Further, it needs to be unusual, evocative, emotional, and incident-based. Let's take a look at each of these imperatives separately.

- *Unusual.* Publishers want stories that they haven't seen before. Think about it...if what you write isn't unusual, it will read as unoriginal, as derivative, the kind of ho-hum storytelling a chatbot can produce.
- *Evocative.* The best writing thrusts you into a memory or a feeling or a mood—it evokes something sensory-based and relatable. Often, what is evocative is thematic (see Chapter Eight).
- *Emotional.* Never neglect story. The best plots marry action and emotion—the more apparent the emotional truth, the deeper the connection with your readers.
- *Incident-based.* Don't start with reflections. Start with action. "Action" doesn't necessarily mean a car chase or shoot-em-up drama; it refers to anything that eases or catapults the reader into an incident that is already in progress.

Your narrative question drives the plot and informs your characters' decisions. While there is no one best way to frame your narrative question, the more you lay out an emotional truth, the more likely your readers are to connect with it. If your narrative question is weak, vague, unclear, muddied, boring, delayed, or missing, you'll lose readers. If it's vivid, clear, compelling, intriguing, and immediate, readers will be hooked from the start.

BEAT THE BOTS

As you read the following examples, ask yourself if these varied openings satisfy all six parameters and the four imperatives outlined above.

Oyinkan Braithwaite's *My Sister the Serial Killer*, a thriller

WORDS

Ayoola summons me with these words—Korede, I killed him. I had hoped I would never hear those words again.

BLEACH

I bet you didn't know that bleach masks the smell of blood. Most people use bleach indiscriminately, assuming it is a catchall product, never taking the time to read the list of ingredients on the back, never taking the time to return to the recently wiped surface to take a closer look. Bleach will disinfect, but it's not great for cleaning residue, so I use it only after I have first scrubbed the bathroom of all traces of life, and death.

Do you see how Braithwaite's opening provides information about the characters, while providing a clear narrative question? How many men has Ayoola killed? Why? Who is Korede and why is she helping clean up? By the end of the book, we expect to get answers to all these questions—and we do—Korede is the killer's sister, and to her, loyalty to her family is more important than life itself.

> ## Chris Grabenstein, *The Island of Dr. Libris*, middle-grade fantasy
>
> The Theta Project
> Lab Note #316
> Prepared by
> Dr. Xiang Libris, Psy. D., Dlit, EGD
>
> I am thrilled to report that, after an exhaustive search, I have found the ideal subject for our first field test, which will commence as soon as Billy G., a twelve-year-old male with a very vivid imagination arrives on site.
>
> His mother will be busy. His father will be away. He will be bored.
>
> In short, Billy G. will be perfect.

Grabenstein's opening inspires reader curiosity while setting a distinctive mood: playful, mysterious, intriguing. We want to know more about the Theta Project and the field test, and we're eager to meet Billy. These emotional truths will surely resonate with a preteen—the benign neglect from busy or absent parents and boredom. The ending, which the *New York Times* remarked featured a "winning generosity and sweetness" fulfills the implied promise of the narrative question.

BEAT THE BOTS

Emily Henry, *Beach Read*, romance

The House

I have a fatal flaw.

I like to think we all do. Or at least that makes it easier for me when I'm writing—building my heroines and heroes up around this one self-sabotaging trait, hinging everything that happens to them on a specific character-istic: the thing they learned to do to protect themselves and can't let go of, even when it stops serving them.

Maybe, for example, you didn't have much control over your life as a kid. So, to avoid disappointment, you learned never to ask yourself what you truly wanted. And it worked for a long time. Only now, upon realizing you didn't *get* what you didn't *know* you wanted, you're barreling down the highway in a midlife-crisis-mobile with a suitcase full of cash and a man named Stan in your trunk.

Maybe your fatal flaw is that you don't use turn signals.

Or maybe, like, me, you're a hopeless romantic.

Henry's narrative question is clear—can a hopeless roman-tic find love? Spoiler alert—yes! The novel ends with a mar-riage proposal from an unlikely suiter that's gleefully accepted.

Note that in all these examples, a major component of the narrative question is surprise. The Mind Wandering creativity tactic (discussed below) is a reliable tool to come up with these deliciously unexpected surprises.

FAQ

Q: Can you spend too much time Mind Wandering?

A: It's important to differentiate between controlled and uncontrolled Mind Wandering. For our purposes in coming up with useful Plot Twists, Plot Reversals, and Moments of Heightened Danger (TRDs, discussed later in this chapter), we'll take a controlled approach. We'll allow our minds to meander at will, but only after determining our core question and for a prescribed amount of time. Controlled Mind Wandering is different from uncontrolled Mind Wandering, which includes idle, pleasant daydreaming, pervasive fantasizing, and anxiety-producing fretting. To answer your question, you'll see below where I discuss how to use this tactic that I recommend ten-minute increments. That's long enough to generate exciting TRDs, but not so long that it will interfere with your productivity.

BEAT THE BOTS

ADAPT JANE'S PLOTTING ROADMAP TO SUIT YOUR STORY

The stories that keep people turning pages are filled with unexpected twists and turns. As novelist Ernest J. Gaines said, "I believe that the writer should tell a story. I believe in plot." To many writers, though, while storytelling is instinctive—plotting is not. Jane's Plotting Roadmap helps you identify pivotal twists and determine where in your through-line plot they should occur. The Mind Wandering creativity tactic guides you in selecting and integrating plot Twists, plot Reversals, and Moments of Heightened Danger (TRDs) at strategically sound moments.

The phrase "plot twists" is an umbrella term encompassing three specific techniques.

1. Plot Twists: something unexpected, but not the opposite
2. Plot Reversals: something unexpected, and the opposite
3. Moments of Heightened Danger: something that adds urgency and dread to the story.

Properly placing Plot Twists, Plot Reversals, and Moments of Heightened Danger (TRDs) ensures your story's pace aligns with reader expectations based on your genre (discussed below).

61

Prompt #9: Select a Favorite Narrative Question

Select a favorite book and identify the narrative question. Share the narrative question and explain why it's a favorite.

For example, I might select *Angel's Tip* by Alafair Burke. Here's how the book begins.

Chapter One

> The man leaned forward on his stool to make room for a big-boned redhead who was reaching for the two glasses of pinot grigio she'd ordered. He asked for another Heineken while the bartender was down his way, figuring he could enjoy a second beer before anyone in the restaurant bothered to take note of him.
>
> He was good at blending into the background in even the most generic settings, but he certainly wasn't going to stand out here, given the commotion at the other end of the bar. Four men in suits and loosened ties were throwing back limoncello shots, their second round with the group of girls that had brought the man to the restaurant in the first place. Actually, his interest was not in all three—just the tall blond one.

> He was used to taking more time with his selections, but he needed to find a girl tonight. This would be his first time on a schedule, let alone a tight one.

Here's why I chose it: This last phrase of the first paragraph alerts the reader that the narrator has a reason to want to go unnoticed. The next paragraph explains why. The last paragraph reveals that this isn't the man's first time doing whatever it is he's planning. The ominous tone creates suspense. By the end of the book, we know we're going to find out what the man does to the tall blonde. We're also going to learn what drives him and why there's urgency tonight, when there usually isn't. This 168-word excerpt meets all the metrics of excellence in narrative questions. It:

- engages readers' interest
- creates a mood
- inspires curiosity
- gets people thinking
- introduces people and a situation that includes an implied question
- offers an implied promise that by the end the implied question will be addressed

Also, it's unusual, evocative, emotional, and incident based.

Now it's your turn! Select a favorite book and identify the narrative question. Share the narrative question and explain why it's a favorite.

To participate in the *Beat the Bots* TikTok community:

- Record a video of your answer and post it, including the hashtag #beatthebots and tag me at @beatthebotsbook
- You can also tag #authortok and #booktok to connect with other writer and reader communities!
- Watch other writers' videos by visiting the TikTok hashtag #beatthebots

Join the conversation!

GET READY FOR A ROAD TRIP!

Jane's Plotting Roadmap offers a graphic representation designed to help you decide where and when to add relevant TRDs.

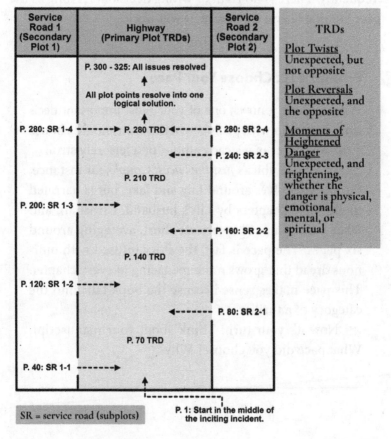

Notice the center highway. This route follows your primary plot, your through-line. Your story will start at the bottom and end at the top. Periodically, something will happen to interrupt the pace of travel—a TRD. Where you place TRDs along the main highway largely depends on your genre. Thrillers, for instance, may feature a TRD every page or two. Some literary novels operate at a much more leisurely pace, with a TRD occurring only every one hundred pages, or even less frequently. There is no right or wrong decision. As long as the pace is suitable and consistent, it will work.

Prompt #10: Choose Your Pace

When writing a novel, one of your most important decisions has to do with pacing, whether you should choose a rip-roaring tear, a steady amble, or a leisurely stroll.

In Mary Kubica's *Just the Nicest Couple*, for instance, the story revolves around Lily and Jake, but is narrated in alternate chapters by Lily's husband, Christian, and Jake's wife, Nina. Chapters are short, averaging around six pages. The pace is fast, the story infused with ominous dread that grows more menacing in every chapter. This pace makes sense because the book falls into the category of a thriller.

Now it's your turn! Think about your manuscript. What pace did you choose? Why?

BEAT THE BOTS

To participate in the *Beat the Bots* TikTok community:

- Record a video of your answer and post it, including the hashtag #beatthebots and tag me at @beatthebotsbook
- You can also tag #authortok and #booktok to connect with other writer and reader communities!
- Watch other writers' videos by visiting the TikTok hashtag #beatthebots

Join the conversation!

You'll also note two service roads running along either side of the main highway, abbreviated as SR1 and SR2. These represent your two subplots. Two subplots work well in most novels; integrate more and you risk confusing your readers; develop fewer and you risk oversimplifying your story. Jane's Plotting Road Map allows you to lay out separate storylines for each. Start by planning your primary plot. Then, after you determine your two secondary plots, repeat the process for each of them. Ideally, each subplot works in tandem with your primary plot and they all come together to create a logical and satisfactory conclusion. Just as with your primary plot, increasing the frequency of incidents that relate to each of your subplots speeds the pace; decreasing their frequency slows it down.

MAKE TRD DECISIONS BASED ON CHARACTER TRAITS

You can't plot in a vacuum. You need to account for all the elements of your story: character, setting, atmosphere, action, dialogue, exposition, and other factors. Some TRDs are apparent, a stunning shift in perspective, or a revelation that catches readers utterly unaware—the man behind the curtain in L. Frank Baum's *The Wonderful Wizard of Oz*, for example. That ending exemplifies an ideal; it showcases what Aristotle described in his *Poetics* as "surprising, yet inevitable." Other TRDs are more nuanced, working well because they're consistent with the character's personality, or otherwise align with the story.

Pro Tip: Read with a Writer's Eye to Become a Better Writer

TRDs do more than help you write productively. They also help you read more analytically, which will, of course, help you write better. In addition to providing forward momentum to your plot, TRDs control pacing. This dual benefit—TRDs inspire curiosity with unexpected incidents and control the pace—demonstrates their power.

In Chapter Two, the exercise invited you to deconstruct a favorite book, one you wish you'd written, looking at character transformations. The same principle works with TRDs. All novels, in all genres, include them, but you may never have thought of analyzing books from this perspective. It can be a revelation to discover the kinds of TRDs the author integrates and how often they appear.

Another interesting phenomenon is that not everyone agrees whether an incident is, in fact, a TRD. In other words, what is unexpected to one person is par for the course to another. This divergence underscores the importance of knowing your genre and your reader expectations.

On the first page of *Seven Years of Darkness: A Novel*, by You-Jeong Jeong, for instance, the protagonist lies, saying he doesn't know where a village is located. Because the lie is apparent to the reader, it's a startling TRD. Why on Earth would someone lie about something so prosaic? This early TRD does more than inspire reader curiosity; it also shows that the protagonist is an unreliable narrator.

A final note about using TRDs: Jane's Plotting Roadmap is intended to be a help, not a hindrance. Feel free to adapt it for your own use. A good place to start is to tap into your inner muse with the Mind Wandering creativity tactic.

Prompt #11: I Hear Myself

Mind Wandering is controlled daydreaming, yet in some quarters, daydreaming has a bad reputation. If you admit to daydreaming, people may think you're lazy or shirking responsibility. Cognitive psychologist and neuroscientist David J. Levitin, the author of *The Organized Mind: Thinking Straight in the Age of Information Overload*, disagrees. He writes: "That daydreaming mode turns out to be restorative. It's like hitting the reset button in your brain. And you don't get in that daydreaming mode typically by texting and Facebooking. You get in it by disengaging." Journalist Carl Honoré, the author of *In Praise of Slow: Challenging the Cult of Speed*, says, "You don't have to work for Google, or any of the other firms encouraging staff to pursue personal projects on company time, to use slowness to unlock your creativity. Anyone can do it. Start by clearing space in your schedule for rest, daydreaming and serendipity. Take breaks away from your desk, especially when you get stuck on a problem."

For me, Mind Wandering, structured daydreaming, lets me run simulations of various TRDs, trying them on for size, as it were. By spending time with the characters who will be executing the TRD, I get a good sense of which one will work best for *that* character at *this* point in the story. When I daydream, I realize what works and what doesn't, and why.

BEAT THE BOTS

Now it's your turn! Complete this sentence: When I daydream, I realize

_____.

To participate in the *Beat the Bots* TikTok community:

- Record a video of your answer and post it, including the hashtag #beatthebots and tag me at @beatthebotsbook
- You can also tag #authortok and #booktok to connect with other writer and reader communities!
- Watch other writers' videos by visiting the Tik-Tok hashtag #beatthebots

Join the conversation!

USE MIND WANDERING TO DISCOVER UNEXPECTED TRDS

The Mind Wandering creativity tactic provides direction while allowing flexibility—two attributes certain to strengthen your writing process, neither of which can be replicated by AI. Mind Wandering uses your intelligence, your humanity, and your ingenuity to come up with curiosity-inspiring TRDs.

Let's start by discussing what Mind Wandering is not—it isn't uncontrolled daydreaming, distracted thinking, or a waste of

71

time. Mind Wandering equips you to do just the opposite: you'll be able to efficiently access ideas that are already in your brain.

While it might seem counterintuitive, letting your mind wander can lead to creative breakthroughs. In an interview with *Forbes*, Dr. Moshe Bar, the former director of the Cognitive Neuroscience Lab at Harvard Medical School and the author of *Mindwandering*, explained that "Creativity requires broad, expansive mind wandering. During creative thinking, we explore our web of memories for new combinations and novel solutions." Professor Ethan Kross, director of the Emotion & Self Control Laboratory at the University of Michigan and author of *Chatter, The Voice in Our Head, Why It Matters, and How to Harness It* concurs, saying that Mind Wandering "facilitates creative problem solving." We're going to use the technique to come up with exceptional TRDs. These five steps will help ensure you optimize your experience.

1. Time

Allocate ten minutes. You'll be amazed how many innovative thoughts will come to you in such a brief period of time. While you can extend the time, you want to avoid open-ended Mind Wandering sessions. We want to approach the process purposefully. I have conducted effective Mind Wandering sessions in as little as three minutes. Set a timer to ensure you're aware of an end point.

2. Environment

Some people find listening to music facilitates the Mind Wandering process; others prefer silence. Some people enjoy thinking while walking; others prefer to sit quietly with a cup

BEAT THE BOTS

of coffee. The environment itself doesn't matter. What does matter is that the environment is comfortable for you. In other words, the more relaxed and content you feel, the more likely the Mind Wandering process is to work for you.

Being exposed to water, be it the ocean, a lake, a river, a stream, or an indoor water fountain facilitates creative thinking. Wallace J. Nichols, a marine biologist, has conducted research that proves that being in or around water reduces stress. In his book titled *Blue Mind*, he wrote, "...our brains are hardwired to react positively to water ... being near it can calm and connect us, increase innovation and insight, and even heal what's broken." Forests provide solace, too. The Japanese Ministry of Agriculture, Forestry, and Fisheries created the term *shinrin-yoku*, which translates to "forest bathing" or "absorbing the forest atmosphere." The ministry explains that the practice encourages people to spend time in nature—no actual bathing required. The goal of forest bathing is to live in the present moment while immersing your senses in the sights and sounds of a natural setting.

Even if you can't leave your home for a walk on the beach or stroll through the woods, you can approximate the mood by playing any of scores of free nature videos widely available on YouTube, the sounds of waterfalls, or birds chirping, or forest creatures cavorting. Experiment with different environments to see what suits you best.

3. Attitude

An article hosted by the National Library of Medicine called "Being Creative Makes You Happier: The Positive Effect of Creativity on Subjective Well-Being," by Cher-Yi Tan et al., starts with this declarative sentence: "The impact of happiness on creativity is well-established." In short, the happier you are, the more creative you're likely to be. Dr. Bar (the author of *Mindwandering*) agrees: "If you'd like to summon some creative meandering, your best chances are while you're in a good mood."

What tools do you already have in your personal toolbox to help yourself adopt a positive mindset? For example, deep breathing, meditation, petting a cat, journaling, and repeating certain uplifting phrases (mind speak) like "You can do it!" and "You're going to come up with fabulous ideas!" have all be shown to support positive thinking.

Prompt #12: My Best Self

What does your ideal creativity-inspiring environment look like? Why? Singer, actress, and screenwriter Michelle Phillips said, "I call my tiki bar my tiki office. This beautiful, open-air space is such a creative environment for me."

Now it's your turn! What does your ideal creativity-inspiring environment look like? Why?

To participate in the *Beat the Bots* TikTok community:

- Record a video of your answer and post it, including the hashtag #beatthebots and tag me at @beatthebotsbook

- You can also tag #authortok and #book-tok to connect with other writer and reader communities!
- Watch other writers' videos by visiting the TikTok hashtag #beatthebots

Join the conversation!

4. Your Goal

Ask a specific question. Say to yourself, "I need a **T**, an **R**, or a **D** about…" then let your mind go. Start by remembering a satisfying or happy experience, the first time you met someone you love, the day you received some good news, the first time you accomplished something you'd been working on. Let this reflection serve as a jumping off point, then let your thoughts roam from there. You'll breeze through memories as your brain seeks relevant ideas that can be combined in new ways, simulating outcomes.

5. Logistics

Listen to your thoughts. Not all TRD ideas will be relevant or useful. That's alright. It's likely that some will be. Don't judge them yet, just track them. Just as we did with coming up with initial ideas, write them down or record them into your phone. When your time has expired, give yourself a pat on the back. You just completed a uniquely human endeavor—you mined your own brain for worthy ideas on that most complex task—identifying the unexpected.

AI Weighs In

I asked a chatbot: Can you give me an example of how to use a character trait to develop a compelling plot twist?

AI said: *Certainly! Let's consider a character trait and how it can be used to develop a compelling plot twist.*

Character Trait: Trustworthiness

Character: Sarah, a trusted and loyal friend

Plot Twist: Sarah's Betrayal

ChatGPT went on to delineate the steps: establish the trait, conflict with the trait, foreshadow, insert a plot twist, and reveal the motivation, consequences and resolution. This structure is helpful. It ensures an appropriate arc for the twist, but notice that it's nonspecific. Yes, AI can help. But it takes your understanding of *your* characters and *your* story and *your* ability to craft evocative prose to make it work.

ASSESS YOUR TRDS

Plotting with TRDs ensures your stories will be suspenseful, creating appealing urgency. To assess each TRD's merit, ask yourself these four questions.

1. *Is your TRD intriguing? Does it inspire curiosity?*
2. *Does your TRD evoke a memory or sensory experience that will resonate with your readers?*
3. *Is your TRD incident based, grounded in action or dialogue?*
4. *Does your TRD reveal an emotional truth?*

If you can answer yes to all four questions, your TRD is likely to work well. If you can't, ask yourself if you can tweak it to add in the missing elements.

And remember the words of the great crime fiction novelist Raymond Chandler: "When in doubt have a man come through a door with a gun."

Exercise

Mind Wandering: Expect the Unexpected

1. Once you're ready, with pen and paper or a recording device at hand, think about what is going on in your story at the point you want to insert a TRD.
2. Think happy thoughts, not about your story. If you're sensitive to environment, let your mind drift to the actual or virtual rolling waves, the sun-dappled lawn, the birds calling to their friends, or whatever gives you pleasure to see and hear.
3. Ask yourself what is the most unexpected thing that could happen here. Go through the options for **Ts**, **Rs**, and **Ds** one at a time. Jot notes as ideas come to you.
4. Complete the four-step assessment process delineated above.

Here's how I might approach the process. Let's say I have a character, Andrea, who shies away from confrontation. By integrating examples of Andrea's disinclination to argue a point or stand up for herself into the story *before* the situation described below occurs, the TRDs will seem fitting, not contrived. The TRD options I suggest wouldn't work if Andrea didn't possess that characteristic, and if readers hadn't already witnessed it in action. Here's Andrea's story:

BEAT THE BOTS

Andrea buys a dress on sale after work. Unfortunately, when she tries it on at home, she discovers it's too tight. She's disappointed because she loves it, but she also feels some anxiety and shame. Returning a purchase is so awkward. And she guesses she must have gained a few pounds, a horrifying thought. She dreads the clerk asking why she wants to return it. Then she realizes she's lost the receipt. And she paid cash. Her fretfulness costs her sleep and by the time she gets to work in the morning, she's exhausted and distraught. She tells herself not to be stupid, that she's a grown woman, not a whining baby, but her self-flagellation only heightens her despair. The clock ticks slowly until her lunch hour finally arrives and she drags herself to the shop.

Now plot it out. Andrea expects to be ridiculed, shamed, or harassed.

- What could happen next that would strike my readers as unexpected, but not the opposite (a **T**)?
- Alternately, what could happen next that would come off as unexpected *and* the opposite (an **R**)?
- And what could happen next that would represent heightened danger, be it physical, emotional, mental, or spiritual (a **D**)?

Andrea assumes she'll be questioned. She anticipates the clerk will ask for the receipt and when she confesses that she doesn't have it—note the language choice—not that she *told* the clerk she doesn't have the receipt or *announced* it or *explained* it; rather, she *confessed* it—she wouldn't be surprised to be escorted by security to a back office to wait for the police. That's in keeping with her personality, isn't it? So as she prepares to confess that she doesn't have the receipt, she expects the clerk will smirk and roll his eyes. Maybe she frets that his gaze will drop to her hips—remember, she's afraid she's gained weight—and she's mortified.

Here's how I might think this situation through.

A Plot Twist

The clerk says, "Darn...I'm so sorry...I hate when this happens. Unfortunately, I don't have the authority to accept the return without a receipt and the manager isn't here. I know this isn't what you want to hear, but I'm afraid you'll need to come back tomorrow."

He's nice, right? He's not accusing Andrea of anything. It's a totally unexpected response and a huge relief.

The clerk goes on to say, "But guess what? I can give you this five-dollars-off coupon for the inconvenience."

This isn't the *opposite* that we expected. It's *different*. It is a Twist.

A Plot Reversal

The man behind the counter says, "No problem." He lowers his voice to a whisper and adds, "Don't quote me, but this brand runs small." He gives Andrea her money back, and she's out the door in thirty seconds flat with her dignity intact and her anxiety a distant memory.

This is a **Reversal**, the exact opposite of what she expected.

A Moment of Heightened Danger

After the clerk explains that she'll need to come back tomorrow to talk to the manager, Andrea accepts the five-dollars-off coupon and walks over to look at a display of sweaters. And boom, in comes a guy with a gun.

That's a moment of heightened **Danger**.

Note that I set myself up for success by following the Mind Wandering creativity tactic steps. Then I role-played options. In the process I came up with three intriguing plot twists, a **T**, an **R**, and a **D**. I did this by working the logic based on my particular character at this particular point in the story. Now let's reflect on the process. What did you discover? I discovered that my TRD had to align with my character's personality.

Now it's your turn! After you finish the four steps of this exercise, complete this sentence: I used Mind Wandering to come up with a **TRD**, and discovered

_____.

To participate in the *Beat the Bots* TikTok community:

- Record a video of your answer and post it, including the hashtag #beatthebots and tag me at @beatthebotsbook
- You can also tag #authortok and #booktok to connect with other writer and reader communities!
- Watch other writers' videos by visiting the TikTok hashtag #beatthebots

Join the conversation!

In this chapter, we discussed the power of a throughline plot, starting with your narrative question and working through the TRD-idea generating process using the Mind Wandering creativity tactic. In the next chapter, we'll discuss setting the stage—how to infuse your settings with vitality and meaning.

Reflection on Creativity

"Creativity is a wild mind and a disciplined eye."
Dorothy Parker

CHAPTER FOUR

CREATIVITY TACTIC #4

CONCEPTUAL BLENDING: CHOOSE SETTINGS THAT INSPIRE READER CURIOSITY

"What gets me going with a story is the atmosphere, the visual imagery, and then I people it with characters, not the other way around."
Ann Beattie

CREATE SETTINGS THAT COMMUNICATE MORE THAN PLACE

Artificial intelligence can generate text to show what a place looks like, but it can't describe how your characters feel about that place. Only you can do that. In this chapter, we'll delve deeply into Conceptual Blending, a creativity tactic that helps you bring together disparate factors such as culture, language, habits, standards, values, customs, food, mores, pace of life, and so on to create a world readers can envision and want to visit.

The Conceptual Blending creativity tactic tracks people's reactions to settings, an endeavor that requires human judgment, not the superficial or derivative output provided by AI—if AI can provide any information at all. For example, when ChatGPT was asked what *Blue Bloods'* lead character, Police Commissioner Reagan, thought about New York City, it only offered general commentary about the character and the city (and warned that its comments may lack relevance because of its time-based "knowledge cutoff"). Here's the bottom line when it comes to creating relevant settings: if you want to know what a character feels about a setting, ask the character, not a chatbot.

FAQ

Q: Any tips for creating a unique fantasy world?

A: Whenever you're creating an all-new setting, the kind of invented environments we see in fantasy, horror, science fiction, and romantasy (a newer hybrid, combining romance and fantasy), world-building is paramount. Three crucial factors to define are:

1. Geography to showcase your characters' strengths and weaknesses

BEAT THE BOTS

2. Your characters' emotional reactions to the setting
3. Societal systems relating to the setting that are consistent and logical

For instance, let's say you're writing a novel about an underwater world. You'd need to integrate grueling terrain, such as caverns and mountain ranges, to enable your characters to demonstrate their athleticism, bravery, or brains (geography). Your protagonist should long for something he cannot have, to live on dry land, perhaps. To create longing through juxtaposition, you could allow him access to a sand bar, where he can see grass and forests. His dream becomes palpable, the terrain he longs for so close, and yet so far away (emotional reaction). In this underwater world, let's create a kind of pecking order, one that provides for warriors to inhabit the deeper environs, relegating the rest of society to the less-desirable surface areas (societal system).

These three factors, taken together, ensure your made-up world is rich with detail, and suitable for your ideas, the people who inhabit it, your through-line plot, and your reader expectations.

Note that all elements of storytelling interrelate. You can't determine your setting without considering your characters' attitudes, and AI can't begin to understand your characters' relationship with those places. I asked Jonathan Santlofer, the bestselling author of international thrillers, how he creates such evocative settings. He explained his process this way:

> Think of your setting as a character, what it looks like, how it feels. What makes a particular country, city, or town distinctive? What are its predominant colors, the buildings, the streets? How does it smell? What are the people like? Every place has something that sets it apart. Amsterdam has its canals and bicycles (something I used in my novel, *The Lost Van Gogh*), New York City its constant noise (identify how it varies from neighborhood to neighborhood, how it affects your characters in a scene or the general mood of a scene). Biggest tip: If you are setting a book in a foreign city, go! Do not think you can get away with visiting it on the internet. You will get things wrong and people who know the place will be annoyed and not trust what you have to say. Plus, you never know what you will discover that will inspire a passage you never thought to write. For smaller interior settings the same rules apply, the feel, the smell, the ambient noise, the light, whether it's two people in a restaurant, or several in a home. Remember, the setting will affect how your characters speak, the tone, the volume, and their body language. People act differently in different settings.

BEAT THE BOTS

CHOOSE SETTINGS FOR ATMOSPHERE

Setting represents a core element of novel writing, alongside plot, characters, theme, voice, and other factors central to storytelling success.

Broadly, setting refers to time and place. Time doesn't mean only the hour of the day or the day of the week, although, of course, that's part of it, and often details are crucial. Timing starts with a much broader decision: the era. Is this the Middle Ages? The Renaissance? The Great Depression? The 1960s? Now? The future?

Likewise, place doesn't refer only to the den, the patio, the pizza joint around the corner, or the boats bobbing in the marina. These are all settings, but they are not *the* setting for your story. Place refers to something grander than a singular location—place has to answer this question: *where in the world* does your story take place? The mountains of Colorado? The Gulf Coast of Texas? The African savanna? A fantasy world of your own invention? Once you establish the geography of your story, *then* you can and should fill in the local details, whether we are in the pizza joint or the marina.

Prompt #13: Setting Should Reflect an Emotional Truth

Larry McMurtry's *The Last Picture Show* uses how characters feel about their hometown of Anarene, Texas, to reveal their innermost needs and desires. Jacy can't wait to get out of Anarene. She goes to Dallas to attend college and

87

never comes home. Sonny decides he'd better get out, too, and drives away, hoping for a fresh start, then realizes everything he wants is in Anarene, if only he'd had the brains to see it. He turns his truck around and returns home.

If you ask Jacy what she truly thinks about Anarene, she'd say, "Good riddance." If you asked Sonny, he'd say, "It's not so bad. It's got a lot going for it."

Now it's your turn! Complete this sentence: If you ask my character what they truly think about where they live, they'd say:

_____.

To participate in the *Beat the Bots* TikTok community:

- Record a video of your answer and post it, including the hashtag #beatthebots and tag me at @beatthebotsbook
- You can also tag #authortok and #booktok to connect with other writer and reader communities!
- Watch other writers' videos by visiting the TikTok hashtag #beatthebots

Join the conversation!

From a writing perspective, your reader should know, from the very first page, if not the first paragraph, when and where this story takes place. Although sometimes implication about place or scope of the geography is sufficient. For example, we don't learn that Charlie, the fifteen-year-old protagonist in Stephen Chbosky's coming-of-age young-adult novel *The Perks of Being a Wallflower*, lives in the Pittsburgh area until around page forty. Or how about Pierre Boulle's science fiction classic, published in the United States as *Planet of the Apes*? In this book, the setting isn't revealed until the end. In fact, the setting revelation is the final twist. Explorers from Earth visit a distant planet and discover that apes are in charge while humans have been reduced to a state of bestiality. When the book was adapted for the screen, Rod Serling (and others) made the ending more explicit by having Taylor (called Ulysses in the book) see an arm jutting up out of the beach. It's the Statue of Liberty. Only then does Taylor realize that he wasn't on a distant planet after all—he was on Earth all along, and apes have taken over. In Emma Donoghue's *Room: A Novel*, a story told from five-year old Jack's point of view, the geography is limited to one room. His mother was kidnapped seven years earlier, and the room where they're imprisoned is all Jack has ever known.

KNOW YOUR READER EXPECTATIONS

As with all decisions relating to key elements, one factor to assess is your reader expectations regarding setting. Readers of historical fiction want to be immersed in the period, for instance, not only to see what was there and what wasn't, but to experience how people lived. In Diana Gabaldon's novel, *Outlander*, for instance, the Scottish Highlands come alive with lush descriptions—but these descriptions occur only as characters interact with the environment. While in the Scottish Highlands in 1945, Claire touches a stone in circular henge and is mysteriously transported back to 1743. Marrying historical romance to time travel, the events feel contemporary. The fields of heather, the craggy rocks, the dark castles, the mysterious stones—every element evokes a sense of time and place. In Mary Kubica's *Just the Nicest Couple* (also discussed in Chapter Three), Lily and Christian's home abuts a public hiking trail with a river beyond. Strangers walk by. The lack of privacy permeates the atmosphere. At the beginning, they're certain that the river view is worth the "small sacrifice." As the story unfolds, however, their exposure makes them feel increasingly vulnerable. You, the reader, are there with them, in the woods, in the open fields, inside their house, where anyone can watch them from behind a tree, secure they themselves won't be seen.

Contemporary romance readers crave the entire romance package, not simply a love story. They want to vicariously experience a grand romance, to be transported to another world. They don't merely want to walk down the Champs-Élysées in Paris—that's a place they feel as if they know well from the countless books, movies, and television shows that have shown it. They want a special experience. Take them someplace they can't go on their own. You could take them to an appointment at the American embassy in Paris or let them attend a party at the ambassador's residence. Don't merely send them into the National Gallery of Art in London; let them sit in on a curatorial meeting with the king's archivist. Don't make them sit passively on the outside patio at Bangkok's swanky Peninsula Hotel, or if you do, be certain they see something remarkable, like a woman in in a tight black dress and stiletto heels jumping onto a commuter boat traveling along the Chao Phraya River. Readers would rather go on an elephant ride through

BEAT THE BOTS

the jungle outside Bangkok or get a sexy soapy massage in the Huay Kwang section of the city than sit quietly in a hotel room. When writing unusual locations, go big. This principle isn't limited to romance readers. Most readers want to spend time in settings they don't know, or settings that, while they may be familiar, are freshly envisioned.

Judith Guest's novel *Ordinary People*, for instance, looks at an affluent family's reactions to a tragedy. The nondistinctive environment—the kind of upper middle–class suburban oasis found in all fifty states—casts the extraordinary events into sharp relief. Dealing with themes of life and death, survival and suicide, trust and betrayal (discussed in more detail in Chapter Eight), this work of literary fiction uses its affluent location as a counterpoint to the desolate emotions the characters must confront.

Prompt #14: Personification Brings Settings to Life

Dictionary.com defines "personification" as "the attribution of human nature or character to animals, inanimate objects, or abstract notions." Personification increases engagement since readers are required to imagine the connection you describe, an active process.

To enhance your theme, add personification to one specific element of setting. In the horror novel *The Haunting of Hill House*, author Shirley Jackson uses personification to bring terrifying menace to the house. Consider this sentence, from page one of the novel: "Hill House, not sane, stood by itself against its hills, holding darkness within." Shel Silverstein personified an apple tree in his picture book *The Giving Tree*. He wrote: "Once there was a tree, and she loved a little boy." In both examples, an element of the setting becomes a device to reinforce the theme—one filled with terror, the other filled with love.

Choose something specific about your setting, an old stone wall, a towering skyscraper, a stained glass window, a solar panel, a corn field, an herb garden in the kitchen window. Ask yourself how *that element* feels about your character. Start by naming the element, then complete this sentence: When the [element of setting] looks at my character, it feels

_____.

To participate in the *Beat the Bots* TikTok community:

- Record a video of your answer and post it, including the hashtag #beatthebots and tag me at @beatthebotsbook
- You can also tag #authortok and #booktok to connect with other writer and reader communities!
- Watch other writers' videos by visiting the TikTok hashtag #beatthebots

Join the conversation!

ALIGN SETTING AND THEME

Theme, which we'll discuss further in Chapter Eight, refers to a dominant idea or unifying principle, often revolving around a central conflict, allegiance versus betrayal, hope versus despair, love versus hate. While theme figures into every aspect of your novel, from characters' longings (see Chapter Two) to your plot (see Chapter Three), it can also add complexity and intrigue to your setting. To maximize this thematic power, you need to ensure your settings highlight your underlying conflicts. To do so, it's important to understand the four kinds of conflict: physical, mental, spiritual, and emotional.

When we think of conflict, we often think of physical altercations, but the other kinds are equally potent. Mental conflict refers to intellectual challenges or difficulties; emotional conflicts relate to feelings; and spiritual conflicts address issues such as self-esteem and faith.

These four categories of conflict are not mutually exclusive. For example, Gary Paulsen's *Hatchet*, a middle-grade adventure novel, considers the plight of twelve-year-old Brian, who is lost in the Canadian wilderness when the pilot of the small-engine plane he's traveling on has a heart attack and dies. Brian, a city kid, finds himself utterly out of his element, totally alone with only the clothes on his back and the hatchet on his belt. Scary. Over the course of the novel, he's forced to call on physical strength, mental acuity, emotional courage, and spiritual confidence he didn't know he possessed. Here are the conflict-based questions he had to face, all related to the unfamiliar and unforgiving setting.

- Physical: What do I eat? Where do I sleep? What predators must I vanquish?

- Mental: How can I keep my bounty safe from interlopers? How can I make fire? How can I avoid getting eaten alive by swarms of insects?
- Emotional: How can I cope with the terror? How do I control my panic? How can I handle the overwhelming feeling of being abandoned, even though I know I wasn't actually abandoned, that the crash was just a horrible accident?
- Spiritual: Can I find the inner strength to do this? Do I have the wherewithal to survive?

Brian's transformation from self-doubting child to confident and capable adolescent is a classic example of character transformation. How he does it is a great example of through-line plotting. The setting is the central element in this tale of survival.

WRITE LEAN

Early novels tended to include lengthy geographic depictions that many of today's readers would find boring. Those writers appropriately painted pictures of places few readers would ever see. With the advent of television and the internet, even dedicated armchair travelers have different expectations today than did readers of generations past.

BEAT THE BOTS

Pro Tip: Immerse Yourself

Beth Vrabel, the award-winning author of nine middle-grade novels, explains how she immersed herself in the setting for her book *When Giants Burn*. The book is an adventure story about two kids whose homemade airplane crashes near a wildfire outside of Pando, a clonal aspen grove in Utah thought to be the oldest, heaviest and largest living being.

I sold the idea, knowing Pando's longevity and expansion would be a central theme, but without having seen the quaking aspen in person. Sure, I spent a lot of time reading about Pando—poetry, essays, articles. I watched countless YouTube videos, and studied Google Map images of Fishlake National Forest and the surrounding small towns.

But nothing in that research compared to the mise-en-scène I gathered during a half-hour in a small-town burger joint outside the park, watching as locals kicked snow off their boots and sat down to their regular order, picking up a conversation where it had clearly branched off the day before (all while studiously ignoring the newcomer scribbling in her notebook). No amount of research could capture what it was like to pull alongside State Highway 25, pick my steps across a stretch of yellow trees, press my spine against the trunk of a slim aspen and ponder how the roots under my feet had survived tens of thousands of years.

Research alone might lead a writer to both overly romanticize and oversimplify. Taking the time to immerse yourself in the setting is a purely human experience, one that allows your setting to grow into a character onto itself. This will root your story, providing a sturdiness into which readers can lean as the story blooms in their mind.

Until you experience the setting, you can't know what you don't know. Even when world-building in, say, fantasy or horror, you need to apply the same principles of immersion. Shut your eyes and picture the world you've created. Peer into corners. Peek through windows. Immerse yourself in your world so you can see what your readers will see.

Contemporary readers don't want labored descriptions of hills and valleys and beaches and cityscapes—they want to read about experiences that could only occur at that place and time of your story, what I call the world in a word (or a phrase). That said, sometimes the prose itself is so spectacular that it works. Consider, for example, the following opening sentences. The authors take profoundly different approaches to sharing information about the settings, yet both are effective.

> ### *Tarzan and the Forbidden City* by
> ### Edward Rice Burroughs
>
> #### Chapter One
>
> The rainy season was over; and forest and jungle were a riot of lush green starred with myriad tropical blooms, alive with the gorgeous coloring and raucous voices of countless birds, scolding, loving, hunting, escaping; alive with chattering monkeys and buzzing insects which all seemed to be busily engaged in doing things in circles and getting nowhere, much after the fashion of their unhappy cousins who dwell in unlovely jungles of brick and marble and cement.

Remarkably, Burroughs' sentence runs seventy-six words. Its sheer length mimics the scope of the landscape. The birds' motivations and the monkeys' motion draw you into the thickly populated jungle. Note the multitude of active verbs, from *scolding* to *escaping*, among other specific and evocative word choices, such as *riot* and *lush*. Note also, the last phrase: "... and getting nowhere, much after the fashion of their unhappy cousins who dwell in unlovely jungles of brick and marble and cement." This comparison of an actual jungle to the concrete jungle of a city is immediately relatable and apt, and at the time of its writing, in 1938, fresh. From this one sentence, we know where we are and how the narrator perceives his environment, and it alludes to the promise of the story—readers, who live in an urban jungle, are going to discover its similarities to the African jungle. That's a narrative question that delivers on all fronts (see Chapter Three for more information about narrative questions). Note that the concrete jungle metaphor required human ingenuity. AI can't innovate; it can only emulate.

While long descriptions of setting are passé, your readers still want to experience the world your people populate. An effective strategy to addressing this expectation is to weave description into action. As you think about how to reveal your setting, keep in mind that you should integrate only the details needed to bring the incidents you're writing about to life. We were just in the African jungle. Now let's go contemporary Boston.

This is from *The Other Woman* by Hank Phillippi Ryan. As you read the following excerpt, notice how little exposition is needed to create a strong sense of atmosphere. A few adjectives go a long way.

The Other Woman by Hank Phillippi Ryan

Chapter One

> "Get that light out of my face! And get behind the tape. All of you. *Now*." Detective Jake Brogan pointed his own flashlight at the pack of reporters, its cold glow highlighting one news-greedy face after another in the

BEAT THE BOTS

> October darkness. He recognized television. Radio. That kid from the paper. *How the hell did they get here so fast?* The whiffle of a chopper, one of theirs, hovered over the riverbank, its spotlights illuminating the unmistakable—another long night on the job. And a Monday-morning visit to a grieving family. If they could figure out who this victim was.

Lean and mean. Don't you love a "pack" of reporters? The "whiffle" of the helicopter? The world in a word.

Ryan does a masterful job of showing the characters interacting with their world. And the way to do that is to use sensory references. For example,

- From *The Quiller Memorandum* by Adam Hall, "The light was strengthening on the far spire and the matte uniformity of the sky was curdling into cloud."
- Or how about this from Peter Swanson's *Eight Perfect Murders: A Novel*? "Outside it was still bitterly cold, but the sun was out, the sky a hard, unforgiving blue."

Prompt #15: Use Sensory Descriptions to Let Readers Connect with Your Settings

When trying to understand a character's attitude, ask yourself what do they see? Smell? Hear? Taste? Touch? Kate White, the *New York Times* bestselling author of seventeen novels of suspense and the former editor-in-chief of *Cosmopolitan*, explains: "Having great settings in your suspense novels makes them even more compelling to readers, but what's even better is to use settings to *subtly* add to the reader's sense of dread—for instance, describing woods with the musky-sweet smell of decaying leaves or a kitchen where the only sound is from a dripping faucet."

This principle applies to all genres. The question to consider is how your character *feels* about the setting, and to express it through a sensory connection. For example, here's what Josie, the protagonist of my mystery series, feels about the New Hampshire beach where she walks most every day. "I loved walking along the craggy shoreline, stepping over and around the slick twisted ribbons of seaweed and selecting silvery gray curls of driftwood for holiday decorations."

Now it's your turn! Write a sentence that reveals something about your character's relationship to the setting, be it dread, allure, dismay, or exhilaration, integrating at least one sensory reference.

BEAT THE BOTS

> To participate in the *Beat the Bots* TikTok community:
>
> - Record a video of your answer and post it, including the hashtag #beatthebots and tag me at @beatthebotsbook
> - You can also tag #authortok and #booktok to connect with other writer and reader communities!
> - Watch other writers' videos by visiting the TikTok hashtag #beatthebots
>
> Join the conversation!

Remember that every character experiences the world differently. You're not merely writing about setting. You're writing about how *that particular character* perceives the setting. Charles Todd, the son in the eponymous mother-son partnership who wrote the Bess Crawford mysteries (alas, Caroline has died), told me: "The character is fourteen. She'll see war-torn France differently from the battlefield nurse." In Laura Lippman's novel *By a Spider's Thread*, the narrator describes the Midwest starting with: "They were in one of the 'I' states when Zeke told Isaac he had to ride in the trunk for a little while."

INTEGRATE SETTING INFO SEAMLESSLY

The best way to share information about the setting is to slip it in one sentence at a time. This tactic helps you avoid dialogue tags, too (discussed in Chapter Seven). Review these two options and ask yourself which is stronger:

Option One:

"I have to go," Mary said. "I'm late."

"Don't go," Tom whispered, kissing her neck.

"I'll get fired."

"No, you won't."

"Pete said one more time and I was out," Mary said.

"He owns the place. He won't fire you."

"I have to go," she repeated.

Option Two:

"I have to go," Mary said. The sun peeked through the broken slats of the old venetian blinds. "I'm late."

"Don't go," Tom whispered, kissing her neck.

"I'll get fired."

"No, you won't."

A cow plodded across the pasture. Same old, same old. Mary tugged up her jeans and leaned over the bed to kiss the man who said his name was Tom. "Pete said one more time and I was out."

BEAT THE BOTS

"He owns the place. He won't fire you."

She sat to pull on her boots, her feet pale in the oblong of dim yellow light, winter sun. "I have to go."

Note that the dialogue is the same, but the extra information in option two changes everything. The cow. The dim winter sun. The man who *says* his name is Tom. We don't know exactly where we are, but we know enough to intuit the location and sense the overall mood.

Prompt #16: Observe Details

To help understand how your character perceives the world, take them somewhere they've never been. They don't have to leave town. They just have to go somewhere new. Think about it—your characters can't know every nook and cranny of their community. No one can. There may be a public parking garage near your character's office, but she doesn't need to use it because she has an assigned parking place behind her company's building. Or perhaps your character drives past a long-since-deserted factory he's thinking about buying or a specialty food store he decides to give a try. Bring your character into that place and ask them to name three specific things that surprise them about the setting. Then add a sentence revealing what your character thinks about the place.

Let's say my character is in a TV studio for the first time. She's been invited to talk about her work—she's a subject matter expert. Here's what she sees and how she feels about it: "It's so dark—until they flip a switch and the spotlights totally blind me. Black cables as thick as my wrist snake around the floor, an accident waiting to happen, if you ask me. The anchor is drop-dead gorgeous, but man, oh, man, she's wearing more make-up than I use in a year. To tell you the truth, I feel like a kid on Christmas morning, I'm so excited!"

Now it's your turn! Bring your character into an unfamiliar place and ask them to name three specific things that surprise them about the setting. Then add a sentence revealing what your character thinks about the place.

To participate in the *Beat the Bots* TikTok community:

- Record a video of your answer and post it, including the hashtag #beatthebots and tag me at @beatthebotsbook
- You can also tag #authortok and #booktok to connect with other writer and reader communities!
- Watch other writers' videos by visiting the TikTok hashtag #beatthebots

Join the conversation!

SETTING AS CHARACTER

In some stories, the setting is so fundamental to the story, it almost becomes a character itself. For example, Stephen King's *The Shining* is set in an isolated hotel. The protagonist is desperate to win the job as winter caretaker of the resort, closed for the season. The remote location and overall eeriness of the place accentuates the characters' inability to connect with one another. As their relationships break down, the isolated setting becomes even more threatening.

AI Weighs In

I asked a chatbot: Can you give me an example of a premise for a romance novel where setting is so important to the story, it almost becomes a character?

AI said: *Certainly! In a romance novel, a setting can take on the role of a character by not only providing a backdrop for the story but also by influencing the emotions and actions of the characters. Here's an example of a setting as a character: Title: "Whispers by the Sea"*

The coastal town of Harbor Haven was more than just a location; it was a character in its own right. Its personality changed with the tides, sometimes gentle and inviting, other times fierce and untamable. The salty breeze whispered secrets to those who dared to listen,

> *and the crashing waves offered a rhythm to life that was both soothing and tumultuous.*
>
> *As the sun dipped below the horizon, casting a warm, golden glow over the harbor, it bathed the quaint, weathered cottages in a romantic light. The town's cobbled streets, lined with colorful fishing boats and cozy cafes, held the stories of generations who had loved, lost, and found themselves in the arms of another.*
>
> This description is clearly evocative, but it's also trite, filled with clichés and common tropes. We need to come up with a fresh take on this familiar seaside town. A few years ago, I read an article about a remote village in Wales located on the Irish Sea. When a resident died, a team of horses hauled the body up cobblestone streets too steep and rutted for cars to traverse to reach the town center, where the only funeral home was located. This process had been the tradition for centuries. Then one day, the government ruled that having horses bear that burden constituted cruelty to animals, so the men had to do it themselves. I don't know about you, but the irony here is, to me, hysterically funny, and the situation isn't trite. Let's set a romance in that town!

In Gabriel García Marquez's *One Hundred Years of Solitude*, the meaning and futility of life is illuminated through the mythical town of Macondo. Here's how the novel opens: "Many years later, as he faced the firing squad, Colonel Aureliano Buendía was to remember that distant afternoon when his father took him to discover ice. At that time Macondo was a village of twenty adobe houses, built on the bank of a river of clear water that ran along a bed of polished stones, which were white and enormous, like prehistoric eggs. The world was so recent that many things lacked names, and in order to indicate them it was necessary to point." The second and third sentences of Chapter One showcase the importance of the setting (and the first presents a clear narrative question, discussed as an element of through-line plots in Chapter Three).

To create this kind of relatable setting, it's crucial you consider not just the time and place, but everything that surrounds the time and place. For that, you need Conceptual Blending.

CREATE RELATABLE SETTINGS WITH CONCEPTUAL BLENDING

Melding various factors, such as geography, weather, music, food, activities, and the like creates a robust setting, one that goes beyond the superficial, beyond the obvious. The Conceptual Blending creativity tactic invites you to look at the intersection of lifestyle elements and geography. This process helps you identify, organize, and synthesize the myriad elements that contribute to your characters' feelings about their settings, and express those perceptions through sensory references. When done well, your readers will feel what your characters feel.

Conceptual Blending helps you drill down into your characters' sensibilities and understand their attitudes toward your setting. An important note—artificial intelligence can't know what your characters' think, feel, or believe—that's up to you to determine. Conceptual Blending facilitates that analysis. To use this tactic, answer the questions in Part One of the Conceptual

Blending creativity tactic from your character's point of view. Note, it's often helpful to answer the questions from two or more characters' points of view to understand their differences. Part Two asks you to write it up. Part Three helps you assess your ideas.

Exercise

What Do Your Characters See?
Perception Is Reality

Part One: Conceptual Blending Chart

- Choose two characters, your protagonist and one other person. In a mystery or thriller, your detective is your protagonist. Your second character could be the killer, the victim, or a suspect. In a literary novel about overcoming addiction, the protagonist is the addict, the person whose struggles are recounted in the book. For the second character, you could choose a drug dealer, a rehab counselor, or a drug buddy.
- For example, let's say I'm writing a novel about a young woman struggling to break free from family expectations and live the life she chooses. Tessa, in her twenties, is coming home to share good news—she's earned her doctoral degree. Tessa's mother, Alice, is in her fifties. She works at a big box retailer. Alice is mistrustful of higher education since the so-called elites just end up lording over everyone else, thinking they know what's best.

BEAT THE BOTS

	Question	Tessa	Alice
1.	Is your story set in the present? If not, name the historical or future era.	1990. I'm twenty-six.	1990. I'm fifty-three.
2.	Where is your story set?	Nantasket Beach, Massachusetts, where I grew up.	Nantasket Beach, the armpit of the South Shore
3.	Summarize your setting's geography.	Our family home is a few blocks from the beach. The sand is tan, the beach rocky, the ocean almost always dark. We're also a few blocks from the bay, where the water is warmer and calmer. Nantasket is flat until you reach Strawberry Hill. The views from the top are super!	An ugly beach. A dangerous ocean. Flat. Dirty. Dull. The rich folk live on Strawberry Hill.
4.	What is the weather like?	We enjoy four glorious seasons.	Mostly cold, even in summer. The kind of cold that gets in your bones.
5.	How hard is it to get around? Is the terrain challenging? Is there easy access to public transportation?	Because it's flat, it's easy to get around. When I was a kid, I biked everywhere. There's an occasional bus, but the public transportation isn't as good as it should be.	Going anywhere is a pain in the neck. You've got to have a car—and I don't. Sometimes I have to wait an hour for a bus. That's real fun in January.

6.	How long does it take to reach an international airport? How long to reach a regional airport?	Boston's Logan airport is the closest international one. To get there takes about two hours driving, three hours using buses and the subway, and an hour and a half by ferry. New Bedford Regional Airport is probably the closest regional airport. It's about an hour and a half away.	How should I know? I never go anywhere.
7.	Are there any annual or periodic community events, such as the Dushore (Pennsylvania) Founder's Day celebration or the Mansfield (Texas) Pickle Parade?	Various community groups organize things like sandcastle building competitions and art shows.	No. Did you say Pickle Parade? We should have one of those 'cause we're all in a pickle around here.
8.	Are there any notable musical traditions, such as the Monterey (California) Jazz Festival or the Glimmerglass Opera Festival in New York?	In summer, there are concerts and shows on the beach.	No.

BEAT THE BOTS

9.	If English is the predominant language, are there communities that speak other languages, such as Spanish, Russian, or Chinese?	When I was a kid, I remember some of our neighbors speaking Italian.	They want to speak to me, they'll be speaking English.
10.	Is the area known for certain foods, such as chili, barbeque, sausages, clam chowder, or fried chicken?	Wonderful steamers! And lobster.	We have good shell-fish in the summer, mussels, clams, and lobster, but only if you can afford it, which I can't.
11.	What other elements of the setting contribute to the mood, feel, or atmosphere of the place?	Paragon Park Carousal. And the boardwalk. There used to be the roller coaster, but they took that away five years ago.	It's fun watching tourists try to swim in the ocean, which even in August tops out at like sixty-eight or seventy degrees. You should hear them squeal!
12.	Does your character like the setting? Why or why not?	Yes. It's home.	No. It's a dump. I'd leave if I could, but I have nowhere to go, so I'm stuck.
13.	How will the setting figure into your story? Is it a subplot? A metaphor? Thematic?	The setting showcases the isolation some people feel, especially once the summer tourists leave.	Living is hard here. Bad weather. No opportunities. It's like lots of towns you hear about, down on their luck, and getting nowhere fast.

Part Two: Write It Up

- Select a specific location from your story to write about.
- Write two scenes that reveal how the two characters you're working with *feel* about your chosen location, one per character. Don't tell us how they feel—we want to experience what they experience. As novelist E. L. Doctorow explained, "Good writing is supposed to evoke sensation in the reader—not the fact that it is raining, but the feeling of being rained upon." This understanding leads to empathy, which, in turn, leads to relatability—a core value that leads to publishing success.
- Don't be heavy-handed. Be subtle. Think sensory descriptions. Think subtext.

Here's my example:

(1) Tessa

"Roller coaster!" I screamed even though I was alone in the old Chevy.

Hollering "roller coaster" as soon as you saw the old wooden monstrosity was a long-standing tradition, and here I was shouting it even though the roller coaster is long gone. When I was a girl, the first person who spotted it on the drive from Boston to Nantasket won. Later, I realized there was no a prize, it was just Mama's way of keeping us busy.

Nantasket Beach came into view, the sand more beige than white, ribbons of slimy bottle-green seaweed tangled with driftwood and rocks. White caps bobbed along the ocean surface. Pewter clouds blew in from the north, bringing in a cold rain and lots of it. I loved a good storm.

I rolled to a stop in front of my old house, the cottage where I'd been born. The house where Grandma had baked bread every afternoon. The house that Mama somehow had made into a home.

I pushed open the screen door. Mama never locked the door.

"Mama!" I called. "I'm home!"

(2) Alice.

Alice wheeled her shopping cart up F Street through the punishing rain. The rickety shack, her home, came into view, paint peeling, the side gutter dangling. Damn place was still standing. Maybe this storm would finally do the dump in and she could escape.

Part Three: Assess Your Ideas

☐ *What did you learn about your characters? Did anything surprise you?*

To Tessa, "home" evokes sweet memories. In writing it out, I realized that she holds a completely romanticized view of a place her mother referred to as a "rickety shack." I felt sad that Alice thought of her home as a "dump." I bet she doesn't have the money to move. It wouldn't surprise me if Alice fibbed to everyone that home was where the heart was or something equally glib because she doesn't want to admit she can't afford anything better. Also, I was disappointed that Alice isn't proud of Tessa, that seeing her own daughter embrace a higher education doesn't move the needle on Alice's negative views about the "elite."

☐ *What did you learn about your setting?*

I learned that beauty truly is in the eye of the beholder. I wonder if I could do more with that concept thematically.

☐ *Have you:*

    o *Painted a vivid picture?*

I think so. I used a minimal approach to describing the ocean, beach, and rain, but I do think my descriptions were clear.

    o *Created a mood that's consistent with each character's perception of the location?*

Yes. Tessa is excited, joyous. Alice is dreary, trudging along in the rain.

> ○ *Added insights about your character/s?*
>
> This was an unexpected benefit. I think I showed Tessa's happiness and Alice's resignation well.
>
> ○ *Moved the plot forward?*
>
> I'm curious what will happen when Alice hears Tessa's news that she earned a Ph. D. Will Alice fake being happy for her or will she let her disdain show? Inspiring curiosity in a solid indicator that I've moved the plot forward.
>
> ○ *Used sensory descriptors to highlight what your characters see, hear, feel, smell, and/or taste?*
>
> Yes, I chose several sensory-based words like "slimy," "bobbing," and "punishing."

Now it's your turn! Spending time with your two characters will help you ensure your setting is fully developed and on point.

Exercise

Part One: Conceptual Blending Chart

Now it's your turn! Choose two characters, your protagonist and one other person.

Question	Character #1 Name	Character #2 Name
1. Is your story set in the present? If not, name the historical or future era.		
2. Where is your story set?		
3. Summarize your setting's geography.		
4. What is the weather like?		
5. How hard is it to get around? Is the terrain challenging? Is there easy access to public transportation?		
6. How long does it take to reach an international airport? How long to reach a regional airport?		
7. Are there any annual or periodic community events, such as the Dushore (Pennsylvania) Founder's Day celebration or the Mansfield (Texas) Pickle Parade?		

BEAT THE BOTS

8. Are there any notable musical traditions, such as the Monterey (California) Jazz Festival or the Glimmerglass Opera Festival in New York?		
9. If English is the predominant language, are there communities that speak other languages, such as Spanish, Russian, or Chinese?		
10. Is the area known for certain foods, such as chili, barbeque, sausages, clam chowder, or fried chicken?		
11. What other elements of the setting contribute to the mood, feel, or atmosphere of the place?		
12. Does your character like the setting? Why or why not?		
13. How will the setting figure into your story? Is it a subplot? A metaphor? Thematic?		

Part Two: Write It Up

Using your answers to these questions, write two scenes that reveal how those two characters *feel* about your chosen location, one per character

(1) Jot notes about your protagonist here

(2) Jot notes about your other character here

Scene One:

Scene Two:

Part Three: Assess Your Needs

☐ *What did you learn about your characters? Did anything surprise you?*

_____

_____

☐ *What did you learn about your setting?*

_____

_____

BEAT THE BOTS

☐ *Have you:*
  ○ *Painted a vivid picture?*

_____

_____

  ○ *Created a mood that's consistent with each character's perception of the location?*

_____

_____

  ○ *Added insights about your character/s?*

_____

_____

  ○ *Moved the plot forward?*

_____

_____

  ○ *Used sensory descriptors to highlight what your characters see, hear, feel, smell, and/or taste?*

_____

_____

As you think about your experience coming up with TRDs using the Conceptual Blending creativity tactic, what did you learn?

Here is how I might answer this question: Using the Conceptual Blending creativity tactic helped me recognize the profound differences between Alice and Tessa. That will help me stick to my through-line plot.

119

> Complete this sentence: Using the Conceptual Blending creativity tactic helped me:
>
> _____.
>
> To participate in the *Beat the Bots* TikTok community:
>
> - Record a video of your answer and post it, including the hashtag #beatthebots and tag me at @beatthebotsbook
> - You can also tag #authortok and #booktok to connect with other writer and reader communities!
> - Watch other writers' videos by visiting the TikTok hashtag #beatthebots
>
> Join the conversation!

Setting: evocative, thematic, grounding...a crucial element of writing success.

Now that we've considered where your story takes place and how your characters perceive the location, it's time to drill down to determining your point of view.

Reflection on Creativity

"A rock pile ceases to be a rock pile the moment a single man contemplates it, bearing within him the image of a cathedral."
Antoine de Saint-Exupéry

PART TWO
YOUR STORY, YOUR VOICE

"Process makes you more efficient."
Steve Jobs

CHAPTER FIVE

CREATIVITY TACTIC #5
DIVERGENT THINKING: DETERMINE YOUR POINT OF VIEW

"You never really understand a person until you
consider things from his point of view."
Harper Lee

CHOOSE YOUR POINT OF VIEW

One of the ways we'll beat the bots is by writing with a voice
that can't be easily replicated. Part of that process is choosing
your point of view (POV), which requires determining whose
story you want to tell and how best to share it. Select the wrong
POV and readers won't connect with your story. Use too many
POVs and readers end up confused, not intrigued. In this
chapter, we'll review your POV options, decide what's best for

125

your project, and see how the Divergent Thinking creativity tactic can help you sort through those options.

FAQ

Q: Some genres seem to always be written in the first person, others in the limited third, and so on. If I want to stand out, shouldn't I mix it up?

A: While there's no hard-and-fast rule about which POV to use in which genre, it's not a coincidence that authors tend to the same POV within a genre—it's all about reader expectations and genre conventions. Simply wanting to mix something up isn't a good enough reason to make a decision about POV. The better approach is to analyze each POV's strengths, discussed in this chapter, and determine which option matches your story.

UNDERSTAND YOUR POV OPTIONS

The most commonly used POVs are first, second, and third person (both limited and omniscient). There are other notable alternatives, too, including breaking the fourth wall and using multiple POVs, which are worth your review and consideration. The following listing explains these alternatives' strengths and offers notable examples. It's important to note, however, that there is no one best option. For instance, you'll

BEAT THE BOTS

see that literary fiction appears in both the first-person and third-person POV listings. Later in this chapter, we'll discuss how best to make the decisions.

FIRST PERSON (I, ME)

Since, by definition, the narrator is speaking directly to the reader, the first-person POV is the most intimate option. If you have one person's story to tell, it may be the best choice. Keep in mind, though, that when you use the first-person POV, you can include only what that one person sees, thinks, feels, and knows. If your character isn't in the scene, there is no scene. A real upside is that this option allows readers to get inside one person's head, to see the world as they see it—or in the case of an unreliable narrator, to see the world as they want you to think they see it. Some examples:

- In a traditional mystery, often called a "fair play" mystery, the reader knows only what the sleuth knows, and the first-person voice ensures that they'll learn it at the same moment.
    - Rhys Bowen's A Royal Spyness series, including *The Proof of the Pudding*
    - My Josie Prescott Antiques mystery series, including *Jane Austen's Lost Letters*
- In science fiction, since everything is foreign, seeing it through one person's eyes, whether happily exploring it or unhappily contending with unfamiliar environments and technologies, requires that readers experience the same things as the narrator.
    - Andy Weir's *Project Hail Mary*

- Ernest Cline's *Ready Player One*
- Middle-grade and young-adult novels examine the dilemmas and challenges of growing up in a confusing and unpredictable world. These stories generally include considerable introspection, so the first-person POV is the natural voice to express these characters' uncomfortable inner thoughts, the kind that are rarely spoken aloud.
  - Suzanne Collins's *The Hunger Games*
  - John Green's *The Fault in Our Stars*
- Literary fiction examines pivotal, life-changing moments, from hiding youthful indiscretions to finding romantic partners to overcoming obstacles to aging gracefully, or not, and the like. Since these stories typically share deeply personal longings and fears, they lend themselves to the first-person POV.
  - Herman Melville's *Moby Dick*
  - Toni Morrison's *The Bluest Eye*

SECOND PERSON (YOU)

The second person voice can be unsettling for readers because it almost feels as if the narrator is accusing you, the reader, of something. It can also foster empathy, since the narrator is sharing an experience directly with you.

- Italo Calvino's *If on a Winter's Night a Traveler*
- Jay McInerney's *Bright Lights, Big City*

THIRD-PERSON LIMITED (HE, SHE, THEY)

The third-person-limited POV is the most frequently used alternative. Your story unfolds through one character's thoughts, feelings, and actions. This POV can be used effectively in all genres.

- J.K. Rowling's *Harry Potter and the Half-Blood Prince*
- Delia Owens's *Where the Crawdads Sing*

Telling your story from various people's perspectives (multiple POV) is common when using the third-person-limited POV, usually differentiated by chapters. But some authors mix POVs within a series, sometimes within a book, occasionally within a chapter, and even within a sentence (which can be head hopping). As with all unconventional writing decisions, you should ensure you have a good reason to vary from the norm.

- SJ Rozan's Lydia Chin/Bill Smith novels. Each novel within the series switches third-person POV. Lydia narrates the odd-numbered books, while Bill narrates the even-numbered books.
- Sally Rooney's *Beautiful World, Where Are You?* The novel is written in both third-person-omniscient POV and first-person email interactions.

Prompt #17: Your POV, Your Happy Place

In his *New York Times* essay, "How a Few Days Sailing in the Aegean Changed My Mind About the Fundamental Nature of Things," author Adam Nicolson explained that, "To be in the places these [Greek philosophers] knew, visit their cities, sail their seas and find their landscapes is to know something about them that cannot be found otherwise, and despite that locatedness and despite their age, the frame of mind of these first thinkers remains astonishingly and surprisingly illuminating today." In other words, these legendary Greek philosophers' points of view were informed by where they lived, by what they saw and experienced. How about you?

Think of the place where you grew up. What's your favorite memory and how did it guide your thinking? For this prompt, describe a favorite memory from where you grew up from three different points of view: first, second, and third limited, integrating information about why that particular memory is a favorite. Then add a thought about what you learned. Here's mine:

- My favorite memory from where I grew up is from autumn. I loved the crackling sound of treading on fallen leaves. I'd walk alone, my head full of dreams and schemes and plans.
- Your favorite memory from when you grew up is from autumn. You loved the crackling sound

BEAT THE BOTS

of reading on fallen leaves. You'd walk alone, head full of dreams and schemes and plans.

- Her favorite memory from where she grew up was from autumn. She loved the crackling sound of treading on fallen leaves. She'd walk alone, her head full of dreams and schemes and plans.

I learned that both first person and third-person limited felt quite natural to me. I wasn't comfortable with second person. It felt judgmental. After all, who am I to declare what "your" favorite memory is?

Now it's your turn! Describe a favorite memory from where you grew up from three different points of view: first, second, and third limited. Then add a thought about what you learned.

To participate in the *Beat the Bots* TikTok community:

- Record a video of your answer and post it, including the hashtag #beatthebots and tag me at @beatthebotsbook
- You can also tag #authortok and #booktok to connect with other writer and reader communities!
- Watch other writers' videos by visiting the TikTok hashtag #beatthebots

Join the conversation!

THIRD-PERSON OMNISCIENT (HE, SHE, THEY)

This narrator knows everything. It is the voice of God. A warning: you need to avoid unattributed "head hopping." Here is an example of "head hopping" that works well because we're identifying the characters. "As the students settled into their cubicles, Susie prayed her eyes did not show her anxiety and Peter silently hoped the money he'd paid for an advance look at the test was worth it." Do be careful, though. Authors often struggle to maintain a consistent omniscient voice and veer into random head hopping (which dips in and out of multiple characters' tight narratives without warning).

- Fantasy includes complex and foreign worlds, offering readers an immersive experience. Being untethered from each character's personal narrative allows for commentary on the world itself, while enabling you to shift smoothly from one character and location to another.
  - Terry Pratchett's *Reaper Man*
  - Diana Wynne Jones's *Howl's Moving Castle*
- Literary fiction: where the author wants to communicate a sweeping world view.
  - Britt Bennett's *The Vanishing Half*
  - Gabrielle Zevin's *Tomorrow and Tomorrow and Tomorrow*

THIRD-PERSON OBJECTIVE (FLY ON THE WALL)

The reader feels like a fly on the wall. They can see, hear, smell, taste, and touch everything the characters do. It is a completely objective narrative perspective. There is nothing subjective provided by the narrator, no comments, no opinions, no judgments, no character's inner thoughts or reflections. Nothing beyond the facts is shared, only what is happening, what is said, who is doing what. For example:

- Ursula K. Le Guin's *A Wizard of Earthsea*
- Shirley Jackson's "The Lottery"

BREAKING THE FOURTH WALL

The term "breaking the fourth wall" comes from playwriting and refers to actors speaking directly to the audience. The technique has been used for centuries, from Greek choruses in classic plays and Shakespearean asides to modern narrators stepping out from behind the curtain.

- Rick Riordan's *The Lightning Thief*
- Lemony Snicket's *A Bad Beginning*

Prompt #18: Multiple Points of View—Reading an Animal's Mind

Georgette Heyer used the third-person-omniscient POV in *Faro's Daughter*. Ms. Heyer is known for her exceptional ability to reproduce the actual communication styles of late-eighteenth- and early-nineteenth-century England—from slang and idioms used by the aristocracy to thieves' cant. This book, a romance, is set in London in the late 1700s. Miss Grantham is the protagonist, and in the scene below, she is out for a ride in the park with Mr. Ravenscar, her love interest, who is driving his team of famous gray horses. The horses are a little frisky since they haven't been exercised in a while. Within a single chapter, the POV switches from Ms. Grantham and Mr. Ravenscar to the team of horses. In the following excerpt, note how Heyer segues in and out of the horses' POV.

> "Don't be alarmed!" Ravenscar told Miss Grantham. "They are only a little fresh."
>
> "I wonder you can hold them so easily!" she confessed, repressing an instinctive desire to clutch the side of the curricle.
>
> He smiled, but returned no answer. They swept around the corner into King Street, turned westward, and bowled along in the direct of St. James's Street.

There was sufficient traffic abroad to keep Mr. Ravenscar's attention fixed on his task, for the greys, thought perfectly well-mannered, chose to take high-bred exception to a wagon which was rumbling along the side of the road, to shy playfully at a sedan, to regard with sudden misgiving a lady's feathered hat, and to decide that the lines of white posts, linked with chains, that separated the footpaths from the kennels and the road, menaced them with a hitherto unsuspected danger. But the gates leading into Hyde Park were reached without mishap, and once within them the grays settled into fine, forward action, satisfied, apparently, to find themselves in surroundings more suited to their birth and lineage.

There were several other equipages in the Park, including some phaetons, and a number of barouches. Mr. Ravenscar touched his hat every now and then to acquaintances, but presently, drawing away from the other vehicles, he was able to turn his attention to his companion.

"Are you comfortable, Miss Grantham?"

There are several notable elements here:

- The verb "chose" marks the switch in POV.
- Readers get to see the street scene as the horses experience it. There's no info dump or banal descriptions.
- Heyer's voice is clear. She writes with wit and social irony.

Replicate this POV tactic by writing a brief scene in which you transition from a person to an animal, then back again.

To participate in the *Beat the Bots* TikTok community:

- Record a video of your answer and post it, including the hashtag #beatthebots and tag me at @beatthebotsbook
- You can also tag #authortok and #booktok to connect with other writer and reader communities!
- Watch other writers' videos by visiting the TikTok hashtag #beatthebots

Join the conversation!

ASSESS YOUR CHOICE WITH A THREE-STEP DECISION-MAKING TOOL

Choosing your POV isn't a binary decision. There will always be more than one viable option. To help you think it through, ask yourself these three questions:

1. What are my reader expectations? Are there specific reasons why most entries in your genre use a certain POV?
   - If yes, should you adhere to the convention?
   - If no, experiment with alternatives.
2. Is there a reason why the reader should see only one POV? (Like an amateur sleuth or an unreliable narrator)
   - If yes, go with the first-person POV.
   - If no, experiment with other alternatives.
3. Do you want to show how different people react or interact?
   - If yes, then you're looking at third person, either limited or omniscient. You might also consider multiple third-person POVs; most experts encourage you to limit the scope to five POVs. Another option is interweaving first and third, with one POV assigned to each person.
   - If no, you're looking at a first-person POV.
   - If you want to involve the reader in the storytelling process, experiment with breaking the fourth wall and talking directly to your reader.

Pro Tip: Your Best Tool for Beating the Bots Is Your Unique Author's Voice

Charles Todd, the mother-son writing team, authors of the *New York Times* bestselling Rutledge novels (also discussed in Chapter Four), told me:

> I am told that I should fear the BOTS. AI is going to replace authors and we will lose our craft. I am not afraid. Yes, someone could feed the Rutledge Books into a computer and crank out a Rutledge novel. I have several reasons not to believe this. Tidbits of research that jump from the page and cause plot changes. Life experiences that come from so many places we have been and things we have seen. At the heart of it all is our storytelling tradition that came from our family heritage.
>
> Caroline and I began our journey listening to the stories of my grandfather. He would sit on his porch and tell his tales to all present who would be enraptured by them. In fact there were some that were my favorites that I would ask him to tell again. I memorized them word for word and yet it was not the same. I learned how much the sound of his voice and the emphasis he put on the words made all the difference. We worked all these

years to create our voice. We told people that books are read for the story and not who wrote which part. Being co-authors made this critical. We had to speak with one voice as the characters would say them. Who Inspector Rutledge and Bess Crawford are, is defined not by imitation, but from a certain feel. The story unfolds in large part from the reactions of the characters. Writing is a craft we learn, but our voice is distinct and develops over time. If a BOT can listen to readers and fans, travel never knowing what is "around the bend," and share a life lived; then I will worry.

FIND YOUR UNIQUE WRITER'S VOICE

It's important that your writing sounds like you and no one else, that it screams your singular you-ness. Honing your uniqueness is one of the most powerful ways you can be assured of beating the bots. You want your prose to stand out for its clarity, vision, eloquence, and verve, and certain POVs are likely to be a more solid match your specific aspirations than others. Experiment. For example, does a first-person POV let your smartass narrator share his cynical reflections on the downlow? Or will readers gain a clearer understanding of his jaded view of the world by witnessing how other characters react to his snide remarks? If so, third-person omniscient might be a better choice. Which option most effectively lends itself to the task at hand and lets you strut your writing stuff? There's no right or wrong answer here, so you need to try both options to gauge their effectiveness.

Prompt #19: Window to the World

Write a brief scene about what your character sees through the window from three points of view, first, second, and third. Which feels right?

For instance, I might write:

- I watched Tony for a few seconds before I went inside. He sat at the bar, so I only had his profile. He was as handsome as I remembered, a big man, broad and tall, a winner for sure.
- You watch Tony for a few seconds before you go inside. He sits at the bar, so you only have his profile. He is as handsome as you remember, a big man, broad and tall, a winner for sure.
- She watched Tony for a few seconds before she went inside. He sat at the bar, so she only had his profile. He was as handsome as she remembered, a big man, broad and tall, a winner for sure.

I learned that I loved writing this from the second person POV. It felt natural, immediate, intimate.

BEAT THE BOTS

> Now it's your turn! Write a brief scene about what your character sees through the window from three points of view, first, second, and third. Which feels right? Why?
>
> ---
>
> To participate in the *Beat the Bots* TikTok community:
>
> - Record a video of your answer and post it, including the hashtag #beatthebots and tag me at @beatthebotsbook
> - You can also tag #authortok and #booktok to connect with other writer and reader communities!
> - Watch other writers' videos by visiting the TikTok hashtag #beatthebots
>
> Join the conversation!

People struggle to define the term "voice" because it's amorphous, atmospheric, and intangible. It's rather like Supreme Court Justice Potter Stewart's explanation when asked to define obscenity: He said he couldn't define it, but "I know it when I see it." Little, Brown and Company editor Ben George put it this way when explaining how he completely fell in love with Nathan Harris's *The Sweetness of Water*. He said that Harris's voice "set my hair on fire." And literary agent Rachelle Gardner says, "Your writer's voice is the expression of you on the page. It's that simple—and that complicated. Your voice is all about honesty. It's the unfettered, non-derivative, unique conglomeration of your thoughts, feelings, passions, dreams, beliefs, fears, and attitudes, coming through in every word you write…It's a process of peeling away the layers of your false self, your trying-to-be-something-you're-not self, your copycat self, your trying-to-sound-a-certain-way self, your spent-my-life-watching-television self."

Your writer's voice is as unique as your thumbprint. It's your personality on the page, expressed with confidence, a special sauce of your own creation, packed with flavor and seasoned just right.

Prompt #20: Write with Abandon

Talk about the process of finding your writer's voice. Was it a struggle? Are you still working on it? Articulating your strengths or what might be holding you back can be liberating. For example, here's what I know about finding my writer's voice: For years, I didn't know I had a writer's voice. I just wrote. Once I realized what the term meant, I spent time thinking about it, and I realized that I needed to loosen my mental grip on how I should sound. How about you? What's holding you back? What will help you find your true voice?

Now it's your turn. Complete this sentence: Here's what I know about finding my writer's voice:

_____.

BEAT THE BOTS

> To participate in the *Beat the Bots* TikTok community:
>
> - Record a video of your answer and post it, including the hashtag #beatthebots and tag me at @beatthebotsbook
> - You can also tag #authortok and #booktok to connect with other writer and reader communities!
> - Watch other writers' videos by visiting the TikTok hashtag #beatthebots
>
> Join the conversation!

AVOID THE SAME OLD, SAME OLD WITH DIVERGENT THINKING

You may be aware of a phenomenon called "groupthink," where people lose their ability or motivation to make independent decisions. From the O-ring debacle that led to the spacecraft *Challenger* exploding to the victims' allegiance to the bank robber who held them hostage (leading to the term "Stockholm Syndrome"), groupthink is the antithesis of creativity. The equivalency in writing is when you mimic the underlying structure, overarching plot, or character arcs from other authors' works. That approach with lead you to produce derivative and formulaic stories—just like a chatbot. You need to diverge from the norm, and the process by which you do that is called "Divergent Thinking." This creativity tactic will help you develop your own writer's voice and choose POVs that correspond to your style within your genre.

The Divergent Thinking creativity tactic is a problem-solving technique. By trying to come up with off-the-wall ideas, you're often able to find unexpected nuggets of pure gold. To better understand the concept, take a look at the example in the chart below.

What It Was Designed For	Alternate Use Ideas
An Umbrella: A tool for keeping dry in the rain	• When held upside down, a sack to carry light parcels • A walking stick • Without the center shaft, a hat • A ball catcher (assuming the balls are lightweight) • A weapon • Part of a photo studio setup, a white umbrella helps diffuse light. • Decoration, for instance, a bunch hung from the ceiling, upside down • A planter, by filling the upside-down umbrella with dirt

Can you come up with any additional ideas? This kind of general divergent thinking exercise is fun and a good warm-up to stretch your brain muscles. Now apply it to your writing. For instance, let's say you want to show that your protagonist, Mark, is struggling with depression. He's determined to hide his condition from well-wishers who do nothing but mouth platitudes that only make him feel worse, including his wife, Marianne. You're debating whether to tell Mark's story from his own perspective or Marianne's perspective—or both, maybe using a first-person narrative for Mark's chapters and a third-person POV from Marianne's chapters. That's an interesting idea, and logical.

Divergent thinking says we need to go a little wild, though, to think big, to add drama. Here are some POV ideas based on two specific scenes designed to show Mark's struggles:

- Mark and Marianne go to a friend's barbeque. Mark becomes the life of the party, hiding his depression behind a mask of joviality.
  - The man next door can't help overhearing what's going on. He puts his eye to a knothole in the fence and watches for a while. How about telling the story from the neighbor's POV? In fact, the entire book could be told from strangers' POVs. A coffee shop customer, for instance, could eavesdrop on Marianne's phone conversation with her sister. Or a grocery store clerk could report on Mark and Marianne's testy conversation about their dinner plans while they're checking out.
- Mark builds a treehouse and sits in it all day, alone. There's an interesting juxtaposition here that is worth noting. Mark is sitting high above the community that he doesn't feel connected to, looking down. Is he looking down on them?

- Maybe Mark talks to a bird who's built a nest on a nearby branch. Or the story could be told from a mouse's POV after the mouse takes up residence in the treehouse.

- Mark pulls out all his flowering plants, telling anyone who asks that he's planning a new garden. A garden might make an interesting metaphor. The barren flower bed symbolizes Mark's current feelings of emptiness. If he finds his way out of his depression, he might plant flowers (immediate gratification) or bulbs (long-term gratification). If he doesn't, he might leave the ground as is, fallow.

  - Each chapter could begin with a brief update on the flower bed, perhaps from a third-person-objective POV, the all-knowing, all-seeing perspective. Perhaps at the start, the flowers are in bloom. The next chapter shows them wilting. Mark is weeding at the beginning of the third chapter. About a third of the way through the book, Mark pulls out all the plants. After that, chapters might begin with a status update: rain pocking the dirt, fallen leaves blowing onto the plants, and so on.

BEAT THE BOTS

> ### AI Weighs In
>
> **I asked a chatbot:** Which POV is best for a thriller?
>
> **AI said:** *The choice of point of view (POV) in a thriller largely depends on the specific story and the effect you want to create.*
>
> True enough—but not helpful. No matter how you phrase the question about choosing POV to a chatbot, you get broad descriptions of the pros and cons of various alternatives. Artificial intelligence can define the terms, but only you, the human, can bring actual intelligence to the decision-making process.

What do you think? Do any of those approaches seem worth trying? It can't do any harm to write a few pages from a mouse's POV or see how the story reads when an update on Mark's garden is written from the third-person-objective POV.

Creativity *requires* divergent thinking—otherwise you'll keep doing the same thing you've always done. Using the Divergent Thinking creativity tactic expands your field of vision to include ideas that go beyond the obvious, ideas you might never have otherwise found, and you just never know where it may take you.

147

Exercise

Choosing the Right POV for Your Story and Your Voice

If, after using the Three-Step Decision-Making Model introduced earlier in this chapter, you still can't decide which POV is right for your story, this exercise will help you sort through your options.

1. Write the first three pages of your story from the first-person POV, the second-person POV, the third-person limited POV, and the third-person omniscient POV.
2. Now try experimenting with off-the-wall POVs. To jump-start this phase of the exercise, here are some possibilities.
   - Your protagonist's car
   - Your protagonist's pet
   - An appliance, like the refrigerator or washing machine
   - The TV
   - A device like an iPhone or tablet
3. When you're done, reflect on your experience.
4. To help you decide, answer these questions.:
   - Which option feels most natural to the story?
   - Which excited you the most?

BEAT THE BOTS

- Which lent itself to bigger, bolder, more dramatic storytelling?
- Which supported your unique voice most effectively?
- Which most fueled your creative energy?
- Which was the quickest for you to write?

Probably the POV that got the highest number of votes is the one you should go with. Think about it. That POV is the one you decided is most exciting, effective, and energizing. Remember, though, there are no right or wrong decisions. If you find yourself flailing partway through and decide to change course, that's okay! Writing is a process—and finding your own process is a crucial step in achieving writing success.

As you think about your experience using the Divergent Thinking creativity tactic to choose your POV, what did you learn?

Here is how I might answer this question: Using the Divergent Thinking creativity tactic helped me come up with off-the-wall ideas! I mean really...who wouldn't want to read a novel told from a mouse's POV?

Now it's your turn! Answer this question: as you think about your experience using the Divergent Thinking creativity tactic to choose your POV, what did you learn?

> To participate in the *Beat the Bots* TikTok community:
>
> - Record a video of your answer and post it, including the hashtag #beatthebots and tag me at @beatthebotsbook
> - You can also tag #authortok and #booktok to connect with other writer and reader communities!
> - Watch other writers' videos by visiting the TikTok hashtag #beatthebots
> - Join the conversation!
>
> Join the conversation!

In this chapter, we examined the complex issues associated with choosing the right POV, which includes finding your unique writer's voice. We put the Divergent Thinking creativity tactic to work to help us come up with fresh takes on familiar objects and options.

Now that you know whose story is being told and have confidence in your ability to tell it like no one else can, it's time to delve into one of the most complex aspects of storytelling success: how and when to reveal your characters' backstories.

Reflection on Creativity

"Creativity is an act of defiance."
Twyla Tharp

CHAPTER SIX

CREATIVITY TACTIC #6
THE SENSORY CONNECTIVE: REVEAL BACKSTORY ARTFULLY

*"Dole out backstory sparingly, a tiny
bit at a time. Less is more."*
Lee Child

LET THE PAST STAY IN THE PAST (MOST OF THE TIME)

Your characters' backstories inform their current actions, so authors need to know them, but readers rarely do. Consider the implications of this imperative—if backstories aren't generally available, a chatbot can't access them when making its predictive recommendations about character motivations and actions. Only you, a human who actually knows the ins and outs of your characters' pasts, can to that. Your decisions about what aspects of your characters' backstories to share, when, and how has major ramifications throughout the storytelling process.

Integrating backstory requires shrewdness and sensitivity, byproducts of real intelligence, not artificial intelligence. In this chapter, we'll discuss the ways and means of sharing backstory, including linking a sensory experience to a memory using the Sensory Connective creativity tactic. In addition, a three-step decision-making tool guides you in determining which aspects of your characters' backstories to reveal and which can stay in the past.

FAQ

Q: Does your idea to present "the world in a word," apply to backstory?

A: Yes! It's an excellent technique to address the challenge of sharing pertinent information without long-winded exposition. Our characters had lives before they stepped onto the page, some of them long and eventful lives. Yet it can be done. Linda Landrigan, editor-in-chief of *Alfred Hitchcock Mystery Magazine*, explains, "Authors of short stories need to rely on 'telling details' to communicate backstory. There isn't time for anything else." And not only authors of short stories. Novelists need this same discipline. What one thing (which could take the form of a comment, a personality tic, a lifestyle choice, or a physical attribute, for example) can

BEAT THE BOTS

> communicate a world of information? Don't tell us the history. Show us that one thing. Author G. D. Peters offers this example: A woman has a tan line on her left ring finger, where, typically, one wears a wedding ring. This one detail inspires curiosity. Since the tan line tells us that she was wearing a ring until quite recently, we want to know why she removed it.

Sharing backstory is tricky because if your share too much information, or if you share it too early, before readers care about your characters, you're certain to lose them. Bestselling author Hallie Ephron, says, "Too much back story at the start of a novel can be lethal. Before you let all hell break loose, you need to make the reader care." Many authors assume the best way to create this needed empathy is to provide historical context—backstory—but they're wrong. To write a page-turner, every sentence must propel the story forward via incident or character interactions, and backstory takes us out of the action, slowing the pace.

Neil Nyren, former executive vice president, associate publisher, and editor-in-chief of G. P. Putnam's Sons, explains, "Just because you may have thought up an exhaustive backstory for each character doesn't mean you have to tell it all to us. It's enough that you know it and can inform their actions accordingly." Lawrence Light, who writes thrillers, adds, "Backstory can overwhelm a book." David Baldacci goes further, saying, "Avoid the backstory dump at all costs. Readers will see it for what it is: laziness and a writer's being unprepared. Better to divide and conquer. So append it to some dialogue, lance it judiciously into a paragraph, affix it to an action scene where it makes sense. Yes, it takes additional time and planning. But remember this: once the passengers sense the captain can't pilot the ship well, they all head for the lifeboats, and they'll never book a second passage." In other words, don't *tell* readers your characters' backstories—*show* those bits of their pasts that readers need to know through incident-based reflections, carefully constructed flashbacks and flash-forwards, and epistolary devices.

KEEP YOUR READERS INTRIGUED

The idea that readers don't need to know much about your characters' backgrounds is jarring to those of us who've spent so much time developing those backstories, but it's true. It's counterintuitive, but sometimes withholding factual information creates a deeper emotional connection with readers by encouraging them to speculate.

Prompt #21: Steer to the Pain

What drives your protagonist to act as they do? Arthur Miller, the great playwright, wrote, "Betrayal is the only truth that sticks." Whatever betrayed your character and why—that's the backstory to reveal. Here's how I would complete this exercise.

You'll recall that Alice (Tessa's cantankerous mother, introduced in Chapter Four) was weighed down with discontent. Why? That part of Alice's backstory may be worth sharing.

BEAT THE BOTS

Alice had been betrayed by her husband. He'd waltzed out the door when Tessa was six after announcing that he was going to become an actor. He'd been so earnest sounding, she'd just laughed and laughed, while he'd floundered for the words to explain.

"I have to try," he'd said.

She'd stopped laughing. "What about us?"

"You'll be fine."

So he'd bought himself a one-way bus ticket to New York City and that was that. She never heard from him again, didn't know if he was dead or alive, if she was still married, or a widow, or what. Some life.

Now it's your turn! Explain who betrayed your character and why, then write a mini-scene. When you're done, I'd love to hear what you came up with.

To participate in the *Beat the Bots* TikTok community:

- Record a video of your answer and post it, including the hashtag #beatthebots and tag me at @beatthebotsbook
- You can also tag #authortok and #booktok to connect with other writer and reader communities!
- Watch other writers' videos by visiting the Tik-Tok hashtag #beatthebots

Join the conversation!

155

Lee Child says, "The first thing any book needs is suspense, because every book must give the reader a reason to keep on going. The way to create suspense is to ask—or imply—a question...and then not answer it until later. Backstory can and absolutely should fit in with that principle. Introduce your protagonist, and make us intrigued by him or her, with present-moment actions and thoughts and behaviors. We'll all ask ourselves, 'Wow, who is this person?' Don't answer us! Make us wait! Make getting to know him or her a part of the suspense. Make it a part of the reason to keep on reading. If she's got a scar, make us wait to find out how. If she's single, make us wait to find out why. Make the reader speculate."

The good news is that you're likely to be pleasantly surprised at how much you can accomplish with just a sentence or two, sometimes with just a word or two. Consider an unplanned pregnancy. Would your character describe it as a surprise? Or an accident? The word choice communicates a world of information. In the thriller *Falling* by T. J. Newman, a character says, "The whoops baby ten years after the first kid..." Backstory in a phrase.

In Adam Hall's *The Quiller Memorandum*, backstory adds intrigue, not merely information, about the eponymous protagonist, a British spy. "Six months in the field had left me sickened and I wanted England more than I had ever wanted her before." That one sentence reveals both Quiller's state of mind and his commitment to his nation. We're brought into Quiller's world, and we find ourselves caring about him. This technique—using snippets of emotionally charged backstory to illuminate your characters' internal drivers—ensures you engage readers' interest without slowing your story's pace. Notice that by sharing the emotional truth (more than facts) behind a character's backstory, you connect with readers on a visceral level.

Prompt #22: Steer to the Pain

As you read the backstory I integrate into every Josie Prescott Antiques Mystery story or book, note all the information I'm *not* sharing. You don't learn whether she was ever married, where she grew up, whether she had siblings, where she went to college, or myriad other facts. What you learn is the caustic emotional truth that led her to move to New Hampshire. Remember—steer to the pain.

Josie worked at a high-end antiques auction house in New York City until she got caught up in a price-fixing scandal that rocked that rarefied world—she was the whistle blower. She was chased out of her job for not being a "team player," then a week later, her beloved father, her only living relative, died, and a week after that her boyfriend dumped her for being a "downer." Her dad always said that when you feel as if you're at the end of your rope, tie a knot and hang on, and if you can't hang on, move on. Josie lasted for a year, then moved on. She moved to New Hampshire to start a new life.

In four sentences totaling 118 words, you learn enough about Josie's backstory to empathize with her and to understand how emotionally fragile she must have been when she first arrived in New Hampshire.

Now it's your turn! Decide what aspects of your protagonist's backstory readers need to know to care about the character or to understand what drives their actions. Remember to steer to the pain. In just a few sentences, tell us about it.

To participate in the *Beat the Bots* TikTok community:

- Record a video of your answer and post it, including the hashtag #beatthebots and tag me at @beatthebotsbook
- You can also tag #authortok and #booktok to connect with other writer and reader communities!
- Watch other writers' videos by visiting the TikTok hashtag #beatthebots

Join the conversation!

It should be noted that some stories rely on backstory for their through-line plot. In both Liane Moriarty's *Big Little Lies* (also discussed in Chapter Six) and Richard Osman's *The Thursday Murder Club*, for instance, revealing the backstory over the course of the novel is intrinsic to the theme and the storylines. Revelations are doled out sparingly as the story unfolds.

USE INCIDENT-BASED REFLECTIONS WITH THE SENSORY CONNECTIVE

Adding in backstory through a character's reflections by recalling an event or an era works well to subtly communicate

BEAT THE BOTS

crucial facts. To use the Sensory Connective, you need to ensure that the memory:

- Relates to a current incident
- Is brief
- Wraps up logically, reconnecting to the current incident

For instance, say a woman walks into a bakery to buy a cup of coffee. While she is waiting her turn, the sweet aroma of cinnamon sugar envelopes her, leading to a memory of the carefree summers she spent at her grandma's house before her father snatched her away. The clerk breaks into her reverie with a cheery, "Hi! What can I get you?" In this example, you can see that the backstory meets our parameters: the memory is bookended by current incidents: it starts with a sensory experience—the evocative aroma, and ends with an abrupt but logical event, the clerk asking for her order. In only a few seconds of the character's time, and only one sentence, we garner a world of information.

Bestselling author Hank Phillippi Ryan explains her use of the sensory connective this way: "I think of parceling out backstory the same way I would if I were having lunch with a person I just met. I only tell what the person needs to know at the time. My editor calls it 'the Hank tucking method.' To begin to set the backstory, I tuck in a phrase, or a memory, or a reference in the midst of something else. Phrases like 'I wished my father was still alive to see this' or 'She reminded me of the poodle we had back in Indianapolis' or 'Since her divorce five years ago, she always…' Those bits add up to a bigger picture."

Pro Tip: In Series—Short and Sweet

New York Times bestselling author Louise Penny says,

> I feel strongly that readers jumping into the middle of a series will accept there are things they just won't know, and don't expect to know, unless they go back and read from the beginning. There's a danger in giving out too much information.

Note that in a series, you need to integrate the same snippet of backstory in every book, changing the wording each time and using new sensory connectives.

This idea—that less is more—applies to even the most complex backstories. Meredith Anthony, an author and book reviewer, says, "Nothing is worse than over-explaining. Instead of lingering on a psychopath's history of abuse, for instance, just mention that they hurt a family pet. Or wet the bed into adolescence. Readers will fill in the rest."

Be mindful of time, too. Fleeting thoughts are fine. But longer thoughts beg the question of how much time has passed. Let's say, for example, that a man is in the park playing with his dog. He spots someone in the distance walking with a distinctive gait that reminds him of his former best friend, now his sworn enemy. That will work. It's the kind of sensory-inspired memory that we all experience—logical and brief. If I went on to detail the event that led to the relationship's

BEAT THE BOTS

metamorphosis, that wouldn't work—don't take your readers out of the here and now for more than a few sentences.

Because people's backstories contribute so heavily to their personalities, preferences, and predispositions, ultimately, they determine what they think and do. For those situations where more information is required, it may make sense to use incident-based flashbacks (or flash-forwards). Proceed with caution, though. Flashbacks can be distracting. There you are, into the story, and boom, your concentration is broken as the author shifts time frames. If you decide to use a flashback or flash-forward, either connect it to a current incident by using the Sensory Connective creativity tactic, as discussed above, or move it to its own chapter. One additional consideration for your review: novelist Allison Amend recommends that authors avoid flashbacks "until the 'now' is well established." She warns that "too much flashback may be an indication that the story has started in the wrong place."

Prompt #23: A Distracting Interruption

Slipping backstory into a scene can be disruptive, interrupting the flow and slowing the pace. An external distraction, however, can be an effective technique allowing you to integrate a small amount of backstory.

For instance, let's say your character is standing in front of a bread display at the grocery store, debating between the healthy multigrain and the buttery brioche. An exhausted-looking woman wheels a screaming infant up the aisle. What memory does the screaming baby or bone-tired woman trigger in your character?

(Remember—share only a few words or sentences of backstory at a time.) Then a man murmurs, "Excuse me," and reaches around your character to snare a loaf of brioche, bringing your character back to the here and now.

Notice we're using the Sensory Connective creativity tactic, bookending the backstory with two sensory events—the screaming baby and the soft-spoken polite man.

Here's an example of how I might write this up. I'll write about Tessa, the young woman who just finished her doctoral program that we met in Chapter Four. Here's my scene:

> *Multigrain or brioche?* Tessa wished she were more decisive. She should be home applying for jobs, not waffling over bread. A high-pitched shriek pierced the air. A baby in a blue onesie wailed, his face all scrunched up. The woman wheeling the baby carriage didn't even seem to notice. She leaned heavily on the carriage handle, trudging along as if she were slogging through ankle-deep mud. Smudges of purple under her eyes told Tessa she was about to keel over, she was so exhausted. Mom used to look like that. Still does, as she thinks about it. Worn to a nub. Out of steam. Out of time. Out of hope.
>
> "Excuse me," a man said, reaching around her to extract a loaf of brioche from the shelf.

BEAT THE BOTS

> Now it's your turn! Use these two sensory events, the screaming baby and the soft-spoken polite man to bookend a bit of backstory about one of your characters. Start with the baby screaming and end with the man reaching for the bread. What happens in between? Remember to keep it brief!
>
> ---
>
> To participate in the *Beat the Bots* TikTok community:
> - Record a video of your answer and post it, including the hashtag #beatthebots and tag me at @beatthebotsbook
> - You can also tag #authortok and #booktok to connect with other writer and reader communities!
> - Watch other writers' videos by visiting the TikTok hashtag #beatthebots
>
> Join the conversation!

ADD DIMENSION WITH DEVICES

Paula Munier, bestselling author and literary agent, says, "Sometimes the best way to weave in backstory is to use a device. Devices like letters, quotes, transcripts, journal entries, news clippings, etc. are tools you can use to tell readers what they need to know without slowing the story down. For a master class in devices, check out *Where'd You Go, Bernadette,* by Maria Semple. She uses more than thirty different kinds of devices in that story."

Prompt #24: Experiment with a Device

In *Defending Jacob* by William Landay, backstory is revealed through court transcripts. This factual recounting of a trial is juxtaposed with a family living with the consequences of the alleged crime. The power of the raw emotion is heightened by the use of hard fact-based evidence.

Now it's your turn! How can you reveal backstory through a letter, newspaper clipping, email, memo, phone or text message, handwritten note, or other written, audio, or video communication? Briefly explain the device and what is revealed.

To participate in the *Beat the Bots* TikTok community:

- Record a video of your answer and post it, including the hashtag #beatthebots and tag me at @beatthebotsbook
- You can also tag #authortok and #booktok to connect with other writer and reader communities!
- Watch other writers' videos by visiting the TikTok hashtag #beatthebots

Join the conversation!

EVALUATE YOUR OPTIONS

This three-step decision-making tool will help you determine whether you need to add in backstory, and if so, how best to approach the task. Ask yourself these three questions:

1. Can you reveal backstory through implications tied to a current event? For instance, can you show a woman sitting alone at a bar drinking too much, rather than recount her history of binge drinking in the past? How about having her be on a first-name basis with her bartender? Or have a stool reserved for her at the end of the bar? Or wake up in a stranger's bed without any memory of how she got there? If so, you don't need to add backstory.
2. Are you using a chronological structure? If so, avoid integrating flashbacks or flash-forwards as they break the narrative flow. If you're using a nonlinear structure, you might find flashbacks or flash-forwards a sound choice.
3. Can you use a device such as a journal, newspaper article, or email to reveal past information organically?

These three questions, taken together, will help you determine if you need to include backstory, and if so, how much. Because there's no one definitive answer, it's important to experiment with different alternatives, assessing your options with objective judgment, something only you, a human, can do.

AI Weighs In

I asked a chatbot: Can you come up with a backstory to explain a woman's coulrophobia (fear of clowns).

AI said: *Certainly!*

Samantha Johnson, a thirty-four-year-old graphic designer, has been terrified of clowns ever since a fateful day at the circus when she was a child.

When Samantha was seven, her parents took her to a circus that had just come to town. It was supposed to be a fun family outing filled with cotton candy, acrobats, and laughter. Everything was going well until the clowns came out to perform. One of the clowns, named Chuckles, startled Samantha by running up and blowing his horn into her face. She screamed and burst into tears and the crowd laughed at her discomfort. The combination of the surprise, the blaring horn, and the crowd's laughter left her traumatized. From that day forward, clowns became a symbol of humiliation and fear for her. Even as an adult, she can't shake the memory of that circus mishap, and the mere sight of a clown triggers her coulrophobia.

BEAT THE BOTS

ChatGPT did a good job recounting an incident that led to a phobia, but as with past searches on various chatbots, the answer is trite, smacking of been-there-done-that familiarity.

Instead of relying on the obvious, aim for something realistic, but unusual. For instance, maybe the girl was out trick or treating one Halloween when she was seven years old. An older boy dressed as a clown jumped out from behind a bush, hoping to scare her. It more than scared her—it traumatized her. The panic faded, but the fear of clowns stayed with her.

The Sensory Connective creativity tactic is a reliable way to weave in backstory. The following three-part exercise will enable you to put this valuable technique to work.

Exercise

Create a Sensory Connective

Part One: Determine Your Backstory's Value

Answer these two questions to help you confirm the backstory you plan on sharing has sufficient merit.

1. Does the backstory reveal an emotional truth that drives your character's actions?
2. Can you steer to the pain, homing in on only the most dramatic revelations?

167

Here's how I might use these questions to think the decision through. You'll remember that Mark (introduced in Chapter Five) is depressed, but we never learn why. Let's add a snippet of backstory to explain the situation. Mark is depressed because he got laid off. He hasn't found a new job yet, and he hasn't told Marianne, his wife. He goes to the library every day, pretending he's going to work. He's applying for every job he can find, but so far, he hasn't got even a nibble. He feels like an utter failure.

1. *Does the backstory reveal an emotional truth that drives your character's actions?*

    Yes. Mark's experience is deep with raw emotion, and will help readers understand why he's acting as he is.

2. *Can you steer to the pain, homing in on only the most dramatic revelations?*

    Yes, the backstory will reveal Mark's reaction to the job loss, not the job loss itself.

Part Two: Segue In and Out

To integrate the backstory smoothly using the Sensory Connective creativity tactic, remember the three parameters—your backstory should:

- Relate to a current incident
- Be brief

- Wrap up logically, reconnecting to the current incident

Write it up:

The wooden chair scraping the tile crashed into the library's typical hush, interrupting Mark's staring into space, seeing nothing. Mark raised the newspaper to shield his face and peeked around the edge to see who'd taken the seat at the other end of the table. Some kid, high school, probably. He glanced at his watch. Three twenty. Another hour and he could go home, tell Marianne another lie. He was such a loser. Who ever heard of an off-work accountant? The kid opened his laptop lid and started tapping away, and Mark resumed his staring, all he was good for these days—nothing.

Part Three: Assess Viability

To determine whether you successfully integrated your backstory, answer these questions:

1. Was the memory (backstory) triggered by something the character saw, heard, tasted, felt (touched), or smelled?
2. Was the backstory specific?

3. Did the backstory reveal a significant emotional truth about the character (as opposed to being merely informational)?
4. Did the backstory end organically, reconnecting to the current incident in a natural and logical manner?

Here's my self-assessment:

1. *Was the memory (backstory) triggered by something the character saw, heard, tasted, felt (touched), or smelled?*

    Yes, Mark heard the chair scraping the floor.
2. *Was the backstory specific?*

    It didn't include a specific incident, but it did account for why Mark was in the library (he no longer had a job to go to), what he was doing (nothing), and the consequences of losing his job (lying to his wife).
3. *Did the backstory reveal a significant emotional truth about the character (as opposed to being merely informational)?*

    Yes, we learned he feels like a loser and that he's inert, unable to do anything, a common symptom of depression.
4. *Did the backstory end organically, reconnecting to the current incident in a natural and logical manner?*

Yes, Mark resumed staring into space, the short scene ending where it started.

Now it's your turn! Complete the three parts of the exercise, then share your thoughts about what you learned regarding revealing backstory.

Part One: Determine Your Backstory's Value

Answer these two questions to help you confirm the backstory you plan on sharing has sufficient merit.

1. Does the backstory reveal an emotional truth that drives your character's actions?
2. Can you steer to the pain, homing in on only the most dramatic revelations?

Part Two: Segue In and Out

To integrate the backstory smoothly using the Sensory Connective creativity tactic, remember the three parameters—your backstory should:

- Relate to a current incident
- Be brief
- Wrap up logically, reconnecting to the current incident

Write it up:

Part Three: Assess Viability

To determine whether you successfully integrated your backstory, answer these questions:

1. Was the memory (backstory) triggered by something the character saw, heard, tasted, felt (touched), or smelled?
2. Was the backstory specific?
3. Did the backstory reveal a significant emotional truth about the character (as opposed to being merely informational)?
4. Did the backstory end organically, reconnecting to the current incident in a natural and logical manner?

If you answered yes to all of them, congratulations! You've successfully used the Sensory Connective creativity tactic to reveal important backstory. If you answered no to any question, you might want to adjust the situation to better integrate the backstory.

When you've finished, I'd love to hear about your experience! Complete this sentence: I tried the Sensory Connective creativity tactic to reveal backstory and learned

_____.

BEAT THE BOTS

To participate in the *Beat the Bots* TikTok community:

- Record a video of your answer and post it, including the hashtag #beatthebots and tag me at @beatthebotsbook
- You can also tag #authortok and #booktok to connect with other writer and reader communities!
- Watch other writers' videos by visiting the TikTok hashtag #beatthebots

Join the conversation!

In this chapter, we discussed how to artfully reveal backstory. We looked at the Sensory Connective creativity tactic, using devices, and whether to use flashbacks or flash-forwards. In the next chapter, we'll talk about how to write dialogue that doesn't merely say something—it does something. We'll also discuss important mechanical issues including using dialogue tags, punctuation, and formatting.

Reflection on Creativity

"You can't use up creativity. The more you use, the more you have."
Maya Angelou

CHAPTER SEVEN

CREATIVITY TACTIC #7

CONFLICT GENERATOR: WRITE DIALOGUE THAT DOES SOMETHING, NOT SIMPLY SAYS SOMETHING

"It's all about language. Once I can figure out what the language inside their head is—that way in which people talk to themselves without saying anything, the stream of what is running in your head—once I can figure out what that language is, I can get the character. It just clicks in."
Francine Prose

HARNESS THE POWER OF DIALOGUE

Dialogue is one of three narrative tools to move the plot along and reveal character attributes (in addition to description and action). By using the Conflict Generator creativity tactic to

BEAT THE BOTS

write dialogue that resonates with emotional truth, your stories spring to life. Once you know the underlying conflicts that drive your characters' actions, and how those conflicts intersect, you'll know what your characters should say, and how they should say it. Only you, the creator of your story, can write dialogue that reveals your characters' personalities, longings, and attitudes through the words they speak and through their silences. The Conflict Generator creativity tactic requires your imagination and wise judgment, not a chatbot's predictive and derivative recommendations.

The spoken word is powerful. To write compelling dialogue, you need to:

- Create credible voices for every character, and each one needs to be different from the others.
- Use dialogue to *show*, not tell, and even when we decide that a summary is better than a conversation, we need to *show*, not tell.
- Layer in deep meaning through subtext—our dialogue needs to *do* something, not merely say something.

Also, your dialogue has to look right. You have to know the mechanics of writing dialogue, including tags, typographical emphasis, and proper punctuation.

CREATE INDIVIDUAL CHARACTER VOICES

To create natural-sounding dialogue, you need to know your characters. That said, don't try to mimic the way people talk exactly. In real life, people use a lot of fillers like "ah" and "um." They litter their conversation with "like" and "well." People hem and haw and take a long time to get to the point. Sometimes they're repetitive. All of these conversational gambits are perfectly understandable—people ramble while getting their thoughts in order. They add in fillers while deciding how frank to be. They're embarrassed or ashamed. That's the way people speak in real life, but if you include those details in your dialogue, you risk distracting and boring your readers.

FAQ

Q: You recommend eliminating fillers like "um" and "ah." But if I want my characters to sound real, shouldn't I let the talk the way actual people do?

A: You raise an important point, but I'd worry that writing belabored dialogue will slow your story's forward momentum and annoy your readers. While as a general statement, I recommend eliminating these kinds of fillers, sometimes you might have a good reason to include them, to show that someone is inarticulate or that a middle-aged woman is trying to talk like her teenage daughter, for instance. Another possible reason to include one or two of these filler words might be to show the character thinking something through. Note that these kinds of decisions require careful thought and assessment—what will you achieve by including them? Don't rely on AI to choose for you. Only you, with your knowledge of your particular character's attributes and your through-line plot, can make this determination.

BEAT THE BOTS

Let's take a look at two questions that will help you create unique character voices. One question is about vocabulary; the other is about usage.

1. Choose words that the character knows and uses.

   For instance, does your character use pedantic, esoteric words because he's an academic with his head in the clouds? Or does he use those words to cover up his insecurity? Look how smart I am! Or does he use those big, arcane words only with other academics, switching to common English with laypeople? Is his attitude patronizing or kind?

2. Does your character know American idioms? (Or if you're setting your book in another country, does your character know local idioms?) If not, why not?

   Maybe English isn't their first language. This character could be an immigrant; an international tourist; a fairy or other character one might find in a fantasy novel; a ghost who knew idioms from when they were alive, but now that they've been reactivated in today's world, they're befuddled; an alien from another planet; a con man; or an unreliable narrator up to no good.

Let's dig into the immigrant example. Your character has been in the United States for decades, but her English isn't perfect. She understands the idiom "It's raining cats and dogs," but when she uses the phrase, she states it as, "It's raining with cats and dogs." Another consideration: do the people interacting with this character find these tiny misstatements charming or annoying?

177

Prompt #25: Idioms at Work

Let's take an idiom and make it slightly off as a way of communicating important information about the character. For example, if a man says he's "feeling under the weather," you know he's feeling a little sick. What do you know about him if he says, "I'm feeling below the weather" instead? The warped idiom tells us something is off, but it doesn't tell us what or why. Remember all the possible reasons reviewed in this chapter. This kind of subtle character reveal is intriguing, certain to engage your reader's interest.

Now it's your turn! Take the idiom "barking up the wrong tree," which means "following a false lead," and write a line or two of dialogue that incorporates that idiom—or a mistake in the expression of the idiom—to communicate something about the person speaking it. What did you come up with?

To participate in the *Beat the Bots* TikTok community:

- Record a video of your answer and post it, including the hashtag #beatthebots and tag me at @beatthebotsbook
- You can also tag #authortok and #booktok to connect with other writer and reader communities!
- Watch other writers' videos by visiting the TikTok hashtag #beatthebots

Join the conversation!

BEAT THE BOTS

Another reliable technique to create unique character voices is to consider the character's attitude toward popular culture. Let's say one of your characters is a fifty-year-old man out to be cool, you know, the kind of fellow who drives a Corvette with racing stripes. He misspeaks, then says, "My bad." Will that sound natural coming from him? Yes, it will, because he's that sort of person. Will his college-age son roll his eyes, embarrassed at his dad who's trying too hard to be cool? Probably? Will his mother know the term? It depends on the mother, right? That's the point—there's no right or wrong answer here—it depends on the person.

The following three examples showcase techniques to reveal character through the spoken word, integrating the style and mores of the era and cultures in which those characters lived.

The first example is from page one of Georgette Heyer's Regency romance *The Corinthian*. From these two sentences, we know everything we need to know about the eponymous character—the Corinthian—and his mother. During the Regency period, the term "Corinthian" referred to a man of perfection—rich, good-looking, athletic, and so on. The protagonist of this book is named Richard. His mother is Lady Wyndham.

Before I share the two sentences, I want to highlight one issue relating to dialogue tags. Ms. Heyer uses the word "complained" as a tag. That certainly tells us Lady Wyndham's attitude, but I suggest to you, it's not needed. Her attitude is apparent from her words. So why would the author have included it? There's no way to know, of course, but I suspect there are two reasons: style and the standards of the day. Ms. Heyer often adds information through dialogue tags and related exposition. Fair enough. That's her style. As to the standards of the day, this book was first published in 1940, when using more descriptive dialogue tags was the norm. I wonder if Ms. Heyer would have skipped it were she writing today.

We'll discuss the proper use of dialogue tags in a little bit, but for now, read this two-sentence, twenty-five-word excerpt with the tag, then without it, and see if you agree that it isn't needed. As you read the first excerpt, note the tag's proper placement—after the first phrase.

> ### *The Corinthian* by Georgette Heyer
>
> "Your poor Papa was always out when one wanted him," complained Lady Wyndham. "It is very affecting to me to see Richard growing every day more like him."
>
> "Your poor Papa was always out when one wanted him. It is very affecting to me to see Richard growing every day more like him."

The words Heyer wrote for Lady Wyndham stand on their own, making her complaining tone evident. That we don't need the tag is a tribute to the author.

My next example comes from the middle-grade novel *Hello Universe* by Erin Entrada Kelly. In this scene, Virgil's grandmother is in the kitchen, slicing a mango.

BEAT THE BOTS

Hello Universe by Erin Entrada Kelly

"Come take one of these. Your mother bought too many again. They were on sale, so she buys ten. What do we need ten mangoes for? They're not even from the Philippines. They're from Venezuela. Your mother bought ten Venezuelan mangoes, and for what? That woman would buy kisses from Judas if they were on sale."

From those fifty-six words, we learn a ton about what Virgil's grandmother thinks about Virgil's mom, and it's not good. Grandma's voice is ironic and witty.

The third example comes from "Home," a short story by George Saunders first published in the *New Yorker*. Almost the entire story is in dialogue. Here is the beginning, which includes over a hundred words of exposition.

"Home" by George Saunders

Like in the old days, I came out of the dry creek behind the house and did my little tap on the kitchen window.

"Get in here, you," Ma said.

Inside were piles of newspapers on the stove and piles of magazines on the stairs

---

181

and a big wad of hangers sticking out of the broken oven. All of that was as usual. New was: a water stain the shape of a cat head on the wall above the fridge and the old orange rug rolled up halfway.

"Still ain't no beeping cleaning lady," Ma said.

I looked at her funny. "Beeping?" I said.

"Beep you." she said. "They been on my case at work."

It was true Ma had a pretty good potty mouth. And was working at a church now, so.

What a great way to show Ma's character!

Prompt #26: Match Personality to Dialogue Style

Think about your character's style. Does she pop gum and shoulder dance to music only she can hear? What would that person's conversation style be like? I bet she'd say things like "Oh, puleeze!" or "Give it a rest," or "In your dreams."

Now it's your turn! Write a one-sentence description of a character that's clear and visual, then write a few examples of a few phrases that particular person would speak.

To participate in the *Beat the Bots* TikTok community:

- Record a video of your answer and post it, including the hashtag #beatthebots and tag me at @beatthebotsbook
- You can also tag #authortok and #booktok to connect with other writer and reader communities!
- Watch other writers' videos by visiting the TikTok hashtag #beatthebots

Join the conversation!

SHOW VIA SCENE OR SUMMARY

Not every incident needs to be experienced in real time. To avoid becoming involved in minutia or slowing the pace, some conversations are better summarized through exposition. Let's say, for example, that for a third of your novel, your character, a college sophomore, has been secretly in love with her roommate's brother. Finally, she confronts him and confesses her love. If you only summarize that conversation, readers will feel cheated. They want to bear witness, to hear your character's actual words and see the brother's reaction. Avoiding a summary is the smart choice here. But it's not a black-or-white decision. Summaries can still show, not tell. It's all in the writing.

Here's a case in point: In a book I wrote some years ago, I had a scene in which two characters were bantering as they discussed trickle-down economics. I had a lot of fun writing it! My first reader's comment was—I'm paraphrasing here: *Shoot me now! Three pages about economics?* I argued that I needed to showcase their expertise—I was *showing*, not telling. Let me read you his editorial note. And you'll see that because he REALLY doesn't give a flying hoot about economics, his example relates to something he does care about—history.

"Sure, I understand you need to display their expertise, quick wit, and friendly banter. All good. But three pages? Shoot me now!"

Okay, I wasn't paraphrasing—he really did write "Shoot me now!" I was quoting. He went on to explain his objection.

"You need to find a way to achieve that worthy goal without all the economic gobbledygook, which interests me zero. If I wanted to read an economic treatise, I would. I don't want to it in my pleasure reading. Instead, write two sentences that do the trick."

. Here was his example: "Once again, Tom and Bob were debating the 'Great Man' theory of history. Tom thought Lincoln was a great man who changed the nation, while Bob argued that it was a nation in crisis that shaped Lincoln to be the leader he became."

So much better, right? This example proves that sometimes summary is the better option. How do you decide? Here is the only question you need to answer to decide which is best: Is the situation part of the story? (Like the young woman

BEAT THE BOTS

in love.) If so, go with the real-time scene. If not (like a discussion of economics designed to reveal character), go with the summary.

LAYER IN MEANING WITH SUBTEXT

Subtext refers to implications or innuendo hidden in the words your character speaks. Adding subtext enables you to share character attitudes and build in context—dialogue should *do* something, not merely *say* something. Subtext should:

- Reveal, exacerbate, or resolve conflict.
- Share character attitudes, reactions, or preferences, or withhold whatever the other character desires: love, empathy, sleep, or food, for example.
- Move the plot along as the characters wrestle with the conflict

Remember that each chapter should show conflict that escalates as challenges become harder, more complex, more fraught. (Raising the stakes in this way is discussed in a later chapter.) Don't squander the opportunity to use dialogue to add this kind of depth.

Consider this 189-word example that features mostly dialogue. Note the difference between the literal content—who's going to pick up the son from the airport and how does the Christmas tree look—and the subtext, the meaning beneath the literal words.

185

Read for the Subtext

Mary reached to the back of the Christmas tree to hang a red ornament. She hated it when the colors weren't evenly spaced. She was nearing the top of the stepladder, but did Mitch care? Oh, no. He didn't even notice. He was too busy snoozing in front of the TV.

"What time is it?" Mary asked.

"Huh?"

"Wake up, sunshine. What time is it?"

"I don't have my watch, but *Jeopardy!*'s on."

"So seven something. You go back to sleep. I'll pick up Sam from the airport."

"I'll go."

"How? Are you going to drive your recliner?"

"Is that supposed to be funny?"

"Do you see me laughing?"

"I said I'd go."

"Sam is my son, too. I *want* to go."

"Why didn't you say so instead of making a federal case out of it? We'll go together."

> "How does the tree look?"
>
> Mitch skewed around to look. "You need more red on the left."
>
> Mary placed two red balls on the left, then used both hands to ease her way down from the stepstool. "Let's go. I don't want to be late."
>
> "Let me just finish my show."

Do you see how this conversation reveals oodles about both Mitch and Mary, and about their relationship?

Here's an example from *Ordinary People* by Judith Guest. In this novel, the mother is cold and emotionally unavailable, yet to an outsider, she's perfect, even charming. After a terrible boating accident results in the death of one of her sons, she finds it impossible to love her surviving son, Conrad. In one scene, she dutifully serves her husband and Conrad French toast. Conrad finally shares his feelings—he's enduring a horrible case of survivor's guilt. She can't bear to hear it. She says: "I'm not hungry," takes the food to the kitchen, and tosses it in the sink. She says, "You can't save French toast." The subtext is heartbreaking: She can't save her love for Conrad just as Conrad couldn't save his brother from drowning.

Pro Tip: The Best Dialogue Is Thoroughly Human

Jessica Strawser, novelist and editor-at-large for *Writer's Digest* magazine, explains:

> The most effective dialogue is full of passion or humor or longing. It's, "You're gonna need a bigger boat," and, "You complete me," and, "I'll have what she's having." It's the loaded emotion of, "Nobody puts Baby in a corner," and the verbal gut punch of, "Frankly, my dear, I don't give a damn." More than anything, it's full of nuance—as much about the words spoken as what isn't said. That's what makes it memorable—and thoroughly human.

For additional examples of subtext, take a look at Ernest Hemingway's short story "Hills Like White Elephants," which is often cited as an example of excellence in adding subtext. The couple never mentions whether the woman will get an abortion or not, yet the issue, the discussion, and the decision, are, most folks agree, apparent. In Jhumpa Lahiri's "A Temporary Matter," we witness how a marriage fails when a couple grieves as individuals. It both cases, the conflicts are grounded in emotional truth.

BEAT THE BOTS

Prompt #27: Subtext—Simmering Anger

Write a few lines of dialogue between a character who is angry and determined not to show it and someone else. The subtext should be clear, although not stated.

You'll recall Alice and Tessa, the mother-daughter duo that I've used in previous examples. Let's say that Tessa is fed up to the gills with Alice. Tessa just earned her PhD, and her mother acts like Tessa got the degree specifically to rub Alice's face in her own inferiority. Tessa doesn't get it, but after years of enduring Alice's nasty little digs, Tessa has had enough. But she doesn't see any benefit in letting Alice know she got under her daughter's skin. Alice isn't going to change, and Tessa has begun applying for tenure-track professor positions. Tessa suspects she's more likely to land a job in a smaller market like North Dakota or New Mexico than Boston, so she probably won't see her mom that often. Here's how I might write dialogue where Tessa is determined not to let her anger show.

> "So why'd you drive down in this storm?" Alice asked. "Just to tell me you finished school?"
>
> "Maybe I should go."
>
> "Suit yourself."
>
> "I'm applying for jobs all over. I doubt I'll end up in Boston."

189

> "Are you going to stay for supper? I've got some leftover chicken."
>
> "I think I'll head back."
>
> Can you feel the chill between them? Tessa's anger and dismay are apparent, despite being unspoken.
>
> Now it's your turn. Write a few lines of dialogue that show your character's unspoken anger.
>
> ---
>
> To participate in the *Beat the Bots* TikTok community:
>
> - Record a video of your answer and post it, including the hashtag #beatthebots and tag me at @beatthebotsbook
> - You can also tag #authortok and #booktok to connect with other writer and reader communities!
> - Watch other writers' videos by visiting the TikTok hashtag #beatthebots
>
> Join the conversation!

IDENTIFY WHO'S SPEAKING

Two reliable ways to indicate who is speaking are dialogue tags and business. Dialogue tags explicitly state who is talking

BEAT THE BOTS

with phrases like "he said" or "she asked." The term "business" refers to an action taken by the speaker that immediately precedes the spoken words. Tags are labels that announce who is speaking—telling the reader so they can follow along. Business gives the character something to do—showing the reader what's happening while that character is speaking. Showing is always better than telling, and this is no exception. Which isn't to say you'll never use tags. You will (unless you decide to eliminate all of them, discussed later in this chapter). Let's review some conventions and discuss your options.

Tags are most needed in large group conversations, those including three or more people. With two people, it should be apparent who's speaking. That said, every four or five exchanges, add business using the character's name, or a tag. Why? So readers don't have to concentrate on keeping track of who's speaking. You don't want to do *anything* that will slow your readers down. Which begs the question: why not use business or tags *more* often? Because doing so slows the reader down, interrupting the forward motion of your story. In other words—use business or tags frequently enough to avoid reader confusion, but no more often than that. The sweet spot seems to be every four or five exchanges.

Since business is showing, I recommend you use it more than tags. To come up with *credible* business, that which flows organically from the situation, ask yourself what is your character *doing* during this conversation. Let's say you're writing about two people in a diner talking. Think about what they do: they sip coffee, add salt, pour ketchup, take a bite of their burgers, push their empty plates aside, signal the server for the check, and so on. The point isn't to get lost in the morass of details. The point is to use these details, a sentence or phrase at a time, as needed, to *show* who's talking. For instance, consider this pair of options:

- "How dare you?" Mary demanded through clenched teeth.
- Mary slapped the table. "How dare you?"

To some extent, this is a style issue, a writer's choice, but I certainly think the "after" example is stronger. It's more active. I, as a reader, jump a little when Mary slaps the table. It feels more vivid to me.

If you need a tag, the prevailing opinion is to use only "said," "asked," and "whispered." I'll add "continued" or "added," to the list, if appropriate. And you can use synonyms for "whispered," like "murmured." Using other descriptive words gets into the problem of telling versus showing discussed above. If I have to label the speech as "exclaimed," (instead of "said"), "challenged" (instead of "asked"), or "joked" (you know you're in trouble if you have to tell people it's a joke)—or if I need to add an adverb, like "he said loudly," that's probably a sign you need to be revising the dialogue itself, either for content or emphasis (discussed later in this chapter.)

If you're going to use a tag, add it after the first clause or sentence. If the dialogue tag comes before the quote, introduce it with a comma. If the tag comes in the middle of the quote, note the punctuation: "Hi, Mary," Jim said, "thanks for coming."

BEAT THE BOTS

Prompt #28: Show the Character's Intention through Business

The following snippet of dialogue uses a tag. Revise it by adding business, showing the reader what Chris (who is three years old) is doing. Remember to add the business *before* the spoken words.

"I don't want to, and you can't make me!" Chris said. Your revision:

_____

To participate in the *Beat the Bots* TikTok community:

- Record a video of your answer and post it, including the hashtag #beatthebots and tag me at @beatthebotsbook
- You can also tag #authortok and #book-tok to connect with other writer and reader communities!
- Watch other writers' videos by visiting the TikTok hashtag #beatthebots

Join the conversation!

SHOW ATTITUDE THROUGH EMPHASIS

There are five typographical options you can use to show emphasis:

1. *Italics*
2. Exclamation point
3. ALL CAPS
4. Ellipsis
5. Em dash

Let's review them one at a time so you can see how to optimize their strengths.

Italics

Italics serve multiple purposes in text, in addition to emphasis. For instance, book, magazine, and newspaper titles are correctly set in italics. So too are foreign words and terms. Copy editor Kate Post explains,

> This one is a bit of a hot topic for debate in the editing world, and the rules vary widely based on the style guide you're using. Most genre fiction and literary fiction use the *Chicago Manual of Style*, which follows this rule *except* for foreign words and phrases that are 1) listed in *Merriam-Webster*, or 2) commonly used in a work. See *Chicago Manual of Style* 7.53 for more details.

In this discussion, though, we're only going to look at using the style to add emphasis.

BEAT THE BOTS

The judicious use of italics can so effectively emphasize certain elements, while downplaying others, the entire meaning of your sentence changes. Say the following sentence aloud seven times, stressing the word set in italics.

I didn't say he stole my money.
I *didn't* say he stole my money.
I didn't *say* he stole my money.
I didn't say *he* stole my money.
I didn't say he *stole* my money.
I didn't say he stole *my* money.
I didn't say he stole my *money*.

Isn't that incredible? One word, set in italics, and everything changes.

Exclamation Point

An exclamation point indicates extreme emphasis or surprise. It's a useful punctuation mark, but it needs to be used with discretion. As with all typographical emphasis options, a little bit goes a long way. Too many exclamation points dilute the element's impact.

Here are two "before" examples of strong dialogue unnecessarily weakened by an adverb and a cliché, followed by an "after" fix, improved by a combination of italics and one exclamation point. Note that the dialogue itself is unchanged.

Before #1:

"Oh, that's a good idea," he said sarcastically. "You're firing on all cylinders now."

195

The adverb is *telling* us about the character's tone of voice. We can do better.

Before #2:

> "Oh, that's a good idea," he said, his voice dripping with sarcasm. "You're firing on all cylinders now."

If you need to *tell* the reader that this dialogue is spoken with sarcasm, then you need to rewrite the dialogue or add typographical emphasis. Plus "dripping with sarcasm" is a cliché.

After:

> "Oh, that's a *great* idea," he said. "You're firing on all cylinders now!"

The dialogue is good. It didn't need revising. What it needed was typographical emphasis. The use of italics (to indicate which word to stress) and the exclamation point (to show intensity) changes everything. Those two modifications point toward the sarcastic tone, which eliminates the need to tell the reader that these words were spoken sarcastically.

ALL CAPS

ALL CAPS communicates a shout. Keep in mind that, from a readability POV, ten words or more set in ALL CAPS becomes onerously hard to read, and we never want to lose readers because they have to slog through our text. Here's an ALL CAPS example from a short story by ZZ Packer called "Brownies," first published in *Harper Magazine*.

BEAT THE BOTS

The story revolves around two Brownie troops in Camp Crescendo, somewhere near Atlanta. One of the Brownie troops is all Black, the other is all white. One of the Black girls says that one of the white girls spoke the "n" word. Note that the word "BAD" is written in ALL CAPS. As you read this one sentence, listen for the character's voice.

The accuser reports what she allegedly heard. "That's a BAD word!" she continued. "We don't say BAD words."

Doesn't this sound like a child? Can't you picture her standing with her hands on her hips? Can you hear the shout? I sure can. And that's the essence of effective storytelling.

Ellipsis

In nonfiction, an ellipsis (three consecutive dots) signals that words are missing from a quote. In fiction, an ellipsis indicates a pause. Using ellipses instead of business offers an alternative to telling words like, "She paused" or "He looked down, thinking."

Just as with all emphasis elements, you can include too many ellipses. I did this in *Jane Austen's Lost Letters*. My editor called it "ellipses run amuck." I used the pausing technique nearly two hundred times. *Oops*. So how did I fix it? I replaced ellipsis with business and revised the text accordingly. For instance, here's Josie asking whether a script is finished.

Before:

> "I was going to read it over one more time, then send it to you, but what the hey...I'll send it to you now."

197

After:

> "I was going to read it over one more time, then send it to you, but what the hey." He tapped a few buttons on his laptop. "Off it goes!"

The "before" example isn't bad, but by adding business, the exchange is more dynamic. The reader is invited into the experience, and the character's voice shines through a little brighter.

Em Dash

An em dash indicates an abrupt change in content, tone, or meaning. It is also used in pairs to indicate a shout-out or an aside. (An em dash is formed by typing two hyphens with no space between them.)

Here's an example of using an em dash to show an abrupt shift in tone—I want to emphasize the speaker's attitude: "William is leaving the company—not of his own choice."

When used in pairs, you're highlighting an intervening modifying phrase. Other alternatives are a pair of commas or parenthesis marks. There's no right or wrong choice here. You make the decision based on your intention. Consider these three options:

- Ms. Walker, the president, made the travel arrangements.
  - Commas, indicating the inclusion of her job title is informational, nothing more.
- Ms. Walker (the president) made the travel arrangements.
  - Parenthesis marks, suggested the inclusion of her job title is a whispered aside or gossipy interlude.

BEAT THE BOTS

- Ms. Walker—the president—made the travel arrangements.
  - Em dashes, signaling it's remarkable that the company president made the travel arrangements.

Employing these emphasis options will help readers understand your intentions, while avoiding telling them.

PUNCTUATE PROPERLY IN DIALOGUE THAT SPANS MULTIPLE PARAGRAPHS

Punctuation's chief job is clarity. The punctuation rule states that you place a quotation mark at the beginning of the character's spoken words and at the end. If the character's conversation extends beyond a paragraph, you place a starting quotation mark at the beginning of each paragraph. You only place the ending quotation mark when the character is done speaking. Because this can be confusing, another option is to insert business between the paragraphs. Depending on how long the business is, you might want to add a tag to the continuation, indicating the same person is speaking, such as "added" or "continued." Let's take a look at an example that shows your options.

Dialogue that Spans Multiple Paragraphs

Let's say Mary and Tom are fighting.

Correct:

"How could you lie to me?" Mary asked. "You must think I'm a fool.

"Years ago, my mother warned me not to trust men like you."

Also Correct (and Probably Easier to Follow):

"How could you lie to me?" Mary asked. "You must think I'm a fool." She picked up her mother's photo, and touched the glass, her mother's cheek. "Years ago, my mother warned me not to trust men like you."

Also Correct (and as Easy to Follow as the Previous Option):

"How could you lie to me?" Mary asked. "You must think I'm a fool."

The doorbell chimed, and Mary hurried to the door. Tom could wait. She brought in the delivery, her new curtains, not that she'd need them now if things went south with Tom. She'd move out in a heartbeat if she had somewhere to go. She walked slowly back

> into the living room. Tom sat in the same chair, his long-suffering expression unchanged. She picked up her mother's photo, and touched the glass, her mother's cheek, then turned to face Tom.
>
> "Years ago," Mary continued, "my mother warned me not to trust men like you."

DECIDE WHETHER TO SKIP USING QUOTATION MARKS AT ALL

Writing without using quotation marks is common in today's literary world, and not only in today's literary world, but throughout history. Here's a (very) partial list of writers who did not or do not use quotation marks:

• Samuel Beckett	• James Joyce
• E. E. Cummings	• Cormac McCarthy
• Junot Díaz	• Marcel Proust
• E. L. Doctorow	• José Saramago
• William Faulkner	• Gertrude Stein
• Charles Frazier	• Virginia Woolf

In fact, Goodreads offers a list of one hundred contemporary books without quotation marks.

Most authors take a different tack, believing that quote marks *enhance* clarity. How should you decide? Here are two questions that will help you decide what's best for you and your project.

1. *Do you write literary fiction or genre fiction?*

If you scan the list of authors who don't use quote marks, you'll note they write literary fiction. Not using conventional punctuation is far more likely (but not in any way required) in literary fiction than it is in genre fiction. Some authors acknowledge that not using quote marks requires the reader to slow down, and they're okay with that. They want readers to savor the prose, not rush through.

2. *What is your reason for not using quote marks?*

In an interview with Oprah, Cormac McCarthy was asked this question. He explained that "his minimalist approach works in the interest of maximum clarity." He referenced James Joyce, adding, "James Joyce is a good model for punctuation. He keeps it to an absolute minimum. There's no reason to blot the page up with weird little marks. I mean, if you write properly, you shouldn't have to punctuate."

Only you, the author, can decide what's best about using quotation marks. If you decide not to, you must ensure there's no ambiguity or confusion about who's speaking. Consider the issue carefully.

AI Weighs In

As discussed in this chapter, the way a character speaks must reflect who they truly are, their desires, intentions, and attitudes. It is your ability to communicate this individuality that sets your writing apart from text produced via a chatbot. The dialogue must also be relevant to the situation, add information about the character or drive the plot forward. AI frequently misses the mark on some or all of those imperatives. Consider, for example, the first two lines of ChatGPT's response to a request to write a new episode of *Law and Order: SVU*, created by Dick Wolf:

> *Detective OLIVIA BENSON, Detective ELLIOT STABLER*
>
> *BENSON: We've been seeing a disturbing pattern, Elliot. Multiple unsolved cases of missing girls, all from different backgrounds, and no leads.*
>
> *STABLER: It's like they vanished into thin air. But we can't give up, Liv. We owe it to these families to find their daughters.*

Olivia Benson was promoted to sergeant two years *after* Elliot Stabler left the show, which occurred at the end of the show's twelfth season, in 2011. Benson made captain during the twenty-first season. Therefore, it's a mystery why ChatGPT would refer to

Benson as "detective" or include Stabler at all in writing a "new" script.

Equally problematic is the weak dialogue. Both characters know the information they're discussing, so it serves no purpose other than to bring viewers up to date, an example of a clunky info dump. This snippet of dialogue *tells* viewers what is happening (static), instead of *showing* the situation (dynamic). This conversational gambit, sharing information via dialogue as opposed to exposition in the mistaken belief that it's more active and thus won't come across as "telling," is a frequently seen writing misstep. Because it's common, it's prevalent in AI's source material. By regurgitating it, the chatbot is simply perpetuating the error. The same principle applies to the chatbot's use of clichés, like "vanished into thin air" and trite conceits, like "owing" a solution to victims' families.

It takes you, a human, to come up with fresh dialogue that doesn't merely *say* something, but also *does* something.

When written well, dialogue can invigorate your story with in-the-moment vitality. To replicate various people's styles of verbal communication, it's crucial that you observe real-world interactions. The following exercise will help you translate those observations into storytelling gold.

BEAT THE BOTS

Exercise

Conflict Generator: Write Dialogue that *Does* Something, Not Simply *Says* Something

Listen for Both Style and Substance

Ask three or five people the same nonloaded, open-ended question. You want to hear what people say, not what they think you want to hear. Of course, you shouldn't ask questions that might make people feel uncomfortable, so I'd stay away from politics, religion, and personal issues. For instance, you might ask:

- If you could travel anywhere, and with all expenses paid, where would you go? Why?
- When you think of comfort food, what comes to mind? Why?
- Think about all the decisions you've made in life— which sports to play (or avoid); which schools to attend (or not); which jobs to take (or pass up). Which is the one you're most proud of? Why?
- Who was your best boss? Why?
- If you could create a map to aid understanding, what would your map show?

Listen carefully to their answers. Listen for both content and style. Are they confident? Glib? Shy? Embarrassed? Proud? Listen to their word choices, phrasings, the cadence of their sentences, their use of idioms, when they hesitate, when they laugh, and so on. To help you remember their answers, consider creating a spreadsheet or a chart like this:

Person asked Demographic Psychographic	Question posed	Content: Words, usage, examples vs. telling or describing or explaining	Process: hesitations, filler words, think first, hem and haw, etc.	Explicit or implied conflict	Thoughts about the conflict

Select an Answer that Intrigues You

After you've completed your survey, consider which answer offers the most fodder for mining conflict to reveal character.

Person asked Demographic Psychographic	Question posed	Content: Words, usage, examples vs. telling or describing or explaining.	Process: hesitations, filler words, think first, hem and haw, etc.	Explicit or implied conflict	Thoughts about the conflict
A woman in her forties, recently divorced	If you could create a map to aid understanding, what would your map show?	"I'd create a map to success. Too many people give wrong information—and stupid me, I listen to them."	She spoke in a defiant tone, her chin up, her arms crossed.	The tug between respecting family and friends and rational judgment	Napoleon Hill, the self-help guru, said "The number one reason people fail in life is because they listen to their friends, family, and neighbors."

Think It Through

Choose two characters and place them in the midst of this conflict. For this example, Mitch, a recent college grad, is up to his eyeballs with his dad's unsolicited advice about which job to take, how much of his salary to put into savings, where to live, whom to date. Mitch loves his father and doesn't want to hurt him, but he wants to make his own decisions. More than that—he wants to tell his dad to shove it, but of course, he never will.

Write It Up

My goal is to have every word, every pause, every piece of business overflow with unspoken meaning as you escalate conflict.

> Mitch swallows ten sips of water. His father stands at the kitchen counter.
>
> "I haven't decided about the job," Mitch says. "The money's good, but the work...I don't know."
>
> "Bird in the hand."
>
> "If I don't take this one, I'll get another."
>
> "You kids." His dad shakes his head. "Cocky as all hell."

"You think this is my only shot?"

"I think good jobs don't grow on trees."

"I'll be fine."

Mitch's dad cocks his head. "It's about time you realize you're just a cog in a wheel."

"You ought to know," Mitch says.

Dad double-taps the counter. "True that." He lowers his gaze to Mitch's Nikes. "Nice kicks." He grabs a Bud from the fridge and pops the top, raising the can for a toast. "You're welcome."

Determine Viability

Once you've drafted your dialogue, it's time to assess whether it's going to work. Ask yourself the following questions to confirm your dialogue is doing all it can do.

- Is each character speaking with a unique voice?
  - Yes. Dad is brusque and sarcastic. Mitch is struggling to be his own man and a little defensive.
- Does the dialogue move the plot along or add information about the characters without relying on an info dump or forced exposition (where the characters are discussing something they already know solely to inform the reader)?

- Yes. I would say the dialogue does both tasks.
- Does the dialogue escalate conflict?
  - Yes. The two men don't see eye to eye, and apparently there's no effort to find common ground.
- Have I layered in subtext? Do readers learn more than merely what they say, but also what they mean and how they feel?
  - Yes. Dad feels unappreciated and Mitch feels dissed, but neither one says so.
- Am I using typographical emphasis judiciously and appropriately?
  - There is none used because none is needed.
- Is my dialogue punctuated properly?
  - Yes.

Now it's your turn! Follow these five steps to create dialogue that resonates with emotional truth.

Listen for Both Style and Substance

Ask three or five people the same nonloaded, open-ended question. You want to hear what people say, not what they think you want to hear. Of course, you shouldn't ask questions that might make people feel uncomfortable, so I'd stay away from politics, religion, and personal issues

Select an Answer that Intrigues You

After you've completed your survey, consider which answer offers the most fodder for mining conflict to reveal character.

Person asked Demographic Psychographic	Question posed	Content: Words, usage, examples vs. telling or describing or explaining	Process: hesitations, filler words, think first, hem and haw, etc.	Explicit or implied conflict	Thoughts about the conflict

Think It Through

Choose two characters and place them in the midst of this conflict.

Write It Up

Aim to have every word, every pause, every piece of business overflow with unspoken meaning as you escalate conflict.

Determine Viability

Once you've drafted your dialogue, it's time to assess whether it's going to work. Ask yourself the following questions to confirm your dialogue is doing all it can do.

- Is each character speaking with a unique voice?
- Does the dialogue move the plot along or add information about the characters without relying on an info dump or forced exposition (where the characters are discussing something they already know solely to inform the reader)?
- Does the dialogue escalate conflict?
- Have I layered in subtext? Do readers learn more than merely what they say, but also what they mean and how they feel?
- Am I using typographical emphasis judiciously and appropriately?
- Is my dialogue punctuated properly?

How did you do? Were you able to differentiate characters' styles of speaking? Add depth to their conversations? Get the mechanics right? I hope you'll refer back to this chapter as you work to reveal emotional truths through dialogue in all your characters' conversations.

To participate in the *Beat the Bots* TikTok community:

- Record a video of your answer and post it, including the hashtag #beatthebots and tag me at @beatthebotsbook
- You can also tag #authortok and #booktok to connect with other writer and reader communities!
- Watch other writers' videos by visiting the TikTok hashtag #beatthebots

Join the conversation!

In this chapter, we discussed how to use the Conflict Generator creativity tactic to home in on the emotional truths that matter to your characters. From those emotional truths write dialogue that does something beyond the literal meaning of the words. In the next chapter, we'll talk about the power of theme and how to use the Random Access creativity tactic to write thematically.

Reflection on Creativity

"Create with the heart; build with the mind."
Criss Jami

CHAPTER EIGHT

CREATIVITY TACTIC #8

RANDOM ACCESS: WRITING THEMATICALLY

"To produce a mighty book, you must choose a mighty theme."
Herman Melville

ADD RICHNESS TO YOUR STORY WITH THEMATIC WRITING

The answer to "What's your story about?" should be thematic, expressing the overarching issue or question your story addresses. While artificial intelligence can generate standard themes, only you can determine which one you want to use to get people thinking in new ways. This chapter introduces the Random Access creativity tactic, which helps you identify innovative takes on worthy themes. We'll also discuss how to add thematic might to your storytelling by integrating symbolic imagery, atmospheric descriptions, and visual and word allegories. You'll be able to create fresh and meaningful prose far beyond a chatbot's capabilities because your themes and your words are specific to your story.

Thematic writing enables your readers to enjoy your story on a deeper level by encouraging them to think about big issues, to reflect on their lives and beliefs. By selecting a theme, then integrating symbols and allegory that support the theme, you'll add dimension and vitality to your writing.

For many writers, though, identifying your theme isn't easy. Sometimes, of course, your theme is clear, purposeful—you set out to write about family values, or bullying, or independent decision-making, a big idea. Other times, the theme becomes apparent only as you draft your story, or even after it's finished. Occasionally, even after you're done, you have no sense at all of your theme or whether you have one. When asked if her novels included a theme, Hank Phillippi Ryan replied:

> Is there a theme to my novels? Yes, indeed, in every one. Do I know it when I begin? Nope. In the middle? Nope. It's only about three-quarters of the way through that the thematic light begins to dawn. I used to worry about this—since I don't outline, sometimes a theme can feel frighteningly elusive. But I have learned to trust the storytelling process, and have writing faith that if I am on the right track, the theme will reveal itself. And when it does, I go back and look at the parts of the book

BEAT THE BOTS

where I didn't think I knew it—and it's always already there.

If Hank's experience reminds you of your situation, ask yourself if this apparent lack of clarity comes from a forest versus trees conundrum. While you're slogging through the metaphorical woods, tripping on plot roots, forging streams alongside your characters—actually writing the book—you don't have a sense of the forest. Only after you're out of the woods, looking at the scope of the forest through a wider lens, does your theme become clear because that's what theme is: a big picture question or declaration fueling the overarching story arc.

FAQ

Q: I like when an author opens the book or chapter with a pithy little quote. Those often seem thematic. How do you choose one?

A: I agree—an apposite quote at the beginning of a book or chapter, called an epigraph—can engage reader interest by highlighting your theme. Epigraphs are typically short excerpts from an existing work, a quote from a novel, a line from a poem, a verse from the Bible. Consider how the following epigraphs foreshadow the books' themes.

- Literary fiction: *To Kill a Mockingbird* by Harper Lee. The theme looks at the battle between

---

215

> righteous honor and virulent injustice in our legal system.
>
> "Lawyers, I suppose, were children once." *Charles Lamb*
>
> - Crime fiction. *The Godfather* by Mario Puzo. The theme focuses on dueling dichotomies: crime and justice and loyalty and betrayal. The epigraph reads:
>
>   "Behind every great fortune, there is a crime." *Balzac*

As with every aspect of writing, all authors must develop their own process. Some, like Hank, rely on the storytelling process itself to reveal meaningful themes. Others, however, find it helpful to choose a theme in advance and write with it in mind. The Random Access creativity tactic, which we'll discuss later in this chapter, will help you choose themes that reflect your storytelling intentions. First, though, let's consider what composes a theme.

CHOOSE FROM TWO CATEGORIES OF THEME

Broadly, there are two kinds of themes: a unifying principle or a dominant idea. A unifying principle refers to a structural element that provides a framework for your story. A dominant idea encourages deep thinking about a universal issue, be it an idea, an attitude, or a belief.

The unifying principle in J. Courtney Sullivan's *The Engagements* is a diamond engagement ring. The book follows four couples linked by a diamond engagement ring. Over nearly a hundred years, the ring was lost, found, and stolen. Woven into the narrative is the story behind the copywriter who crafted diamond producer De Beers's iconic tagline "a diamond is forever," Mary Frances Gerety. In *Shelf Life*, by Livia Franchini, the unifying principle is a shopping list. Thirty-year-old Ruth, a nurse, has to find her way as a single woman after her fiancé dumps her, leaving her with nothing but the list they'd created for their next shopping trip. Chapters are titled after the items on the list. By the end of the book, Ruth has written a new shopping list, including only those items she wants.

Prompt #29: Choose a Theme

Name a theme that interests you. Say why.

For instance, a theme I'm interested in is how people act when driven by a burning desire to find community, to belong. Why? Because I was a late bloomer. I was that girl who struggled to find her place in the world.

If you haven't yet settled on a theme or want to experiment with another one, try working with one of these options:

- Survival—what will your characters do to survive an internal or external danger?
- Courage—how will your character win the battle, whether that battle is physical, emotional, mental, or spiritual?

- Identity—why does your character struggle to make independent decisions?

Now it's your turn! Name a theme that interests you. Say why.

To participate in the *Beat the Bots* TikTok community:

- Record a video of your answer and post it, including the hashtag #beatthebots and tag me at @beatthebotsbook
- You can also tag #authortok and #book-tok to connect with other writer and reader communities!
- Watch other writers' videos by visiting the Tik-Tok hashtag #beatthebots

Join the conversation!

Unifying elements can establish the structure of the novel, in addition to informing its theme. Frederick Forsyth did just that in *The Day of the Jackal*. The novel is divided into three parts: "Anatomy of a Plot" (nine chapters), "Anatomy of a Manhunt" (nine chapters), and "Anatomy of a Kill" (three chapters).

How about naming each chapter after a wildflower? "Rosemary for Remembrance," for example, based on Ophelia's famous speech in Shakespeare's *Hamlet*. According to Isabel Steven, writing for the Rosenbach Museum and Library, "The flowers, herbs and plants that Ophelia mentions and gives to the other characters are similarly full of symbolic meaning. Pansies represent sadness, love, and tender feelings, fennel flattery, columbines fidelity in marriage, and rue bitterness and regret. Daisies symbolize innocence and purity, and violets truth, loyalty and humility, or with their withering, the lack thereof." You can select any category that ties the threads of your narrative together, thus providing a theme. Maybe your story will be enriched if you name parts or chapters after constellations, football plays, or pies, among myriad other options.

Integrating a dominant idea, a global reflection, throughout your story is another effective approach to thematic writing. *In the Time of the Butterflies* by Julia Alvarez focuses on the choice between cowardice and courage in the face of soul-annihilating oppression. Set in the Dominican Republic in the decades leading up to the 1960 murder of three of the four Mirabal sisters, this based-on-fact novel showcases the cost of cowardice and the price of courage. In *My Sister's Keeper*, author Jodi Picoult considers the ethical complexity of being required to save someone's life. The story revolves around two sisters, one dying, the other conceived as a bone marrow match to keep her older sister alive. Anna, now thirteen, is expected to endure her umpteenth surgery, this time to donate her kidney, without having any say in the matter. She refuses and sues for emancipation. This tale of life and death, loyalty and betrayal, and obligation and independence challenges readers to witness impossible choices.

A dominant idea can examine any aspect of the human experience. Socrates said, "An unexamined life is not worth living," and one of literature's chief purposes is assisting in that examination. Some dominant ideas consider the biggest of questions, such as:

- What is the meaning of life?
- Why me?
- Why not me?
- How can I find love?

Other dominant ideas look at issues of self-determination, including whether assisted suicide should be legal, or major public policy considerations, such as whether sixteen-year-old children should be allowed to vote.

Whatever big-picture issue you select, the best way to tell the story is through a small-picture experience. Bestselling author Richard Price put it this way: "You don't write about the horrors of war. No. You write about a kid's burnt socks lying in the road." Don't write a novel about autistic children. Instead, select one autistic child and write her story. That's what Siobhan Dowd did in her middle-grade mystery *The London Eye Mystery*. Thirteen-year-old Ted's mother explains that Ted's brain works on a "special operating system." His fifteen-year-old sister, Kat, just finds Ted annoying. Yet when their cousin Salim steps onto the Ferris wheel (called the London Eye), but doesn't get off, Ted and Kat work together to solve the mystery. Although Ted's autism is clear from his behavior (compulsive counting, using the cheat sheet his therapist gave him to recognize what various facial expressions indicate, and so forth), the word "autism" is never mentioned. Readers gain an understanding of Ted's condition by spending time with him, and from that experience, they're able to reflect on the larger truths inherent in Ted's situation, including how some autistic people

BEAT THE BOTS

interact with other people and the world, and the impact of their condition on their families. By extrapolating meaning from one experience to another, then another, we can achieve understanding across the board, and one hopes, empathy.

You'll note that as all these examples demonstrate, the most powerful themes, both unifying and dominant, are those that radiate with emotional truth—the opportunities we confront, the decisions we make, and the consequences we have to live with, whether joyous or fraught.

Prompt #30: Select an Epigraph

Once you've chosen your theme, or selected one to experiment with, decide on an appropriate epigraph. Good sources of epigraphs include BrainyQuote and Lib Quotes. (Of course, be certain to double-check that the attribution is correct.)

Complete this sentence, then explain your choice: To reinforce my theme of [name your theme], I chose this epigraph [recite the epigraph]. Here's why: [insert your explanation]

Continuing with my example of my character wanting to find where she belongs, I chose this epigraph:

"Fitting in is the greatest barrier to belonging because fitting in says, 'Be like them to be accepted.' Belonging says, 'This is who I am. I hope we can make a connection.'"
Brené Brown

I decided to use this epigraph because it's so clear. It speaks to me on a deep, emotional level.

Now it's your turn! Complete this sentence, then explain your choice: To reinforce my theme of [name your theme], I chose this epigraph [recite the epigraph]. Here's why: [insert your explanation]

To participate in the *Beat the Bots* TikTok community:

- Record a video of your answer and post it, including the hashtag #beatthebots and tag me at @beatthebotsbook
- You can also tag #authortok and #booktok to connect with other writer and reader communities!
- Watch other writers' videos by visiting the TikTok hashtag #beatthebots

Join the conversation!

Once you have your theme and epigraph set, it's time to ensure you're layering in thematic references that support and reflect your theme. One of the most effective ways to do this is through symbols, whether expressed as imagery or text.

ADD SYMBOLIC IMAGERY AND TEXT

A symbol is a material thing that represents a nonmaterial thing, usually a tangible item that illuminates an intangible concept.

Let's say that your theme is "family first." You might select an acorn and an oak tree to visually represent this abstract concept. An acorn, the tiny seed that spawns a mighty oak, is a frequently used symbol representing the concepts of deferred gratification and long-term potential. This image works well because an oak tree, while sturdy, with deep roots and expansive, spreading branches, takes a long time to grow. One of the world's most successful investors, Warren Buffet, the chairman and CEO of Berkshire Hathaway, puts it this way: "Someone is sitting in the shade today because someone planted a tree a long time ago." You find acorns on door knockers, family coats of arms, fences, and the like. Add in sensory-based language to illustrate the experience of sitting under an oak tree to reinforce your theme.

Pro Tip: Old + Old = New

Innovation comes from what Isaac Asimov called a "cross-connection," the ability to take information about one thing, link it to another thing, and come up with a whole new thing. In his essay, "On Creativity," Asimov explained that the cross-connection process is scary because it's unconventional, opening the writer up to judgment, so many people shy away from the process. It requires what Asimov referred to as "daring." Be bold and be open to opportunity. We'll create reader-centric and inspiring thematic writing by using a form of cross-connection called Random Access, discussed later in this chapter.

For symbols to work in supporting your themes, it's important that you adhere to the generally understood meaning of the symbol. A dove, for instance, represents peace; a heart, love; an owl, wisdom; rain, sadness, and so on. Consulting reliable sources such as The Noun Project and Visme can help guide your selection.

The weather offers multiple opportunities to add thematic gravitas. In Iris Murdoch's *The Sea, the Sea*, for instance, a famous playwright leaves his glittering London life for an isolated house on the sea to write his memoir and finds himself haunted by dark and frightful memories. The weather reflects the theme of regret amid the lies we tell ourselves. "The rain came down, straight and silvery, like a punishment of steel rods." This powerful image allows readers to experience the punishment alongside the protagonist. In Jewell Parker Rhodes's middle-grade novel *Ninth Ward*, we watch the effect of Hurricane Katrina on Janie, the twelve-year old protagonist. In addition to experiencing the driving rain and relentless wind (the literal experience), we witness a hurricane's symbolic meaning as Janie realizes that life itself is as tumultuous as a hurricane. In *Men We Reaped*, author Jesmyn Ward also wrote about being powerless in the face of a hurricane's untamable wrath. A hurricane's fury isn't personal—it has no conscience, no intention, no empathy. "Life is a hurricane, and we board up to save what we can and bow low to the earth to crouch in that small space above the dirt where the wind will not reach."

CHOOSE WORDS AND PHRASES THAT SUPPORT YOUR THEMES

Weaving words and phrases that support your theme allows you to subtly reinforce your ideas.

Let's say you're writing a middle-grade novel about Gavin, a young boy who has to grow up fast after his parents' divorce leaves him rudderless. His parents are immersed in their own affairs, picking up the pieces of their lives, licking their emotional wounds. Metaphorically, Gavin finds himself adrift in roiling seas and has to navigate his way to solid ground on his own.

You select an epigraph from National Geographic fellow Elizabeth Kapu'uwailani Lindsey: "True navigation begins in the human heart. It's the most important map of all."

By selecting words that relate to navigation, your theme will be woven into the story with a light touch. Notice the words I've already used to describe Gavin's situation: rudderless, choosing your own path, adrift, roiling seas, navigate, solid ground. This strategy enables your readers to travel alongside Gavin as he charts his course, enhancing reader engagement.

Getting these concepts in my head *before* I write helps me ensure that I embed my theme as I write, both a time-saver and a smart way to infuse my prose with meaning.

Prompt #31: Choose Thematic Words

State your theme (or name one you want to experiment with), list words and phrases that support it, and explain why you chose those terms.

> *If I were working with a theme of finding where I belong, for example, I might think about peeling away my mask, stepping out of my role, coming down from the stage, turning off the footlights, all in an effort to let my true self shine through. I chose these terms because when you're trying to fit in (as opposed to finding where you truly belong), I think of it as acting a part, so my language relates to someone in the theater.*

Now it's your turn! State your theme (or name one you want to experiment with), list words and phrases that support it, and explain why you chose those terms.

To participate in the *Beat the Bots* TikTok community:

- Record a video of your answer and post it, including the hashtag #beatthebots and tag me at @beatthebotsbook
- You can also tag #authortok and #booktok to connect with other writer and reader communities!

BEAT THE BOTS

> - Watch other writers' videos by visiting the Tik-Tok hashtag #beatthebots
>
> Join the conversation!

CONSIDER ALLEGORIES

An allegory is a literary device that can add thematic import to your stories. Allegories help deliver broader messages about the human experience, teach moral lessons, and address controversial issues in a nonconfrontational way. They're similar to metaphors in that both illustrate an idea by making a comparison to something else. However, allegories are complete stories, while metaphors are brief figures of speech.

An allegory is an engaging way to reveal a hidden meaning without explicitly stating it. Toni Morrison, in her Nobel Prize acceptance speech, recounted an African folktale as she warned about the frailty of language—if you don't want to lose a language, you must protect it. In the allegory, a bird represents language. It's up to people to safeguard the bird lest it die or fly away. According to scholar Dr. Michael Austin, writing in *Reading the World: Ideas that Matter*, "The folktale at the heart of Morrison's speech functions rhetorically much as the parables of Jesus do in the New Testament." Morrison's story works on two levels, literal and figurative. On the one hand, the parable is about a bird—a literal narrative. On the other hand, the story about the bird was designed to get us thinking about a culturally sensitive issue (our language) in a

227

new way—a figurative interpretation. This duality adds thematic depth.

In *American Born Chinese*, an allegorical graphic novel examining the complicated issues surrounding identity, author Gene Luen Yang tells three stories that come together at the end. In the first story, the Monkey King represents an idealized man, someone who works diligently to improve himself so he can strengthen his kingdom and become a worthy god to his subjects. However, he was turned away at a gods' party because he was a monkey. The second story follows Jin Wang, an American-born Chinese boy. The teacher who introduces him to the new class does not even ask where he is from, telling the class that Jin just arrived from China, though he actually came from San Francisco. In the third story, Jin, who wants to fit in, to be a regular American boy, decides his name is part of the problem—people mispronounce it all the time. Jin decides to take what he called "an American one," Danny. It doesn't help, since changing your name doesn't change who you are. This allegorical examination of stereotypes and perception showcases the thorny issues related to identity.

Allegories are also used to drive home moral lessons. Aesop's fables, for example, teach children that slow and steady wins the race ("The Hare and the Tortoise"), no act of kindness is wasted ("The Lion and the Mouse"), and necessity is the mother of invention ("The Crow and the Pitcher").

Sometimes, your theme revolves around a hot-button issue. A good technique to helping your message get across is to use anthropomorphism, attributing human traits to nonhuman things. In addition to easing readers into your theme, anthropomorphism increases engagement since readers are required to imagine the connection you describe, an active process.

Clarifying the Terms Anthropomorphism versus Personification

Anthropomorphism differs from personification in one essential way: When something nonhuman is described as having human characteristics, you're personifying it. When you refer to a nonhuman entity knowingly acting like a person, you're anthropomorphizing it. In other words, if the humanlike traits are figurative, it's personification; if they're literal, it's anthropomorphism.

We anthropomorphize all the time. When you tell a pot of water "hurry up and boil," you are anthropomorphizing it (as if the pot of water has intentionality and might respond to prodding).

According to Harvard professor and fairy-tale scholar Maria Tatar, Jeanne-Marie Leprince de Beaumont's 1756 fairy tale "Beauty and the Beast" used anthropomorphism to comfort young girls. Tatar, the editor of *Beauty and the Beast: Classic Tales About Animals, Brides, and Grooms from Around the World*, describes how Madam de Beaumont's story addressed the troubling issue of child marriage. During this era, girls as young as twelve were routinely married off to much older men. Naturally, they were fearful. In *Glamour Magazine*'s "The Real Story Behind *Beauty and the Beast* Is Not What You

Think," author Elizabeth Logan explained that these affluent and privileged men "kept [their young brides] in their castles and dressed them up and made them come down to dinner and…well, you know the rest." The fairy tale was intended to reassure girls that just because you find someone ugly on the outside, a monster, doesn't mean you'll find them ugly on the inside. Tatar commented that "Beauty and the Beast" delivered "a beautiful message about the power of love and the importance of valuing character." The monster, after all, was eminently lovable. Linda Woolverton took anthropomorphism even further in her screenplay for the Disney film of the same name (directed by Gary Trousdale and Kirk Wise). Woolverton created an array of quirky characters imbued with human characteristics: Lumière, a suave French candelabra; Cogsworth, a neurotic clock; Babette, a sassy feather duster; Mrs. Potts, a matronly teapot; and Chip, Mrs. Potts' son, the playful teacup. Cloaking this charged issue—child marriage—with anthropomorphic characters made the difficult reality less frightening.

ATMOSPHERIC DESCRIPTIONS CAN SUPPORT YOUR THEME

Atmospheric descriptions translate your theme into palpable depictions so your readers experience the setting in the same way the characters do. In Chris Pavone's *The Accident*, we experience the paradoxes between darkness and light, safety and danger, and good and evil:

> Isabel stares across the room, off into the black nothingness of the picture window on the opposite

BEAT THE BOTS

wall, its severe surface barely softened by the half-drawn shades, an aggressive void invading the cocoon of her bedroom. The room is barely lit by a small bullet-shaped reading sconce mounted over the headboard, aiming a concentrated beam of light directly at her. In the window, the light's reflection hovers above her face, like a tiny sun illuminating the top of her head, creating a halo. An angel. Except she's not.

This excerpt is laden with symbolic imagery. At first the mood is heavy, hard, frightening. The imagery remains stark until the abrupt shift at the end, where fear turns to hope. Consider the underlying thematic driver revealed in this brief description—is Isabel merely human in a nonangelic sense? Or is she the devil incarnate?

Prompt #32: Write an Atmospheric Description

Write a brief atmospheric description. To help you see how to translate intention into words on the page, explain what you're trying to achieve. Analyzing other authors' approaches to achieving rich experiential descriptions will help you master the techniques yourself.

Here's an example from *Jane Austen's Lost Letters*, one of my Josie Prescott Antiques Mysteries, followed by an explanation of what I was trying to achieve. The books and short stories, which are set on the rugged coast of New Hampshire, are written in the first person from Josie's POV.

My example: I entered Mimi's Copse. The air was cool and dry, a perfect autumn day. The birch and poplar leaves glowed like spun gold. A month earlier, the packed dirt path had been obscured by soft pine needles, and I'd swished as I'd walked. Today, the needles were covered with crackly fallen leaves, and I crunched my way along.

Explanation: I wanted readers to feel as if they were walking alongside Josie. I considered adding details about the scent, too, but decided feeling (cool and dry), sight (spun gold), and sound (swish and crunch) were enough.

Now it's your turn! Write a brief atmospheric description, then explain what you're trying to achieve.

To participate in the *Beat the Bots* TikTok community:

- Record a video of your answer and post it, including the hashtag #beatthebots and tag me at @beatthebotsbook
- You can also tag #authortok and #booktok to connect with other writer and reader communities!
- Watch other writers' videos by visiting the TikTok hashtag #beatthebots

Join the conversation!

BEAT THE BOTS

I Let You Go by Clare Mackintosh tells the story of a woman whose five-year-old son dashes into the street on their walk home from school. He's hit by a car—a hit-and-run—and he's killed. She runs away, to escape the memory, the horror, her guilt. This excerpt explains what she sees in the place she now calls home. "The road continues to narrow, and I can see the swell of the ocean at the end of the lane. The water is gray and unforgiving, white spray bursting into the air from the wrestling waves. The gulls sweep in dizzying circles, buffeted by the winds that wrap themselves around the bay." The narrowing road and the gray, unforgiving water mirrors her view of herself, of her future. This hopelessness is reinforced by the birds flying in circles in a futile search for sustenance.

AI Weighs In

I asked a chatbot: Please give me an example of thematic writing focusing on a theme of reinventing oneself.

AI said: *Certainly! Here's an example of thematic writing centered around the theme of reinventing oneself.*

Title: "Metamorphosis of the Phoenix"

In the quiet corners of a bustling city, where the hum of life resonates with the echoes of forgotten dreams, there exists a tale of resilience and rebirth. It is a story not told in the grandeur of success, but in the quiet moments of personal transformation. Meet Lily, an ordinary woman navigating the labyrinth of life, who found herself standing at the crossroads of stagnation and reinvention.

The first chapter of Lily's life unfolded in the predictable cadence of routine. A job that paid the bills but failed to ignite her passions, relationships that held no spark, and a sense of self slowly eroding like a stone sculpted by the ceaseless waves of conformity. But within her, a quiet rebellion simmered, a desire to shed the layers that obscured the essence of her true self.

The catalyst for Lily's metamorphosis came in the form of a personal crisis—a wake-up call echoing through the chambers of her soul. Instead of succumbing to despair, Lily saw an opportunity for reinvention. It was time to turn the page, to author a narrative that resonated with authenticity.

The first step was shedding the expectations others had placed upon her. Lily embarked on a journey of self-discovery, unearthing passions long buried beneath the rubble of societal norms. An artist emerged from the cocoon of convention, brushstrokes on a canvas mirroring the vibrant hues of her newfound identity.

The professional sphere witnessed a revolution as well. Lily, once confined to the rigid walls of a cubicle, spread her wings in the entrepreneurial sky. A venture that spoke to her soul, a manifestation of the courage to pursue dreams that had long lingered in the shadows.

In matters of the heart, Lily's reinvention was equally profound. The relationships she forged were no longer compromises but collaborations, each connection a testament to the strength found in vulnerability. The scars of past heartbreaks became badges of resilience, proof that one could emerge from the ashes of shattered illusions.

As Lily embraced the changes within, the external world responded in kind. Like a phoenix rising from the ashes, she soared to heights previously thought unattainable. Her story became an inspiration, not because of grand accomplishments, but because of the courage to dismantle the old and construct the new.

"Metamorphosis of the Phoenix" is a tale of reinvention—a reminder that within every individual, there lies the power to shed the old and embrace the new. It invites us to question the narratives we inherit and

> *empowers us to script our own stories of transformation. In the quiet corners of a bustling city, where the hum of life resonates with the echoes of forgotten dreams, Lily's story echoes—an anthem of reinvention, a melody of rediscovery.*
>
> *Fortifying your theme by introducing symbols to create atmospheric descriptions serves to deepen the reader experience.*

First, I'm disappointed the chatbot didn't actually provide an example of thematic writing; instead, it gave me an outline for a story based on my theme. I tried again and asked for a sentence showcasing thematic writing, and it continued to overwrite. (See my analysis below.) Second, the outline is simultaneously overly general and underdeveloped. It's also overwritten and trite.

- *Overly general and underdeveloped:* People don't just decide to go reinvent themselves. Why did Lily embark on this major life change now? It is the consideration of "why now" that ensures your story will be grounded by one specific person's experience, not a generic examination of a process. Where is Lily getting the strength to initiate these changes? What is the precipitating event? How does she know enough to navigate the innumerable challenges associated with becoming an entrepreneur? The outline's broad arc ignores all these vital questions.

- *Overwritten:* Many of the phrases are florid, what is called purple prose. For example, "An artist emerged from the cocoon of convention, brushstrokes on a canvas mirroring the vibrant hues of her newfound identity." This metaphor doesn't make sense. One emerges from a cocoon as a butterfly, not an artist, but okay, let's not be overly literal. The implication, though, is that, by definition, artists aren't conventional, an unwarranted and uncited generalization. (And it's a cliché.) The bot also used a form of "echo" four times, followed by sound-based language like, "an anthem of reinvention, a melody of rediscovery." Whew.
- *Trite:* Phrases such as "bustling city," "the hum of life," and the metaphor of the phoenix rising from the ashes, among many others, are all clichés. (And some are repeated, adding redundancy.)

Here's the sentence the bot wrote when I asked it to focus on sentence-level thematic writing: "In the crucible of self-discovery, she embraced the art of reinvention, sculpting a new identity from the raw clay of her experiences." To me, this sounds as cringeworthy as the outline, equally overwritten and trite.

> We can write far better than this by asking ourselves what we're trying to express, then striving for clarity. Add in the specific thematic words, phrases, and imagery you know will resonate with readers, interweaving appropriate symbols, and your unique vision will come alive.

When writing atmospheric descriptions, remember to show your character interacting with the place you're writing about, integrating sensory references.

USE RANDOM ACCESS FOR A "CROSS-CONNECTION"

The five-step Random Access creativity technique takes a methodical approach to implementing Isaac Asimov's "cross-connection" concept (this chapter's Pro Tip). The goal is to help you come up with words, phrases, images, and ideas that support and amplify your themes.

Two considerations before we jump in. First, the Random Access creativity technique is deceptively simple. You may find yourself thinking *Is this all there is to it?* and the answer is a resounding *Yes!* The tactic works as well as it does because it's quick, and that's the second consideration. Don't spend longer than a few seconds to a minute on a word or image unless your ideas are flowing. If nothing comes to you, that's okay! Move on to another one.

There are two ways to use the Random Access creativity technique, both involving a random selection, one focused on

BEAT THE BOTS

text, the other on an image. Neither option is better than the other—they're both effective. Some writers feel more comfortable working with text. Others prefer the visual pop that comes from an image. I encourage you to experiment with both options. Here are the five steps:

1. *Write down your theme.*
2. *Randomly choose your word or image.*
3. *Come up with a definition.*
4. *Ask yourself what you could write about relating to your theme and linked to your word or image as you've defined it.*
5. *Assess your cross-connections.*

As you experiment with the Random Access creativity technique, you'll see that the five steps can be adapted to other elements of the storytelling process, including plotting, character development, setting selection, among others. Let's take a look at two examples, one based on text, the other based on an image, so you can see how the process works.

RANDOM ACCESS: TEXT-BASED EXAMPLE

Write Down Your Theme

For this example, I'm going to focus on the concept of reinventing oneself. Sometimes, the resulting change is even better than you could have hoped for. Other times, you forge ahead, and only after you become the new you, do you realize that it wasn't what you expected. I'm interested in writing about why some reinventions yield great success leading to happiness and revitalization, and others fall flat.

Randomly Choose Your Word

Here's how I approached the challenge. I opened an issue of *Consumer Reports* that happened to be near at hand and pointed to the word "growth." The fact that it came from a sidebar on mold growth is irrelevant. "Growth" is my word.

Come Up with a Definition

If you know the word, don't look it up in the dictionary. Free associate what your word means to you at this moment in time. About "growth," I wrote: "To move forward, expand, increase, or improve."

Ask Yourself What You Could Write about Relating to Your Theme and Linked to Your Word or Image as You've Defined It

Here's how my train of thought evolved:

- Right away, thinking about reinventing yourself and "growth," the concept of expansion caught my interest. My character wants to reinvent herself because she's bored. It's as simple as that. She doesn't know what she wants. She just knows there has to be more to life than the ho-hum existence she's stumbled into.
- Then a metaphor related to "growth" occurred to me. At the start of my book, my character could have a black thumb—she can't grow a plant to save her life. By the end of the book, her thumb has turned green, her garden lush.
- The next idea that came to me was the movie *The Frisco Kid* starring Gene Wilder and Harrison Ford (written

by Michael Elias, Frank Shaw, and Gene Wilder). The movie, which is set in 1850, follows a Polish rabbi as he travels from Poland to San Francisco to lead his new congregation. He meets con men and burglars, an Amish community that befriends him, Native Americans that nearly burn him alive, among others. From each encounter, he learns life lessons he couldn't have learned any other way. Regarding my story, maybe my protagonist wants to meet classier guys than those that run with her usual crowd, so she attends an art gallery opening on her own, without telling anyone where she was going. She doesn't meet classy guys, but she does meet some bohemian types and finds herself drawn to their free-spirit attitude. She doesn't get the outcome she expected; she gets another outcome that may be even better.

- As I considered the concepts of reinvention and growth, I jotted these notes, too:
  - *My character's thoughts:* Get out of town, start over, start fresh, change my name, change the spelling of my name, redo my backstory (which might require fudging details, or lying, or even setting out to bamboozle people)
  - *My character's plans:* Act the part, change my look, buy new clothes, fake it till you make it
  - *My character's promise to herself:* Do things I've never done before, have adventures, take risks, go for it, be daring, be brave
  - *My character's fears:* Scaredy cat, grow a spine, show some backbone, I can't, I will, I can't, I

will, I'll fail, people will laugh at me, I'll laugh
back, I'll cry

Note: I'd keep going until I was totally out of ideas.
Sometimes you get on a roll—don't stop! Other times, your
ideas peter out quickly. That's fine. Move on!

My biggest takeaway here is that I need my language to be
more explicit than I anticipated. I need to have her think about
packing a bag and leaving. Just get out of town, take the train
to the end of the line, and see what there is to see. I have to
have her go to a department store and try on different looks,
from *Town and Country* preppy to naturalist simplicity to goth
darkness to modern-era hippie New Age. I have to show her
being bold, even though she's scared. Her character is becoming more complex and real. The story is becoming less linear.
The language I should use to reinforce my theme is clearer.

When thinking about "reinvention," the word "growth" is
pretty easy. I opened the magazine again and this time, my
fingertip ended up on the word "plum." My definition is: "A
purple fruit that, when dried, becomes a prune. Also the color
of the fruit, a mixture of red and blue." I free associated.

- A prune. Withered. Dried up. Lonely. Isolated. An
  unhappy young woman meets a dried-up old battle-ax
  and sees her future self.
- Professor Plum from *Clue* comes to mind. Quick-witted. Scholarly. More pedantic than street smart. Sort of
  the opposite of my gal.

And I'd continue on from there until I ran out of ideas.

Assess Your Cross-Connections

Now that you have a bunch of thematic words, perspectives, and concepts, it's time to evaluate their merit. It's important to note that we're talking only about whether your idea will work in your particular story. Sometimes you come up with material that has great merit, just not here. To help you make that determination, ask yourself these questions:

- Did anything surprise you? If so, that might indicate you're taking a new approach, something only we humans can do.
  - I was surprised that of all the words I came up with defining "growth," the one that interested me was expansion. Not change—expansion.
  - My character's mixed emotions surprised me. I thought she was way more confident than she is. I also wondered what kind of lies she'll tell.
  - I really warmed to the idea that came to me with "plum" about her meeting her future self, a cautionary tale. That totally came from out of left field. I think opposites often lead to interesting themes.
- Thinking of your through-line plot, how do these thematic ideas come into play?
  - I know I want to show my character having many false starts. She'll run into obstacles she didn't even know existed. With each experience, she learns something specific that she can apply to the next obstacle. Her knowledge base is expanding. (There's that word again!)

243

Now let's go through the process again, this time using an image.

RANDOM ACCESS: IMAGE-BASED EXAMPLE

Another way to use the Random Access creativity tactic is to access thematic ideas from images, not words. You can choose something you see outside your window or during a walk around the block. Or you can use an outside source, such as the New York Public Library's Picture Collection. Founded in 1915 as a resource for people working in the visual arts, the collection includes one and a half million images across twelve thousand subject headings. Forty-five thousand are available in the library's online digital collection. You name it, they've got it. You might want to simply poke around and see what image catches your interest, or you can search for options within a category. What I did is go to the letter F, I don't know why, and scan through the subject headers. "Fencing" caught my attention.

Write Down Your Theme

For this exercise, I'm going to continue with the concept of reinventing oneself.

Randomly Choose Your Image

The first few pages of fencing images fascinated me. Sure, I knew fences came in a variety of colors and styles, but I had no idea how many colors and styles. I saw ornate black-iron fences and industrial chain link and mesh fences. I viewed a picket fence surrounding a charming cottage and a ranch-rail fence encircling a working paddock. I saw fences made of wire, plastic, wood, steel, and stone. I even saw some made of less traditional materials, like sandbags and wine bottle corks.

Come Up with a Definition

A fence is a physical barrier designed to keep you in or out.

Ask Yourself What You Could Write about Relating to Your Theme and Linked to Your Word or Image as You've Defined It

As I thought about it, I realized that fences can also exist in our heads. I think the concept of a fence could be symbolic of my character's dueling needs to break out of her routine and meet her parent's expectations. Other words and phrases that came to include:

- Stop, climb, tunnel, over or around, break through, the grass is always greener on the other side of the fence, Robert Frost's line about good fences making good neighbors, privacy, shielding me, build one, tear one down, rickety, solid, impenetrable, peek through to see the other side

Assess Your Cross-Connections

- Did anything surprise you? If so, that might indicate you're taking a new approach, something only we humans can do.
  - I was surprised at the dichotomies associated with fences. For instance, fences ensure

privacy for celebrities who've spent their careers striving to become famous. People long for the solitude that comes from keeping people on the other side of the fence, but dread the loneliness that comes from being fenced in and alone.

- I like the idea of fences in your mind. I don't know where I might go with that, but there's something there that interests me there.

- Since there are so many different styles of fencing, I can see how this symbol can be used in various ways over the course of the book. Maybe my character will lean against a fence. It's providing support. Later, she'll have to climb over a fence. It's an obstacle.

- Thinking of your through-line plot, how do these thematic ideas come into play?

  - Fencing represents keeping someone in or out, but it also can come into play through its absence. A lack of a fence allows creatures to run free, but it also might leave them unprotected, vulnerable. I know I can use these ideas to fortify my theme.

The most effective way to use the Random Access creativity tactic is to get into your characters' heads. Let them share their emotional truths.

Exercise

Random Access—Write Thematically

You can complete this exercise for one character or for all your characters. That's an interesting idea, isn't it? To examine your characters' varying reactions to a word or image? Or how about yourself? Mine your own feelings about your text or image prompt to gain insights that can inform your characters and will help you share *your* story.

Now it's your turn! Try practicing the Random Access creativity tactic using both text and images to add thematic flair to your writing in innovative ways that come solely from your mind, not a chatbot.

1. Write down your theme (or select one to work with that interests you).
2. Randomly choose your word or image.
3. Come up with a definition.
4. Ask yourself what you could write about relating to your theme and linked to your word or image as you've defined it.
5. Assess your cross-connections.
   - Did anything surprise you? If so, that might indicate you're taking a new approach, something only we humans can do.

- Thinking of your through-line plot, how do these thematic ideas come into play?

How did it go? Were you able to come up with some surprising ideas? Do they support your plot? Strengthen your characterizations? I'd love to hear about your experience with the Random Access creativity technique. Complete this sentence: I tried Jane's Random Access creativity tactic to write thematically and

_____.

To participate in the *Beat the Bots* TikTok community:

- Record a video of your answer and post it, including the hashtag #beatthebots and tag me at @beatthebotsbook
- You can also tag #authortok and #booktok to connect with other writer and reader communities!
- Watch other writers' videos by visiting the TikTok hashtag #beatthebots

Join the conversation!

In this chapter, we examined the attributes of thematic writing and how to use the Random Access creativity tactic to help you write unique, thematic prose. We're now ready to move onto Part Three, Polish to Perfection, and we'll start that process by considering how to raise the stakes for your protagonist—and yourself.

Reflection on Creativity

"Imagination is the beginning of creativity."
George Bernard Shaw

PART THREE
POLISH TO PERFECTION

"I have rewritten—often several times—every word I
have ever published. My pencils outlast their erasers."
Vladimir Nabokov

CHAPTER NINE

CREATIVITY TACTIC #9
MINDSET STRUCTURES: RAISE THE STAKES ON YOUR PROTAGONIST—AND YOURSELF

"All literature is longing."
Dan Pope

THINK REENVISION, NOT MERELY REVISION

When we think about revision, often it's the small issues that come to mind, tightening the prose, ensuring our verbs and nouns are powerful, confirming we're showing, not telling. All of those elements are crucial to writing success, and we'll discuss them in Chapter Ten. But that's not the only way to think about the revision process. In this chapter, we'll take a wider

253

lens view, to think of revision as "reenvision." In other words, the revision process encompasses two parts—micro and macro. Microrevision addresses the complexity of ensuring your prose is strong and unambiguous. Macrorevision considers big picture issues like identifying plot contrivances (discussed in Chapter Two) and character anomalies (discussed in Chapter Three)—and an issue that often slips through the cracks—determining whether your stakes are high enough, and seeking out ways to raise them ever higher.

When writing fiction, the term "stakes" refers to what your protagonists have to lose if they fail. What's the worst that can happen? Can you add additional pressure? Is the worst that she'll die? Would it be worse for her if she lost not just her life, but her family, her friends, her work, her lover? What about if she lost her mind? What if she lost her very soul? If most, if not all, of those potential losses are not among the stakes, you need more.

You'll notice the title of this chapter connects raising the stakes for your protagonist with raising them for yourself. I linked these two priorities because, in my experience, a lot of us pull our punches in our writing, and maybe in our lives. We don't write raw. We consciously or unconsciously worry what people will say if we write the bald emotional truth, so we write tame. We worry about standing out, but you must because conforming is the antithesis of creativity. We need to get our attitudes straight so we can write with innovative flair and authorial power, illuminating those emotional truths that resonate with our readers. It's one of the most reliable ways to beat the bots. You've heard that adage, "Build a better mousetrap and the world will beat a path to your door." Well, I think people are hungry for truth, for emotional truth. Write the emotional truth and they will come.

It's important to note that AI can't make decisions about which verb or noun best suits your character, the incident, and your author's voice any more than it can decide whether and how to raise the stakes for your particular characters. These decisions require judgment—your judgment.

REVISE WELL WITH THE MINDSET STRUCTURE

To succeed at reenvisioning, you need to be willing to look at your work with steely eyed objectivity. This sounds self-evident, but it isn't. And even if you acknowledge reenvisioning's importance, it's often easier said than done. It's hard to admit that your best efforts might not be good enough. As Michael Crichton, the author of *Jurassic Park* and *Andromeda Strain*, among other bestselling titles, put it, "Books aren't written—they're rewritten. Including your own. It is one of the hardest things to accept, especially after the seventh rewrite hasn't quite done it." This is where the Mindset Structure creativity tactic comes into play. Adopting a can-do, optimistic mindset is central to bringing forth your helpful internal editor, the kind and supportive ally who's dedicated to helping you succeed, and quashing the snarky internal critic who hopes you fail.

FAQ

Q: I'm writing a young-adult fantasy novel. I have high stakes, from mythical beasts to desperate humans. How do I express that in a query letter?

A: You've already overcome the first hurdle—your story features high stakes, and you understand the importance of putting that information into your query letter. As literary agent Roma Panganiban of Janklow & Nesbit explains, "I see a lot of pitches that contain interesting details, but don't include the stakes. Every book needs something to justify its existence, whether that's the search for a missing person or a protagonist overcoming an obstacle to reach a goal." The best approach is to show what the stakes represent to the protagonist. For instance, does the protagonist have to save her mother from a diabolical beast? Become a tribal leader to help reduce humans' desperation? Now add a detail or two—the world in a word. Are the beasts carnivorous and hungry? Why are the humans desperate? Adding specificity will go a long way to clarifying just how high those stakes are.

The Mindset Structure creativity tactic is based on research conducted by medical professionals, advertising executives, and cognitive neuroscientists. Adopting the following four mindsets will enable you to tackle your work with optimism, energy, and enthusiasm.

VISUALIZE SUCCESS

Imagine the satisfaction you'll feel when you finish your manuscript. Tell yourself that the reenvisioning process is one step along the path to reach that finishing line. Mind speak truly affects your outlook and your ability to be productive. Think encouraging thoughts, and you're more likely to accomplish your goals. Think about failure, and you're more likely to fail. This truism, colloquially referred to as "fake it till you make it," has an official place in the psychology of success. The technique is called "behavioral activation." According to Dr. Sue Varma, the author of *Practical Optimism: The Art, Science and Practice of Exceptional Well-Being* and a distinguished fellow of the American Psychiatric Association, "When you put one foot in front of the other, voilà! You start walking. Just like exercising, you may not initially be in the mood, but you end up feeling good afterward and are glad you did it."

LEARN FROM OTHERS

Welcome differing perspectives. Experiment with new strategies. Don't allow yourself to be locked into ideas that don't work because you've always done it that way or it works for someone you admire. Doing the same thing over and over and expecting a different result is a frequently cited definition of insanity. Get out of your rut. Feed your brain by reading outside your usual genre, listening to music that's new to you, or trying a new hobby or leisure activity. Apply this commitment to trying new things to the reenvisioning process. Follow the steps outlined in this chapter and see where they take you.

BE GENTLE WITH YOURSELF

We writers tend to be a sensitive lot. Ernest Hemingway said, "There's nothing to writing. All you do is sit down at the typewriter and bleed." As you undertake the reenvisioning process, be aware that you may feel resistance to making changes, and that resistance may lead to procrastination. But being gentle with yourself doesn't mean giving yourself a pass. Napoleon Hill, the author of the legendary tome *Think and Grow Rich*, wrote, "Nothing is more tragic—or more common—than mental inertia." He also said, "Create a definite plan for carrying out your desire and begin at once, whether you ready or not, to put this plan into action." Acknowledge your antipathy to admitting your manuscript might need work, and get going anyway.

SMILE MORE

Simply smiling, even if you aren't feeling friendly or happy, has enormous health and wellness benefits. Nicole Spector's essay, "Smiling Can Trick Your Brain into Happiness—and Boost Your Health," published on NBC's blog, *Better by Today*, reported on a University of Kansas study that found smiling reduces blood pressure, even in highly stressful situations. Salespeople routinely place signs near their phones reading, "Smile while you dial," reminding them that it's hard to feel grumpy while smiling. On the contrary, when you smile, you come across as warm and accessible. For our purposes, know that in addition to health benefits, smiling induces positive feelings. Ron Gutman, the author of *Smile: The Astonishing Powers of a Simple Act*, explains, "British researchers found

BEAT THE BOTS

that one smile can generate the same level of brain stimulation as up to two thousand bars of chocolate." (Don't you want to know what happened to the person who ate two thousand bars of chocolate?) Positive feelings motivate you to do good work, and when you do good work, you feel proud of yourself and optimistic, which, in turn, creates more positive feelings. One smile can lead to success.

Prompt #33: Smile Your Way to Productivity

Smile for a full minute and think about how you feel, then complete this sentence: When I smiled for a full minute, I felt:

_____.

To participate in the *Beat the Bots* TikTok community:

- Record a video of your answer and post it, including the hashtag #beatthebots and tag me at @beatthebotsbook
- You can also tag #authortok and #booktok to connect with other writer and reader communities!
- Watch other writers' videos by visiting the TikTok hashtag #beatthebots

Join the conversation!

TAKE AN OBJECTIVE LOOK
AT YOUR STORY

Once your attitude is in good shape thanks to the Mindset Structure creativity tactic, it's time to take an objective look at your story. Sometimes, you're so close to your characters and plot and you've wrestled so hard with the language, you lack objectivity. Spend some time thinking about the following questions. Your thoughtful and objective answers can guide your revision by alerting you to potential opportunities to raise the stakes.

1. *What emotional truths are you trying to express in the book?*
2. *Does every chapter relate to that underlying emotional truth?*
3. *What does your protagonist long for?*
4. *What are the consequences of your protagonist's failure to achieve his or her goal?*
5. *What obstacles does your protagonist face?*

Here's how I'd answer the questions regarding T. J. Newman's *Drowning* (also discussed in Chapter Six). This book, a thriller, starts when a commercial airplane is forced to ditch in the Pacific. A small cadre of passengers and crew are trapped inside the cabin, two hundred feet underwater. They have enough oxygen to last six and a half hours.

BEAT THE BOTS

Prompt #34: What's the Worst that Can Happen?

You'll recall that "stakes" refers to what protagonists have to lose if they fail. In Sandra Brown's *Tailspin*, if the doctor fails in her mission, the only dose of a life-saving medicine goes to a criminal, not the child who desperately needs it.

Now it's your turn! What are the stakes in your novel? Complete this sentence: If my protagonist fails,

_____.

To participate in the *Beat the Bots* TikTok community:

- Record a video of your answer and post it, including the hashtag #beatthebots and tag me at @beatthebotsbook
- You can also tag #authortok and #booktok to connect with other writer and reader communities!
- Watch other writers' videos by visiting the TikTok hashtag #beatthebots

Join the conversation!

The broad narrative question in *Drowning* is whether the passengers will be rescued. But it is mostly the story of one man, Will, and his quest for redemption. Will and his wife are about to divorce. The couple's daughter, Annie, drowned six years earlier, and they find themselves unable to let go of their grief. If they moved forward, that "would mean they'd be leaving Annie behind. And neither of them was ready to do that." Will is on the plane with their other daughter, Shannon, escorting her to camp in California. The narrower narrative question is whether Will can redeem himself, thus saving Shannon and his marriage.

1. *What emotional truths are you trying to express in the book?*
   - To be loved, you have to give love. To forgive others, you need to forgive yourself. Telling the people you love that you love them rings hollow unless you also show them you love them. Being emotionally available is the only factor that leads to genuine intimacy.

2. *Does every chapter relate to that underlying emotional truth?*
   - Yes, Will's fierce determination to save Shannon is paramount and central to everything he does in every chapter. His transformation from stoic loner to accessible team player directly results from his own actions, from interacting with his fellow passengers, including Shannon, and by trusting his wife's expertise and commitment.

3. *What does your protagonist long for?*
   - Will longs for the release of the crippling grief that's left him frozen in time, rendering him emotionally unavailable to his wife and overly anxious about Shannon.

BEAT THE BOTS

4. *What are the consequences of your protagonist's failure to achieve his or her goal?*
   - At best, isolation and loneliness. At worst, death.
5. *What obstacles does your protagonist face?*
   - The obstacles are numerous, and they grow more dire and increasingly seemingly insurmountable with every setback. For instance:
     - As the oxygen begins to run low, the risk of carbon monoxide poisoning grows.
     - Ocean water leaches into the cabin, leaving the survivors with less and less space to stand and breathe.
     - A rescue diver on a reconnaissance mission dies.
     - After one passenger successfully escapes in a special navy survival suit, another dies, and all the rest of the passengers refuse to attempt the risky trip to the surface.
     - The plane slips deeper in the ocean.
     - Additional leaks are discovered.
     - Their communications system fails.

And so on.

As each obstacle is overcome, another one, tougher and more unexpected, appears. This progression ratchets up the tension while raising the stakes. You'll note that telling Will's story—how a family came together to survive—also tells a larger story about humanity: the power of empathy and forgiveness. By following Will's transformation, readers find themselves ruminating on the importance of rebuilding frayed relationships before it's too late.

> **Pro Tip: Focus on the Story to Raise Meaningful Stakes**
>
> Yasmin Angoe, Anthony Award–nominated novelist, says,
>
> Raise the stakes for not only your protagonist, but all your characters (even the secondaries) by giving your characters purpose and agency in the story. This means that all your characters, the antagonist, and secondary characters, are in it to serve the story, not to highlight your protagonist. Each character should have their own motivation for their actions, even if it's never explained on the page...even if that character is only mentioned once. Knowing what drives them helps you to elevate the stakes and level up your protagonist.

RAISE THE STAKES ON YOURSELF

If your stakes stay stubbornly low or banal or if you find yourself avoiding writing scenes that are crucial to the story but that might offend people, the issue might not be the protagonist's stakes. The issue might be you. I ran into this situation, and it caught me by surprise. I didn't think an experienced writer like me would fall into an abyss of self-doubt so deep.

In a stand-alone I was working on, I had one of my gals, thirty-two and single, thank you very much, decide to go get herself some lovin'. She describes it this way: *A few drinks. A few laughs. A good-natured man with slow hands, that would be a fitting end to a blissful day.* I planned on having her meet a man, and that plunges her into all sort of trouble—high stakes.

Prompt #35: What Stops You from Writing Raw

It's no fun being judged. I'm especially sensitive to the word "should." When someone tells me I should do this or I shouldn't do that, I find myself bristling. Even when they're right. What stops me from writing raw is my antipathy toward being judged, toward being told what to do.

How about you? What stops you from writing raw? Complete this sentence: What stops me from writing raw is:

_____.

To participate in the *Beat the Bots* TikTok community:

- Record a video of your answer and post it, including the hashtag #beatthebots and tag me at @beatthebotsbook
- You can also tag #authortok and #booktok to connect with other writer and reader communities!
- Watch other writers' videos by visiting the Tik-Tok hashtag #beatthebots

Join the conversation!

265

As it happened, my first reader got a little prudish on me. He asked, "Do you want her to seem a little slutty?" Hello? In this day and age? A single woman in her thirties who wants a little fun—that's slutty? I don't think so! But wait! It would be have been easy to dismiss his reaction as *his* problem. Before I did so, I needed to consider all the options. To catch an error, you need to know it's an error, and that requires objective consideration, not defensiveness or a knee-jerk dismissal based on my personal opinion. Here are three questions that helped me identify whether my view was realistic, and if not, what I should do to fix it.

1. The problem: Maybe I didn't develop her character properly, so letting this red-blooded American woman aim for a one-night stand reads out of character.
   - The fix: Add an incident or two before she goes out showing her free-wheeling spirit or her longing for sex or whatever drives her to go and pick up a man for some celebratory sex.
2. The problem: Perhaps I did develop her character properly, and—whoops!—she would never do such a thing.
   - The fix: Revisit her characterization if I want her to go and have some fun. Which begs the question—why do I? If her doing so supports the story—for instance, if she meets someone who figures into the plot—that's a good reason. If I need her to act a little wild later in the book, that's another good reason. If I wanted to show I was "with it" despite being…let us say…out of my thirties and happily married…

well, that's not a good reason to include this scene. Include incidents that relate only to your story. No tangents. No rambling. No babbling. No sidetracks.

3. The problem: It's possible that my first reader is simply a little prudish.

- The fix: Recognize that some readers will be offended by some of your writing. You need to give yourself permission to offend people. Not gratuitously, of course, but if your story requires a scene that may upset some people, you need to recognize that you can't please all the people all the time, and move on. Steer to the emotional truth and let the chips fall where they may.

I spent some time thinking the issue through, and I decided the character *had* been developed properly and that she *would* do such a thing. Which meant my first reader was a little prudish. That's okay! It was incredibly helpful to receive his feedback and make an independent decision about what was best for the story.

I had trouble writing that scene. I was worried that I would be judged. (And you note that I was right, by the way.) As an aside, I should mention that I'm not writing porn or anything. No one even kisses onstage. It was the implication that bothered my first reader (and me). It was her intention that made him uncomfortable (me too). But I wrote it anyway, despite my discomfort. I can write real. I can write raw. Not to oversimplify the issue, but to write the story, I *had* to raise the stakes on myself.

Prompt #36: How Do You Deal with Naysayers?

Everyone has someone in their life who seems to want them to fail, or at least, to not succeed. How do you deal with those people? I walk away, and if I can't walk away because I'm seated next to them at a lunch meeting or something, I smile and say as little as possible.

Now it's your turn! Complete this sentence: To deal with negative people, I:

_____.

To participate in the *Beat the Bots* TikTok community:

- Record a video of your answer and post it, including the hashtag #beatthebots and tag me at @beatthebotsbook
- You can also tag #authortok and #booktok to connect with other writer and reader communities!
- Watch other writers' videos by visiting the TikTok hashtag #beatthebots

Join the conversation!

Ask yourself what frightens or intimidates you. Those are the scenes you're most likely to struggle with. Amanda Jayatissa, the award-winning author of *My Sweet Girl*, explains:

It's hard to look inside yourself to see what truly frightens you, to admit what inspires you, to subject these personal emotional truths to public scrutiny. To produce work that can't be duplicated by AI, though, you must. It's easy to write generalities, but any chatbot can do that. Writing about what scares you most is what will give you a leg up when competing with AI.

How about you? What are you afraid of? Are you afraid of being judged? Ridiculed? Being bullied? Being chastised for writing outside your lane? (Or whatever other metaphor speaks to you.) Losing friends? Losing love?

Have you asked yourself what you'll do if your fear becomes reality? Preparing yourself to handle something in advance is empowering—and of course, your worst fears may never come to life. This is in keeping with the adage of "Expect the best, but prepare for the worst." I want to add a note here, a kind of disclaimer. You don't get extra points for breaking rules, ignoring norms, insulting people, or writing about offensive or hateful people or incidents. That's not what I'm talking about—not at all. I'm talking about allowing yourself to write with purpose and clarity, telling the story you want to tell. If rules need to be broken, and you're prepared for the potential fallout, go for it. But don't break rules simply because you're feeling rebellious. This begs the question, how do you know which stakes to raise?

CONSIDER WHICH STAKES TO RAISE

Integrating obstacles that most directly threaten your protagonists' ability to achieve their goals is the most effective way to raise stakes. Remember that the essence of conflict is warring goals—what does your protagonist long for and what is the antagonist willing to do to stop them from getting it? That's a good starting place to begin your consideration of how to raise stakes. Even if you think the stakes are high, take another look. Can you ratchet them even higher? If so, do.

Remember to prepare for the reenvisioning process using the Mindset Structure creativity tactic detailed earlier in this chapter. Once you're ready, consider the nature of the process. Specifically, when it comes to elevating stakes, there are two broad categories ripe for picking: internal obstacles and external obstacles.

Internal obstacles link directly to your character's longings, values, beliefs, emotions, and objectives. External obstacles challenge your characters to rise to the occasion as they combat factors outside their control. One important consideration, however, is that an external obstacle that might stop one character cold is, to another character, no more significant than a mildly annoying gnat. It is only when an external situation is perceived as an obstacle that the story moves forward. It is people's reactions to an incident, not the incident itself, that represent stakes. In other words, all obstacles, and by extension, all stakes, are internal. The following checklist will help you develop high-stakes incidents that propel your story forward and lead to real character transformations.

Raising Stakes Checklist	
Context	**Plot and Character Implications: Identify Pressure Points**
Societal Issues	• What is happening in the world that serves as the backdrop to your story? Is there a war? The aftermath of war? A contentious political cycle? A cruise ship under attack? Is Wall Street booming? Or crashing? • What do these factors mean to the society? How can you make things more dangerous, more dramatic, more dire?
Personal Issues	• What is your protagonist's role in this world? Is he a leader? A victim? Is she a savior? A perpetrator? How do your other characters fit within this world view? • What does this role mean to them? How invested are they? How satisfied are they? Do they have alternatives? Do they want alternatives? What can you do to threaten their role, their ability to fulfill their responsibilities, or challenge their rights?
Opposing Forces	• Who or what is out to thwart your protagonist? Why? • Is the opposing force personal? Global? Random? Is it bureaucratic, regulatory, or standard operating procedure?

Cultural Implications	• What group- or community-based belief systems might become obstacles? • Is there a shared language not everyone knows? How about a specialized language, like Morse code? (Consider US Navy pilot Jeremiah A. Denton's use of Morse code to overcome an obstacle. When Denton was a prisoner of war in North Vietnam, he was forced to make a propaganda film stating he and his fellow prisoners were being well-treated. Pretending to be blinded by the camera operator's bright lights, he blinked his eyes in Morse code, spelling out "T-O-R-T-U-R-E," thus alerting navy intelligence to the situation.) Does the culture avoid new technology as is the norm in some Amish communities? How might food options, limitations, or preferences create obstacles? What other aspects of culture might come into play, for instance, music, traditions, or norms?
Illicit Relationships	• How might interpersonal relationships create obstacles? • Is there an unyielding social stratification that keeps certain groups apart? Are there standards of morality that might be compromised or challenged?

BEAT THE BOTS

Oracular Predictions Note: Oracular predictions can come across as contrived or coincidental if you haven't previously laid the groundwork through incident, character belief, ancestry tradition, or some other means.	• Is there something that foreshadows events, such as dream sequences, tendrils of recovered memory, or drug-induced revelations? Is there something or someone that predicts the future, be it a medium, tarot card reader, palmist, or oracle? • Does the revelation expose an obstacle or disclose a way to overcome the obstacle?
Environmental Obstacles	• Are there geographic elements that present obstacles? • Is there a mountain that is subject to avalanches? Streams that must be forded? Cold or heat that must be endured? Is there a polluted river in town? Fire ants on the march?
Other Internal Obstacles	• What emotional truths drive your characters to act, and what stops them from acting? Remember to steer to the pain.
Other External Obstacles	• What external conditions, such as a blizzard or tornado, create obstacles for your characters? How prepared and capable are your characters?

Let's go through an example so you can see how to think it through. You'll recall my allegory idea about cats and dogs

273

forming some kind of power-sharing arrangement, with cats running the backroom systems and dogs being the face of the government. What if cats become the leadership class and dogs their servants? Let's say I go with the latter story—I think there's likely to be more potential for conflict if dogs are relegated to a servant class. Here are some ideas that showcase the potential obstacles cats and dogs might face.

Raising Stakes Checklist	
Working Title	**Reigning Cats—and Dogs**
Context	**Plot and Character Implications: Identify Pressure Points**
Societal Issues	• In a societal system where certain cat breeds hold higher status than other breeds, some kinds of cats are doomed to be devalued. One of the higher-valued breeds could be the leader class, another the celebrity class, a third, the professional class, and all the rest of the breeds, including mixed breeds, are lower in the pecking order, and struggle to better their positions in life. • Dogs are required to wear tags identifying their owners. They can't travel more than ten minutes from their homes. • My protagonist is a mixed-breed cat named Bella trying to pass as a purebred. She's always on edge, hoping not to get caught, determined to provide the best future for her kittens.

	• Dogs band together to protest the restrictions, but can't form a cohesive group. • The stakes rise further when cats institute new policies limiting dogs' rights to free speech (barking is limited to inside spaces only) and free assembly (all dog runs are closed).
Personal Issues	• The emotional toll can be elevated by focusing on how the new rules limiting independence affect specific cats and dogs. For instance, some cats relish the power, while others feel sad and empathetic. Some dogs feel cowed; others become rebellious. • Bella is anxious, but determined to protect her status in order to safeguard her kittens' future.
Opposing Forces	• After several false starts, a group of dogs bands together, forming an organized resistance movement determined to overthrow feline rule. • The leader of the resistance, an appealing and charismatic golden retriever named Rocky, becomes the face of the endeavor. The stakes increase as this group grows from a ragtag gang to an organized guerrilla army. • Rocky's army works to disrupt the status quo. As a result, they find themselves facing discrimination and harassment. • The stakes grow ever higher as their fight for equality (or, to add an additional

	twist, supremacy) builds momentum, threatening to topple the cat-centric government.
	• Bella, seeking to protect herself and her babies no matter the outcome of the rebellion, ingratiates herself with both sides. She goes on a charm offensive with the cat leadership team and surreptitiously befriends Rocky. • Among her cat community, she's known as sweet and effervescent, but not very bright. Because Bella isn't perceived as a threat, she gets to hang out in the background, unnoticed, and as such, she picks up all sorts of information. • After passing Rocky a bit of intelligence that allows his army to prepare for resistance (but won't hurt cats), Bella earns a reputation among Rocky's leadership team as a pragmatist.
Cultural Implications	• The more success the resistance movement enjoys, the more the cats counterattack, developing a diabolical plan to eliminate or suppress dogs' cultural heritage. • The stakes rise as dogs face the loss of their language (no barking is allowed) and traditions (interaction with humans is prohibited). • Bella is outraged at the cats' latest edicts and continues feeding Rocky tidbits of information she picks up during the cats' meetings.

BEAT THE BOTS

Illicit Relationships	• The stakes further increase when Bella and Rocky's clandestine relationship is revealed. They have to outwit both their cat and dog persecutors as they endure the retribution they face by defying societal norms—cats and dogs can't be friends. • When the cat leaders discover Bella has revealed classified information, she's charged with treason.
Oracular Predictions Note: Oracular predictions can come across as contrived or coincidental if you haven't previously laid the groundwork through incident, character belief, ancestry tradition, or some other means.	• If I have a character (cat or dog) who had a relationship with another creature (cat, dog, human, or a supernatural entity of some sort) that predicted the future, I could raise the stakes by having the predictions grow increasingly threatening as the story unfolds. • These dark predictions lead to anxiety, fear, and depression, which serve as additional obstacles to overcome.

277

Environmental Obstacles	• I could create an environmental crisis that endangers both cats and dogs. The crisis could be a thousand-year flood, a drought, a wildfire, or some other life-endangering event. • To manage the impending calamity that threatens their mutual survival, cats and dogs must set aside their differences and work together. Rocky must convince his army to agree to a cessation of hostilities. The cat at the head of government must do the same with her cats. • When Rocky learns that Bella's kittens are in imminent danger from the calamity, he risks his own life to rescue her family.
Other Internal Obstacles	• I would think about how to parlay pride, guilt, and shame into meaningful obstacles.
Other External Obstacles	• I would look to geography-specific factors based on where my story is set.

Note how raising the stakes helps me plot out incidents. In an allegory in particular, you need to write with a dual focus. On the one hand, *Reigning Cats—and Dogs* explores the fantastical world of cats and dogs, a literal interpretation of the narrative. On the other hand, my story uses a figurative approach to delve into universal themes of power versus rebellion, individual identity versus assimilation, and societal values versus personal needs and desires. By raising the stakes in these ways, the novel becomes more intense and emotionally charged, keeping readers invested in the outcome.

BEAT THE BOTS

AI Weighs In

I asked AI whether external factors or internal factors were stronger when raising stakes in a novel.

Its answer was so generic it was meaningless: *Ultimately, the choice between emphasizing external or internal factors depends on the story's genre, themes, and the author's intent. Some stories may thrive on high-stakes external conflicts, while others may derive their power from the internal journey of the characters. The key is to integrate both aspects seamlessly for a rich and immersive reading experience.*

Well, yes, but this isn't helpful in planning actual incident-based stakes in an actual book. A better tactic is to use the Raising Stakes Checklist in this chapter as a tool to develop meaningful stakes for your characters.

No matter what you're writing, the higher the stakes, the more compelling the story. Introducing obstacles that challenge your readers without seeming heavy-handed or coincidental requires an understanding of your people, an assessment only you can do. There is simply no way that AI can replicate your insights and judgment. Give the process a try!

279

Exercise

Mindset Structures: Raise the Stakes

1. Go through the Mindset Structure creativity tactic to get yourself in the right headspace to delve into this crucial reenvisioning exercise. Take your time. Tell yourself you can do it, that you will do it, that you're ready to succeed.
2. To ensure you keep your narrative question top of mind, write it here (see Chapter Three):

   _____

   _____

3. Remind yourself about your protagonist's longings. What emotional truths drive them to act?

   _____

   _____

With your narrative question and protagonist's core motivation in mind, complete the Raising Stakes Checklist. The more ideas about obstacles your protagonist needs to overcome, the better. You may not use them all, but it's incredibly useful to have a list to consult as you go through the writing process. You never know when an obstacle you originally thought might work in an early chapter actually fits better in a later chapter.

BEAT THE BOTS

Raising Stakes Checklist	
Working Title	
Context	**Plot and Character Implications: Identify Pressure Points** Note: Use as many or as few bullet points as you need. There is no right number.
Societal Issues	• •
Personal Issues	• •
Opposing Forces	• •
Cultural Implications	• •
Illicit Relationships	• •
Oracular Predictions	• •
Environmental Obstacles	• •
Other Internal Obstacles	• •
Other External Obstacles	• •

281

How did it go? Were you able to come up with some challenging obstacles? Do they offer your characters the opportunity to showcase their smarts or skills? Did anything about the process surprise you?

I'd love to hear about your experience with the Mindset Structure creativity technique. Complete this sentence: I tried Jane's Mindset Structure creativity technique to help me identify obstacles and raise the stakes for my characters—and myself—and:

_____

To participate in the *Beat the Bots* TikTok community:

- Record a video of your answer and post it, including the hashtag #beatthebots and tag me at @beatthebotsbook
- You can also tag #authortok and #book-tok to connect with other writer and reader communities!
- Watch other writers' videos by visiting the Tik-Tok hashtag #beatthebots

Join the conversation!

In this chapter, we focused on identifying obstacles to raise the stakes for our characters—and ourselves. High stakes resonate with readers, creating urgency and meaning. To create those high stakes, you need to identify what your characters

BEAT THE BOTS

long for. Artificial intelligence can't know your characters' innermost desires, the ones that drive their actions but never appear on the page—only you can know that. When you raise the stakes by tapping into your characters' emotional truths, you'll create more interesting characters, a more dynamic plot, which, taken together, is certain to keep readers on the edge of their seats. In the next chapter, we're going to move to sentence-level revision. You'll discover proven revision strategies certain to help you express your ideas eloquently and unambiguously.

> ### Reflection on Creativity
>
> "You can be cautious or you can be creative, but there's no such thing as a cautious creative."
> *George Lois*

CHAPTER TEN

CREATIVITY TACTIC #10
CREATIVE ANALYSIS: REVISE YOUR OWN WORK

"I work slowly, page by page, revising and polishing."
Dean Koontz

TAKE A CREATIVE APPROACH TO REVISION

In the last chapter, we discussed revising on a macro level, specifically on raising the stakes. In this chapter, we're going to look at revising on a micro level, drilling down to consider sentence structure and word choices, the genesis of elegant prose.

BEAT THE BOTS

Just as writing isn't a synonym for typing, revising isn't a synonym for proofreading. Proofreading is a vital step in the writing process, but before you delve into the nitty gritty of grammar, punctuation, formatting, and other mechanics, you need to:

- Avoid Uncited Generalizations and Vague Terminology (UGVT)
- Choose powerful, active verbs
- Beef up your sensory references

To accomplish this, you need to bring creative judgment and astute insights to the task, which requires your human eye, not AI's generic recommendations. Only you can determine the best style and substance for your work. This chapter provides a detailed roadmap through the revision process. As we proceed, we'll use the Creative Analysis creativity tactic as our guide.

FAQ

Q: I find revision nearly impossible. I procrastinate endlessly. How can I motivate myself to do what I know is a crucial part of the writing process?

A: Many authors don't like revision, so while you're in good company, it's terrific that you understand the need to revise your work.

To overcome procrastination, you need to first identify why you're procrastinating. Here are three common reasons authors cite for avoiding revision, followed by suggestions on what to do about the issue.

285

- *The issue:* You're so emotionally attached to your work, you bristle at the mere idea that your manuscript needs revision.
  - *The fix:* Change how you frame the issue. Remind yourself that you're a professional. Just as all photographs need cropping and color correction to highlight certain elements, sharpen the focus, and tell a compelling visual story, so too do all manuscripts need revising for the exact same reasons—to highlight your theme, escalate your conflicts and the corresponding stakes, and tell a captivating story. The goal of revision isn't to gut your work; rather, it's to enrich it.
- *The issue:* You've read through your manuscript so many times you can recite whole passages from memory. You can't bear the thought of going through it one more time.
  - *The fix:* Read it aloud. Have you ever noticed how tough it is to catch a typo when you're the one who made the mistake? The same principle applies to revision. We get so close to our own work, it's tough to spot weak passages or errors. Sometimes, you know so much about your intentions, your brain skips over anything that isn't in keeping with that intention. A nifty trick to overcome

this is to read your work aloud. Mignon Fogarty, host of the long-running Grammar Girl podcast and author of the *New York Times* bestseller *Grammar Girl's Quick and Dirty Tips for Better Writing*, says:

> I read every piece I write aloud—it's an essential step in my editing process. It's almost like magic in the way it surfaces problems you didn't catch on the page. Typos? Gone. Awkward sentences? Gone. A description that doesn't make sense. Gone (perhaps after some tough rewriting). My favorite trick is to have a computer read your draft to you. Not only is it faster—allowing you to jot down notes or highlight troublesome text as it goes along—but also enlightening: listening to a simulated "someone else" read your work gets you out of your own head and helps you consider the writing in a whole new way.

Editor Karen S. Conlin, an ACES: The Society for Editing Robinson Prize laureate concurs: "Use your computer's 'read aloud' function to do at least one editing pass. That does wonders for helping you catch missing/extra words, clunky constructions, and 'What on earth was I thinking here?' areas."

Note that Conlin refers to an "editing pass." Some authors find it helpful to review their manuscripts several times during the revision process, addressing only one issue at a time. For instance, perhaps you want to do one editorial pass to ensure character motivations align with your plot, another to confirm your use of sensory language is strong and consistent, a third to check the dialogue subtext, and so on. By isolating factors, it's easier to catch missteps than when you're trying to focus on the entire manuscript at once.

- *The issue:* You feel overwhelmed. You don't know where to start.
  - *The fix:* It sounds like you don't have a reliable process, so the fix here is to develop a revision plan customized for your style and needs. Once you have a plan, the process becomes more manageable. We'll talk about designing a revision plan later in this chapter.

PUT THE CREATIVE ANALYSIS CREATIVITY TACTIC TO WORK

As the name implies, the Creative Analysis creativity tactic relies on your judgment. As you consider your revision options, answer this one core question:

What are you trying to express?

This tactic is deceptively simple. First you determine what you want to communicate, then you assess whether your wording will achieve that goal. In the examples that follow, you'll see how revision decisions are easier to make and result in stronger work when viewed through the lens of intentionality.

AVOID UNCITED GENERALIZATIONS AND VAGUE TERMINOLOGY (UGVTs)

UGVTs are the antithesis of good writing. There are two broad categories of UGVTs: quantities and modifiers. Let's look at each category, discuss why UGVTs are a problem, and consider how to address the issues.

CLARIFY QUANTITIES

Let's start with words or phrases that express quantities. The chart that follows shows a sampling of commonly used words relating to quantities, and the meaning or context they imply. As you review the list, note how understanding the literal meaning of a word is easy: look in the dictionary. Understanding the figurative implications and their potential to confuse readers is far trickier.

UGVT: Quantities	Meaning or Implication
Couple	Two
Several	More than two, but fewer than many
Few	Not many, but more than one
Many	Not most, but more than a few
Most	More than half

Generation	Roughly twenty-five years (the average age of a woman when she has her first child)
Myriad	Ten thousand or a number of that ilk
Dozen	Twelve
Gross	A dozen dozen, 144 units
Smidge	A tiny amount
Pinch	The amount of a granular substance, like a spice, that you can hold by pinching your thumb and index finger together
Soupçon	A slight trace, as of a particular flavor
Dollop	A lump or blob of some substance; more broadly, a small quantity
Ream	A standard quantity of paper, consisting of five hundred sheets; often "reams," meaning a large quantity of writing, for instance, she's written reams of poetry
Score	Twenty; from President Lincoln: Four score and seven years ago, meaning eighty-seven years earlier
Spate	A sudden, almost overwhelming, outpouring
Plethora	Overabundance, excessive, from Dictionary.com: "A plethora of advice and a paucity of assistance"
Copious	Abundant, plentiful
Sheaf	One of the bundles in which cereal plants, as in wheat or rye, are bound after reaping; used to indicate a collection of documents

Finding the right word to express quantities serves to convert amorphous terms into concrete references—adding credibility and understanding to your work. If you write the word "many," for example, use the Creative Analysis creativity tactic to ask what you're trying to express. Say you have an elementary school teacher who drags herself home at the end of a long day and tells her husband, "What a day. So many

BEAT THE BOTS

problems." That sounds natural, doesn't it? But is the sentence doing its job? Posing the Creative Analysis creativity tactic question *What am I trying to express?* Tells me that it's not. I want her to describe the magnitude of the situation and how she feels about it, and I don't think "many" does the job. Here are some alternatives:

1. "What a day. Four thousand two hundred and twelve problems, and I'm not done counting yet."
2. "You may be the only person in town who isn't mad at me. What a day."
3. "If I escape with only a letter of reprimand today, I'll call it a win."

These options differ dramatically, and that's the point. They're all good (and they're all better than "many"), but how can you decide? You can't until you know your intentions. Did you simply want to communicate that she had a whopper of a bad day? (Option 1) Or did she have a horrible day because an altercation that mushroomed into her standing alone in the face of a group's anger? (Option 2) Or is the issue that she did something wrong? (Option 3) Until you know what you're trying to express, you can't make an informed decision. Once you clarify your intention, your choice becomes clear.

ADD SPECIFICITY WHEN USING ADJECTIVES AND ADVERBS

To ensure clarity, you need to choose adjectives and adverbs carefully. Modifiers should be used only when they change the meaning of the noun, not merely to add emphasis. For example,

291

if I have a character specifying a meeting place ("the house with the green door"), the adjective "green" is necessary. Certain adjectives, though, like "very," "really," and "pretty," just add emphasis. You see these words all the time, and using them occasionally in dialogue might be appropriate, but as a general rule, you should avoid them. Instead of adding a word to reinforce the noun, find a stronger noun or let the existing noun stand alone. Consider this excerpt from the movie *Dead Poets Society*, written by Tom Schulman: "So avoid using the word 'very' because it's lazy. A man is not very tired, he is exhausted. Don't use very sad, use morose. Language was invented for one reason, boys—to woo women—and, in that endeavor, laziness will not do." Mark Twain also warned against using the word "very." Twain wrote: "Substitute '*damn*' every time you're inclined to write 'very'; your editor will delete it and the writing will be just as it should be."

Using the Creative Analysis creativity tactic will help you choose the best adjective or adverb, or decide the noun or verb is strong enough on its own. For instance, instead of writing, "Mary prefers very colorful furniture!" how about simply "colorful," or depending on your voice and Mary's personality, "glamorous," "psychedelic," or "flamboyant"? Instead of writing that the task is "very difficult," write "arduous," or depending on your voice and the situation, "back-breaking," "killer," or "grueling." Notice the first step is to use the Creative Analysis creativity tactic and answer that one central question: *What am I trying to express?* If I write "walk quickly," I should ask myself what that movement looks like. Do I mean "jog"? "Lope"? "Sprint"? "Scamper"? "Dart"? "Dash?" Don't write "walked angrily" if you mean "stomped." Don't write "walked slowly," if you mean "strolled," "sauntered," or "ambled." Try doing a search for "ly," and see how you use adverbs. Not all

BEAT THE BOTS

adverbs end in "ly," but most do. You may be stunned at how frequently they slip into your writing.

Another reason to use the Creative Analysis creativity tactic when choosing modifiers is that unless they're narrowly defined, they're open to interpretation, which, by definition, violates a crucial metric of writing excellence—to write unambiguously. After all, one person's beautiful is another person's not so much. One person's fantastic is another person's yawn.

Let's say a real estate agent shows a client a house that meets her specifications: three bedrooms, two baths, and a den. After viewing a property, Teresa, the client, exclaims, "This house is gorgeous!" Do you see the problem? How do your readers know what Teresa finds "gorgeous"? When you picture a "gorgeous" house, what image comes to your mind? Is it an all-glass contemporary? A midcentury ranch? A tiny house? Asking yourself what you're trying to express equips you to use that information to select the most appropriate words. And don't forget—as we discussed in Chapter Seven, you want your dialogue to do something, not merely say something.

To revise the UGVT, I need to know what Teresa means by "gorgeous." For instance, I could write: "The brick colonial's center entrance appealed to Teresa's love of symmetry." Or how about this? "The walls of windows simultaneously excited and terrified her." (The next sentences would explain the duality— the expansive view thrilled her, yet the exposure scared her.)

Prompt #37: Choose the Right Adjective

If someone tells you the food is delicious, do you know how it tastes? Of course not. One person's delicious, is another person's bland. You need to be explicit. Is it refreshing, sweet, tart, spicy, smoky, crispy? The more specific, the better.

Now it's your turn! How would you describe the aroma when you first walk into a bakery? Use the Creative Analysis creativity tactic to decide what you want to express. Then complete the sentence below, focusing on your sense of smell. Remember to avoid generic terms like "good" or "wonderful."

Complete this sentence: When I walk into a bakery, it smells:

_____.

To participate in the *Beat the Bots* TikTok community:

- Record a video of your answer and post it, including the hashtag #beatthebots and tag me at @beatthebotsbook
- You can also tag #authortok and #booktok to connect with other writer and reader communities!
- Watch other writers' videos by visiting the TikTok hashtag #beatthebots

Join the conversation!

BEAT THE BOTS

Another approach to curing UGVTs is to find (or in fiction, create) examples, statistics, facts, or quotes that serve as evidence. Consider this UGVT: domestic cats and tigers are alike. Can you see the issues?

- The word "alike" is vague.
- From a writing POV, note also the word "are." Later in this chapter, we'll talk about eliminating as many "to be" verbs as possible.

How about this revision: "According to *The Christian Science Monitor*, 'The biggest and perhaps most fearsome of the world's big cats, the tiger, shares 95.6 percent of its DNA with humans' cute and furry companions, domestic cats.'" Specificity increases believability, a key to reader engagement.

AIM FOR PRECISION

When a word is commonly used, sometimes its meaning gets watered down. See if you can replace it or add examples to illuminate your meaning. Consider the word "nice," which broadly describes someone or something pleasing, agreeable, kind, or more formally, discriminating. "The sommelier offers a nice selection of wines" implies the wine list was chosen with care and discernment. I want to share an excerpt from an introduction I wrote for *Alfred Hitchcock Mystery Magazine*. Periodically, they publish classic short stories. A few years ago, they published one by my mother, Ruth Chessman, called "Poor Sherm," and they invited me to write the introduction.

My mother was a walking dictionary and I was reared to think that precision in language was a calling. I recall the day she told me I was using "nice" improperly.

I'd just come home from school and I found her in the kitchen, scouring a pot. I was about ten.

"I met a new girl at school today," I said, foraging for nibblies. "Her name is Karla, and she's really nice."

"The word nice means discriminating," my mother said, "so I assume you're saying that Karla has good taste."

"Huh? No. All I meant was that Karla was really open, and chatty, and, you know, fun to be around."

My mother nodded as she placed the pot in the drying rack. "Better."

Nice, right? (That was a joke…did you catch my use of the word "nice"?)

The lesson here is to add specificity. I spend a lot of time with the dictionary and thesaurus open, considering the nuance of language.

Three Important Revision Tips, and Advice from Dr. Seuss

- Don't use numbers in dialogue.
  - 9 mm gun
  - $1 million
- Don't use two words if one will do, unless you love the cadence, or there's a clue hidden

BEAT THE BOTS

inside, or you have some other good reason to include it. Also, notice in the examples below that I'm eliminating labeling words. Labeling words (e.g., see, hear, smell, feel, taste, think, realize, know, understand) indicate I'm telling, not showing.

- o Two words and she felt her courage falter. vs. Two words and her courage faltered.
- o She knew he was lying vs. His air of studied nonchalance told her he was lying.

Multiple award-winning author George Saunders explains:

> I write, "Jane came into the room and sat down on the blue couch," read that, wince, cross out "came into the room" and "down" and "blue" (Why does she have to come into the room? Can someone sit UP on a couch? Why do we care if it's blue?) and the sentence becomes "Jane sat on the couch—" and suddenly, it's better (Hemingwayesque, even!), although...why is it meaningful for Jane to sit on a couch? Do we really need that? And soon we have arrived, simply, at "Jane," which at least doesn't suck, and has the virtue of brevity.

297

- Keep a list of frequently used words, and for one of your last editorial passes, search for each one, revising as needed. Whether you're echoing words unconsciously, or using a certain word as a placeholder, it's important to find fresh ways to express familiar ideas, situations, descriptions, thoughts, and incidents.

Consider this writing advice from Dr. Seuss:

Writing simply means no dependent clauses, no dangling things, no flashbacks, and keeping the subject near the predicate. We throw in as many fresh words we can get away with. Simple, short sentences don't always work. You have to do tricks with pacing, alternate long sentences with short, to keep it vital and alive…Virtually every page is a cliffhanger—you've got to force them to turn it.

CHOOSE POWERFUL, ACTIVE VERBS

Reducing the number of "to be" verbs and smothered verbs will dramatically improve your writing. Choose active, powerful verbs to draw readers in.

"To be" verbs (which include *is, are, was, were, am, be, being, been*) refer to a state of being, mere existence. I can hear the naysayers now: "But wait! Shakespeare had Hamlet say 'To be or not to be, that is the question'—that's three 'to be' verbs

BEAT THE BOTS

right there." Yes, but in the entire soliloquy (thirty-five lines, 276 words), there are only nine "to be" verbs, just above 3 percent, a reasonable metric.

Here are three reasons why you should limit your use of "to be" verbs. "To be" verbs:

1. Claim absolute truth and exclude other views. "The best vacations are the ones spent on a beach." Few would agree that the best vacations are *always* spent at the beach.
2. Are UGVTs. A father may tell his child, "Be good at school today." The more specific "Don't talk when the teacher talks today" serves to define "good."
3. Often confuse the reader about the subject of the sentence. For example, "It was nice of him to stop by." Who or what is the "It"?

The better option is to revise sentences that contain a "to be" verb using our Creative Analysis creativity tactic. For example, instead of writing "In China, red is a symbol of good fortune," ask yourself what you're trying to express. You might answer: "In China, red symbolizes good fortune." Using active, powerful verbs adds pep to your writing.

One especially pesky issue related to "to be" verbs occurs when you start sentences with "There is," "There are," "There was," "There were," or "These are." When revising one of these sentences, add specificity.

For instance, how might you "cure" this UGVT? "There are many herbs that last through the winter"? How about this? "Thyme, sage, and rosemary last through the winter." Or: "Thyme, sage, and rosemary, among other herbs, last through the winter."

299

Prompt #38: Revise to Replace the "To Be" Verb

Using the Creative Analysis creativity tactic helps ensure your revisions do more than simply replace the "to be" verb. Knowing what you want to express can guide your choice of an active verb. For instance, instead of "The tiger is behind the rock." I could write, "The tiger crouched behind the rock." Scary!

Now it's your turn! Let's say you have a character who's passionate about art. You wrote: "There is an exhibit I want to go see." How can you revise it? Ask yourself what you're trying to express—write that!

To participate in the *Beat the Bots* TikTok community:

- Record a video of your answer and post it, including the hashtag #beatthebots and tag me at @beatthebotsbook
- You can also tag #authortok and #booktok to connect with other writer and reader communities!
- Watch other writers' videos by visiting the TikTok hashtag #beatthebots

Join the conversation!

USE VERBS TO STRENGTHEN CHARACTERIZATIONS

You'll recall that we discussed how each character should speak with a distinctive voice (see Chapter Seven), and one of the best ways to achieve this is by choosing active verbs that reflect their personalities, education, attitudes, and intentions. For example, consider this sentence:

- The child was behind the sofa.

  The sentence is informative but flavorless. Let's put the Creative Analysis creativity tactic to work. What am I trying to express? That this two-year-old boy is having a blast playing hide-and-seek? Or that he's terrified? All we know so far is that the boy is two (so I'll call him a "toddler," a more specific word than "child").

- The toddler hid behind the sofa.

  "The toddler hid behind the sofa" is accurate, but not unambiguous. We still don't know if he's hiding because he's playing hide-and-seek or afraid. If he's playing, I need to add information to specify his attitude, not by telling the reader that he's having a ball, but by showing him having a ball.

- The toddler hid behind the sofa, pressing his chubby little fingers against his lips to keep from laughing.

  That revision ensures clarity.

But what if the toddler is, in fact, hiding because he's terrified. I don't want to *tell* the reader the boy is afraid. Can I find an active verb that nails my intention, while adding information about the boy's attitude?

301

- The toddler cowered behind the sofa.
  And that's the power of an active verb.

In the last chapter, you'll recall that literary agent Roma Panganiban of Janklow & Nesbit stressed the importance of including the stakes in your query letters. About word choices, she says, "I pay a lot of attention to the verbs in a pitch: 'wants' is less compelling than 'must decide,' 'thinks' less than 'confronts.' Adjectives and adverbs are the same way: the more precise they are, the more easily I can tell if this is a manuscript I want to see."

Precision in language—that's the surest way to write unambiguously.

Active Options to Replace Weak Verbs

Here's a partial list of active verbs: assembled, balanced, basked, bent, blanketed, blocked, burrowed, choked, collected, colonized, convened, covered, cowered, cozied up, crouched, curled up, crammed, crowded, dawdled, dozed, drooped, existed, filled, floated, flocked, flooded, gathered, harbored, heaped, hid, hovered, huddled, hung around, idled, inhabited, inundated, jammed, kneeled, knelt, lay, lazed, lined, lingered, lived, lodged, lolled, lounged, massed, met, mine, mounded, nestled, occupied, quelled, packed, perched, piled, poised, populated, posed, postured, reclined, relaxed, remained, reposed, resided, rested, reunited, roomed, roosted, sagged, sat, saturated, settled, sheltered, slept, slouched, slumbered,

BEAT THE BOTS

> slumped, snoozed, sojourned, sprawled, spread-eagled, squished, squeezed, stacked, stayed, stood, stooped, stretched out, stuck, sunned, swamped, swarmed, tapped, teemed, tenanted, thronged, unwound, waited, wallowed, wedged, wilted...

STAY WITH THE ACTIVE VOICE (MOST OF THE TIME)

Sentences written in the active voice use a subject-verb-object (SVO) structure, placing the subject, the doer of the action suggested by the verb, up front. This contrasts with the passive voice, which places the object (the person, place, or thing receiving the action from the verb), up front.

The active voice is more engaging, but the passive voice has its place in writing. It allows you to focus on what is most important to your reader when the subject is distracting or irrelevant. For instance, a businessperson probably wouldn't tell a customer "Pat messed up your invoice." He'd be much more likely to say, "Your invoice was issued incorrectly." This passive structure accomplishes two things. First, it allows you to hide responsibility, which sounds bad, but is often the right thing to do. Why highlight Pat's error? Second, most likely, your customer doesn't care that it was Pat who messed up the invoice. She just wants it fixed. I call this consideration the "hot issue." Focus on what matters to the people involved. Here's another example: "Albert walked into the stockroom, selected the books you ordered, packed them, affixed the

303

label, and gave them to the shipping clerk yesterday." Whew! To the customer, the "hot issue" is that "Your books shipped yesterday." Yes, it's passive, but it's better writing.

Pro Tip: Inspiration and Authenticity Through Etymology

Jess Zafarris, the author of *Words from Hell* and *Once Upon a Word*, and the creator of www.UselessEtymology.com, explains,

An understanding of etymology—the study of words' origins and the evolution of their meaning—can help you wield your words with greater precision, accuracy, creativity, and intention.

For instance, did you know that the word "hello" didn't become a standard greeting until the introduction of the Bell telephone in 1876?

It appeared a bit before that in a couple of records from the 1820s and '30s, but it wasn't commonly used—and it didn't quite mean the same thing as it does today. These records suggested that if you were approaching a remote property or a distant ship, you might announce yourself by shouting "hello a house!"—though "hallo," "halloo," or "hollo" are more commonly found in this context.

Initially, Alexander Graham Bell proposed using "Ahoy!" as a telephone greeting, but Thomas Edison

BEAT THE BOTS

suggested the word "hello" instead. Some historians have suggested that Edison's spelling was based on a mishearing of "hullo." The term was initially so deeply associated with telephones that call operators in the late 1800s were known as "hello girls."

The lesson: if your story is set in a past century and historical accuracy is important to you, you might want to double-check when common terms first surfaced in English.

The *Oxford Dictionary of English Etymology* and Etymonline.com are both reliable online resources that explain how, when, and why English words came to be. These resources can be gold mines for ensuring that the words you use existed in the time period in which your story takes place.

But there's far more to be found in these resources than historical accuracy. They can also be used to:

- Understand roots and stems—not just from Latin and Greek, but also Germanic and indigenous languages—to build character and place names for your story.
- Explore how word meanings have evolved over the years, and find secret meanings hidden within them, such as the word "electric," which has more to do with amber than with shocking energy.

- Gain a new respect for biases hidden in words, such as the word "hysteria," which was applied primarily to women's mental illnesses and whose root is the Greek *hystera*, "womb."
- Learn about the historical figures and authors who coined words and phrases, from Chaucer and Shakespeare to Mary Wollstonecraft Shelley and James Baldwin.
- Discover how events throughout history have shaped the words we use today, such as the way the Napoleonic Wars inspired the word "chauvinism."

Mine for now-obsolete terms that historical characters might choose and use, such as the Middle English term "balter," which means "to dance with joy, but not with grace."

AVOID SMOTHERED VERBS

When you smother a verb, you convert a perfectly good verb into a noun. Instead of "make a decision," why not write "decide"? Instead of "issue an invitation," how about "invite"? Here are some additional examples to help you see how much stronger the writing is when you let the verb do the work.

1. I'm glad they've come to an agreement.
   - I'm glad they agree.

BEAT THE BOTS

2. We're here to conduct an investigation.
   - We're here to investigate.
3. He didn't give an indication of his plans.
   - He didn't indicate his plans.
4. Professional writers make revisions to their work.
   - Professional writers revise their work.
5. They agreed to give consideration to his proposal.
   - They agreed to consider his proposal.

Smothered verbs sap the power that comes when you let the verb do its job, diminishing its impact and watering down your text.

Prompt #39: Revise to Eliminate the Smothered Verb

Let's say I have two college pals who decide to buy a cabin on a lake together. One of the friends, Angela, is technical, methodical, and literal. The other, Matt, is a free spirit, impulsive, and creative. My first draft reads: Angela said, "It's important that we take the cost of electricity into consideration." Here's my revision, applying several of the tactics discussed this far in the book:

> Angela looked up from her computer monitor. "We need to consider the cost of electricity."
>
> "It'll all work out. It always does."
>
> "No, it doesn't. Lots of people get in over their heads."

307

Matt laughed. "I don't know the water depth. Do you? Can we even get in over our heads?"

"Come on, Matt!"

"Lighten up, Angel-Puff."

I changed "into consideration" to "consider." I added several lines of dialogue using business to indicate the speaker, not tags, and integrating plenty of subtext. You'll note that I included no "to be" verbs.

Now it's your turn! Revise the sentence below to eliminate the smothered verb. Add in some extra information, too, maybe a sentence or two to expand on the thought. Use only active verbs—no "to be" verbs! Aim to add specificity, too! Use the Creative Assessment creativity tactic to analyze the problem and develop a relevant scenario. Ask yourself: *What are you trying to express?*

All applicants interviewed via Zoom with the exception of Lauren.

To participate in the *Beat the Bots* TikTok community:

- Record a video of your answer and post it, including the hashtag #beatthebots and tag me at @beatthebotsbook

BEAT THE BOTS

> - You can also tag #authortok and #book-tok to connect with other writer and reader communities!
> - Watch other writers' videos by visiting the Tik-Tok hashtag #beatthebots
>
> Join the conversation!

BEEF UP YOUR SENSORY REFERENCES

In Chapter Four, we discussed the power of experiential writing, describing incidents by integrating sensory references. Specifically, what do your characters:

- See as they look around (or see in their mind's eye)
- Hear, including ambient noises, ringing in their ears, and voices in their heads
- Feel when they touch something or when something touches them, literally or figuratively
- Smell, including what memories or feelings the aroma might evoke
- Taste, including nonfood tastes, such as the bitter taste of adrenaline or the sour taste of bad breath

Note the imagery in this excerpt from Fran Littlewood's *Amazing Grace Adams.* "One of the ponds is just across the path and Grace almost breaks into a run to reach it. Crouching down, she places the cake box on a brown patch of grass, fills the plastic pistol, watches the water bubble and turn blue-jeweled. The vivid sky above her, the egg-yolk sun, light hitting the pond like flung crystals, all of it is the hope in her as she presses the rubber trigger, dousing her neck, her face, her arms, down the front of her shirt, the top of her scalp. The feel of the cold spray on her skin is indecent. The relief, the release a bright epiphany."

From the "brown patch of grass" and the "egg-yolk sun" to the "flung crystals" and "bright epiphany," this description exemplifies the power of sensory references. Interestingly, this excerpt is 108 words long, and includes three "to be" verbs, in keeping with our 3 percent max metric.

Prompt #40: Add More Sensory References

Now it's your turn! Your character finally gets inside to cozy warmth after freezing outside.

1. Answer the Creative Analysis creativity tactic question: *What are you trying to express?* as it relates to this particular character in this particular situation.
2. Write a sentence or two that incorporates as a deeply felt sensory reference—what does your character see, hear, feel, taste, or smell, and how do they feel about it?

To participate in the *Beat the Bots* TikTok community:

BEAT THE BOTS

> - Record a video of your answer and post it, including the hashtag #beatthebots and tag me at @beatthebotsbook
> - You can also tag #authortok and #book-tok to connect with other writer and reader communities!
> - Watch other writers' videos by visiting the Tik-Tok hashtag #beatthebots
>
> Join the conversation!

DEVELOP A REVISION PLAN

In this chapter, we looked at eliminating UGVTs, choosing powerful verbs, and adding in more sensory references. Using those three imperatives as a starting place, let's create a revision plan. For instance, in revising the paragraph about Charles waiting for Ace (see the example below), I looked at:

- UGVTs
  - References to quantities
  - Adjectives
  - Adverbs
- Verbs
  - "To be" verbs
  - Smothered verbs
  - Active vs. passive voice
- Sensory references

311

> ### AI Weighs In
>
> I asked ChatGPT how to eliminate "to be" verbs. Here's its answer:
>
> > *Replace "to be" verbs with gerunds (-ing form) or participles (-ed form) when appropriate. Example:*
> >
> > - *Weak: The situation is confusing.*
> > - *Strong: The situation is confusing everyone.*
>
> I trust you find this as amusing as I do.

Before:

Charles is at the mouth of the alley, waiting for Ace to show up. To block the cold north wind, Charles lifts his jacket collar. He is tired. Exhausted. He is also tired of waiting. He spends a lot of time waiting, and he's supposed to be patient, but he's not. He is tired of life, when it comes right down to it. He is ready to move on to something new. He is going to finish this deal with Ace and get out of town.

Analysis:

1. Eighty-six words with eight "to be" verbs, more than 10 percent. I think I can replace several of them with more active verbs.

BEAT THE BOTS

2. "A lot" is vague. So is the "alley." I can't picture it. Ditto, "the mouth." Overall, there's a lack of specificity that makes the paragraph banal.
3. The cold wind is the only sensory reference. I can add more.

Using the Creative Analysis creativity tactic, I asked myself what I was trying to express. I want to show Charles's dissatisfaction with his life, his plans, and add more suspense—what is the deal he's doing with Ace?

After:

Charles leans against the rough brick of the old warehouse, long since closed, its windows boarded up. From his vantage point, he can see into the cobblestone alley and up and down Main Street. Empty at this hour. Quiet. Too quiet for his taste. Charles prefers action over tranquility, a crowd over solitude. He waits for Ace to show. He flips up his jacket collar to block the bitter north wind. He's tired. Exhausted, actually. He's tired of waiting, too. He spends hours waiting. Waiting for someone to drive by and hire him to mow the lawn or install drywall. Waiting to get paid. Waiting for Ace. His patience has run thin. Now that he thinks about it, he's tired of life. Life here, anyway. Time to get out of town, start over somewhere new. One last score with Ace, and he'll be on his way.

Analysis:

1. One hundred forty-seven words with three "to be" verbs, 2 percent. I went verb by verb asking myself

what I wanted to express. I replaced boring verbs with active verbs.

2. I replaced "a lot" with "hours." I added details about the location. I integrated specific examples about what Charles was waiting for, his preferences, and how he feels about his situation.

3. I added a variety of sensory references.

I think I achieved my objectives, clarifying the situation and Charles's reactions to it. I added details to highlight Charles's attitudes, perceptions, and intentions. If I hadn't used the Creative Analysis creativity tactic, I'm not sure I would have realized what was lacking in the original paragraph. This methodical process helped me add vigor to this paragraph, and I'm confident it will work for you, too.

Exercise

Creative Analysis: Revise Your Own Work

Now it's your turn to develop a revision plan and give the process a whirl!

1. Choose a paragraph to work with. You could select a paragraph from your current work in progress or write one for this exercise.

2. Ask yourself the Creative Analysis creativity technique core question: *What are you trying to express?*

3. Analyze your paragraph:

BEAT THE BOTS

- How many words are in your paragraph? How many "to be" verbs did you use? What is the percentage? (To calculate the percentage, divide the number of "to be" verbs by the word count.) Do you need to reduce the number you're using to get your usage below the 3 percent mark?
- Check for UGVTs, assessing references to quantities. Also look at your adjectives and adverbs. Can you eliminate any UGVT, substituting specific words and phrases?
- Check all your verbs. Choose the strongest, most precise, most active verbs. Eliminate smothered verbs.
- Are you writing in the active voice, unless you want to hide responsibility or focus on the "hot issue"?
- Can you layer in more sensory references?

4. Revise your paragraph, using the answers to the bulleted questions above as a guide.
5. Analyze your revision using those same questions to assess whether your revision was successful.

How did it go? I'd love to hear about your experience using the Creative Analysis creativity technique

315

to establish your revision plan. Complete this sentence: I used Jane's Creative Analysis creativity technique to create and use my customized revision plan, and I discovered:

_____.

To participate in the *Beat the Bots* TikTok community:

- Record a video of your answer and post it, including the hashtag #beatthebots and tag me at @beatthebotsbook
- You can also tag #authortok and #booktok to connect with other writer and reader communities!
- Watch other writers' videos by visiting the TikTok hashtag #beatthebots

Join the conversation!

In this chapter, we discussed using the Creative Analysis creativity tactic to create a sentence-level customized revision plan. Focusing on the sentence level ensures your writing is innovative, exciting, and brimming with meaning. This accomplishment is certain to separate you from the bots. As Jason Farago put it in his *New York Times* essay, "A.I. Can Make Art That Feels Human. Whose Fault Is That?": "A.I. cannot innovate. All it can produce are prompt-driven approximations and reconstitutions of preexisting materials." Only you

BEAT THE BOTS

can create new material. In the next chapter, we'll delve more into the logistics of the writing process by considering organizational techniques.

Reflection on Creativity

"If you're not prepared to be wrong, you'll never come up with anything original."
Ken Robinson

CHAPTER ELEVEN

CREATIVITY TACTIC #11

JOURNEY MAPPING: GET ORGANIZED

"Organizing is what you do before you do something
so that when you do it, it is not all mixed up."
A. A. Milne

CHART YOUR COURSE

So far, we've talked about elements of craft, getting your book from idea inception to polished perfection using creativity tactics to ensure the finished product is fresh and exciting. In this chapter, we're going to take a broader view of the writing process. We'll discuss specific organizational techniques used by bestselling and award-winning authors and do a deep dive into the Journey Mapping creativity tactic. Don't fall in the trap of thinking organization is a waste of time. Benjamin Franklin wrote, "For every minute spent in organizing, an hour is earned." Moving

BEAT THE BOTS

forward, we'll review three organizational tips designed to help you track time, your progress, and everything (all at once).

When you embark on a writing project, you're navigating unknown terrain. AI can offer routine organizational tips, but the Journey Mapping creativity tactic helps you chart your particular course with confidence. Having a workable organizational system in place can be liberating, freeing your mind to experiment without fear of losing track of your work or going off on tangents. That the Journey Mapping creativity tactic is adaptable to your writing style and organizational needs is what sets it apart from the run-of-the mill tactics that might be recommended by a chatbot.

FAQ

Q: How can I be creative when using organizational tactics that, by definition, fence me in?

A: Organization should support your work, not inhibit it. If you're feeling fenced in, it's possible you're using tools that aren't a good fit for you. *New York Times* best-selling author Jean Kwok explains, "The more I plan my story, the plot, character motivations, the details of my setting, the more creative I can be. I know this seems like an oxymoron, but it's not. Planning allows you infinite creativity, with guard rails." I encourage you to experiment with the tools and tactics discussed in this chapter to see which ones align with your needs and writing style.

319

Keep in mind, there's no one writing process that's best. You need to experiment with various options until you find the process that's right for you. For example, National Book Award winner Don DeLillo writes on an old typewriter. In a *Paris Review* interview, he said, "I devised a new method—new to me, anyway. When I finished a paragraph, even a three-line paragraph, I automatically went to a fresh page to start the new paragraph. No crowded pages. This enabled me to see a given set of sentences more clearly. It made rewriting easier and more effective. The white space on the page helped me concentrate more deeply on what I'd written." To save paper, how about experimenting with this idea on your computer?

Whatever system you develop for yourself, gauge its appropriateness by whether it fosters, not impedes, creativity.

ORGANIZATIONAL TIP #1: TRACK TIME

Time doesn't always refer to the hour of the day or the day of the week, although, of course, that's part of it, and often details are crucial. In my mysteries, for instance, I have to track days, hours, and sometimes even minutes—alibis are involved. To ensure I'm accounting for each suspect's whereabouts during key events (like the murder), I created what I call Jane's Timing Grid. There are plenty of digital tools to do this, which we'll discuss later in this chapter, but for now, I'll show you what I

BEAT THE BOTS

created in case it might be useful for you to adapt to your own work. I find its simplicity beneficial.

In the chart below (which you'll also find in Appendix Three), I'm tracking chapter length, how many consecutive pages are written from each point-of-view character's perspective, the relative page count for each POV character, and to-the-minute timing along with key incidents that occur in each chapter.

JANE'S TIMING GRID

Chapter	Pages	Chapter Length	POV	Day/ Date	Time
1	1	1	Don	Wed, Jan 15	• 9:14, a.m., stakes out Sue's house • 9:37, a.m., follows Sue
2	2-7	6	Don	Mon, July 15	• Etc.
3	8-13	6	Don	Mon, July 15	•
4	14-18	5	Don	Wed, July 17	•
					• Don, 18 consecutive pages
5	19-25	7	Sue	Wed, July 17	•
6	26-32	7	Sue	Thurs, July 18	•

7	33-37	5	Sue	Thurs, July 18	•
					• Sue, 19 consecutive pages
8	38-42	5	Don	Thurs, July 18	•
Etc.					•

This grid creates a visual map showing the elements of timing and pacing that make my fair-play mysteries work.

Prompt #41: Tracking Time

One of the time-tracking details that I find challenging is time zones. For instance, a character based in New York City might need to call someone in Tokyo. Tokyo is fourteen hours ahead, so five in the morning in New York is 7 p.m. the next evening in Tokyo. Getting businesspeople on the phone during regular business hours is impossible.

The most confusing time zone issue I ever ran into was tracking time in both New York City and Adelaide, Australia, which is fifteen and a half hours ahead. Fifteen and *a half*? Oh, my.

Another one that got me scratching my head was adjusting for daylight savings time in parts of Arizona. Arizona doesn't switch to daylight saving time. However, the Navajo Nation in northeastern Arizona does observe daylight savings time so time will be consistent

BEAT THE BOTS

with other parts of Navajo territory in Utah and New Mexico. Complicated!

Alibis, backstory, historical events—they all need to be tracked with time in mind.

Now it's your turn! What's the hardest part for you when tracking time over the course of your story?

To participate in the *Beat the Bots* TikTok community:

- Record a video of your answer and post it, including the hashtag #beatthebots and tag me at @beatthebotsbook
- You can also tag #authortok and #booktok to connect with other writer and reader communities!
- Watch other writers' videos by visiting the TikTok hashtag #beatthebots

Join the conversation!

Jean Kwok, the bestselling author who discussed how planning facilitates creativity (see above), writes about the Chinese-American immigrant experience. She takes an even more detailed approach to monitoring timing. "I always want my books to be propulsive, page-turning reads so they might seem deceptively simple to the reader but in order to make my twists work, my novels have very complex underlying architectures. To ensure that I keep my characters' timelines organized, I use a large-scale timeline tracker like Aeon Timeline, where I enter events like births, deaths, graduations, marriages and the ages of all my characters at those points. I also track historical events that are relevant to my story, like the development of the one-child policy in China, for example, so that I understand the specific political arena my characters must navigate at each point of the story."

The screenshots below show two views from Aeon Timeline's home page, which tracks the timeline of Agatha Christie's *Murder on the Orient Express*. The program uses various shapes and colors to indicate activities, characters, and actions. One screenshot shows a timeline. The other tracks the same information on a spreadsheet.

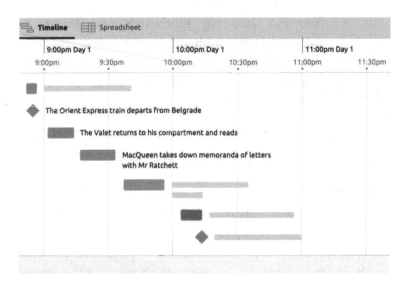

BEAT THE BOTS

Label	Start Date	Participant	Tags
The Orient Express train departs from Belgrade	Day 1 9:20pm	TV HM MR	Train m
The Valet returns to his compartment and reads	Day 1 9:20pm	TV	
MacQueen takes down memoranda of letters with Mr Ratchett	Day 1 9:40pm	HM MR	Hector

New York Times bestselling author Maria Semple also finds that paying careful attention to her timeline enhances her creativity. "I keep an elaborate calendar for my characters detailing on which dates everything happens. I'm constantly revising this as I go along. It gives me the freedom to intricately plot my story, knowing it will at least hold up on a timeline."

ORGANIZATIONAL TIP #2: TRACK YOUR PROGRESS

Many authors find tracking their progress, output, ideas, and snafus increases their productivity. Some use journals, others, spreadsheets or online tools. For example:

- *New York Times* bestselling author Sue Grafton kept what she called a "novel journal." This online journal tracked her progress with each book. Whenever she sat down to write, she noted the date, the weather, and maybe a sentence or two about what was going on in her life. Then she notated where she was in the book and what she needed to figure out for that workday to be productive.

325

- Another *New York Times* bestselling author Ed McBain also kept a journal. He called it his work record. He tracked how many words he wrote each day and whether there were any issues in the story.

Some authors work on a quota system, writing x number of words a day, or working for y number of hours. Thinking of your writing in this methodical way can be especially helpful when you're trying to fit writing into a busy schedule. When I was transitioning to a new career—from corporate training to teaching at the college level—I didn't have the luxury of writing all day or even for an hour or two at a stretch. The only time that wasn't earmarked for grad school or teaching as an adjunct was the twenty minutes between the three classes I was teaching. What I discovered was that I could take ten of those minutes and write. I'd reread the last paragraph I'd written, revising a bit as I went, then write a new paragraph. Guess what? If you do that three times a day, you've written a page. Do that every day for a year—you have a first draft of a book. This tactic worked for me because I was disciplined, determined, driven, and deadline-focused, the four *d*'s of writing success. It's important to note, however, that as with every aspect of the writing process, there is no one best approach. Each writer has to find his or her own best practices. Some authors, like bestselling author Jonathan Santlofer, hate the idea of writing to a quota. He says he'd find it "paralyzing."

BEAT THE BOTS

Prompt #42: Working to a Quota

Now it's your turn! What do you think about the idea of writing to a quota? Would you find the discipline of writing to a quota enabling or debilitating? Complete this sentence: When I think of writing to a quota, I:

_____.

To participate in the *Beat the Bots* TikTok community:

- Record a video of your answer and post it, including the hashtag #beatthebots and tag me at @beatthebotsbook
- You can also tag #authortok and #booktok to connect with other writer and reader communities!
- Watch other writers' videos by visiting the TikTok hashtag #beatthebots

Join the conversation!

ORGANIZATIONAL TIP #3: TRACK EVERYTHING (ALL AT ONCE)

Especially with book-length projects, it's easy to get lost in the manifold details that need to come together. Here's my organizational process:

327

- When I start, I create two Word documents. I label one "[working title], working copy, [date]." For instance, if my work in progress's working title is *Secrets*, and I start it on January 7, my document would be labeled: "Secrets, working copy, 1-7-20xx." The second document is labeled: "Notes—Secrets." This is where I stash all my research, ideas, extra text (sections I decided to delete from the working copy, but don't want to get rid of), and the like.

Pro Tip: Get Your Novel an Email Account

New York Times bestselling author Jean Kwok explains,

"I have an extra gmail account on Google that I created for my writing. I use it for day-to-day plotting on Google calendar. I enter all of the events in my novel so that I can make sure I'm not having my protagonist go to work on a Sunday or making other mistakes like that. It's very easy to get mixed up, especially when your editor asks you to add an extra scene showing your heroine's home life, for example. You write in an afternoon of domestic coziness and before you know it, the office scene that happened 'the next morning' is actually occurring a day later, and that might fall in the weekend. It's reassuring to know that your novel is built upon a rock-solid foundation."

BEAT THE BOTS

- I keep a folder on my desktop with the work in progress's name, say, "Secrets." Inside that folder, I keep another folder, labeled "Old Working Copies— Secrets." That way, if I want to see if I like a previous draft better than the current iteration, I can go to the folder and find it. Additionally, these old versions provide a historical record should I ever need to document my work product.
- I use a cloud storage system that automatically backs up my work. However, with documents of the same name, it overwrites previous versions, so whenever I get up from my computer, I email both my working copy and notes to myself. This redundancy protects me in case my computer crashes and I lose everything. I never delete these emails. Instead, I stash them in a folder where they're always accessible. Yes, I can always access the most recent version on my cloud backup system, but this way, I can easily locate an older version if I want to revisit a scene or sentence or whatever.
- Every week or so, I rename the working copy document using the "save as" function, changing only the date. I then move the previous version into the "Old Working Copies" folder.
- I keep the "Notes" document on my desktop, too.
- At the end of my working copy manuscript, I create an inventory of pending issues called "Plot Threads," a numbered list that helps me be certain that all my plot points are properly addressed by the end of the story. Let's say, for example, that in Chapter Four I have my sleuth ask a helper to check out a suspect's finances. I'll add that note to my Plot Threads listing. At some point

in the novel, I have to include the results of that investigation, and this way, I don't have to rely on memory. Periodically, I review my list to see if I've addressed the issues. When I reveal the financial information my sleuth asked for (say, in Chapter Twelve), I delete the note from the Plot Threads listing. When there's nothing left on the list, I know my first draft is done, and what a moment of euphoria that provides!

- I never get up from my computer without leaving myself a note about what to write next. Sometimes, my note is a paragraph detailing the next scene. Other times, it's simply a one-line reminder of where I was headed. This tactic allows me to go on to other tasks or activities without worrying that I'll forget where I left off.

This process has evolved over the years. While I am comfortable with my process, some writers prefer specialized digital platforms like Evernote or Scrivener. Only you can decide whether low tech (pen and paper), medium tech (writing directly into the computer), or high tech (using software designed for writers) is best for you. If you aren't comfortable with what you're doing now, try other options. Don't be intimidated by technology. Intimidation can lead to inertia, and inertia is among the greatest forces in the world, sometimes allowing writer's block to rear its nasty head. (See the Afterword for thoughts about taming writer's block.) But for those of you who want to experiment with software options, remember that they're designed to support your creativity, not replace it.

BEAT THE BOTS

Prompt #43: Organizing and Technology

Now it's your turn! Do you warm to technology or resist it? Shying away from technology doesn't mean you can't succeed as a writer. After all, Shakespeare, Dickens, Jane Austen, and Agatha Christie did just fine without computers. Obviously, you will need to use a standard word processing program like Microsoft Word since that's how you'll submit your manuscripts to agents and editors, and you'll need to be comfortable using the tracking function—that's how you'll receive your editorial notes. But you can choose your own organizational tools. What frees you up to be your creative best?

Complete this sentence: When it comes to organizing with pen and pencil, a word processing system, or an online platform, I prefer

---

because _____.

To participate in the *Beat the Bots* TikTok community:

- Record a video of your answer and post it, including the hashtag #beatthebots and tag me at @beatthebotsbook
- You can also tag #authortok and #booktok to connect with other writer and reader communities!

331

JANE K. CLELAND

- Watch other writers' videos by visiting the Tik-Tok hashtag #beatthebots

Join the conversation!

Literary writer G. D. Peters uses Scrivener to help him stay organized. He says he uses the app's features for compiling information, organizing it, and writing. Consider this screenshot from his current work in progress, *The Loose End*, a story revolving around the dissolution of Connie and Leland's marriage (also shown in Appendix Four).

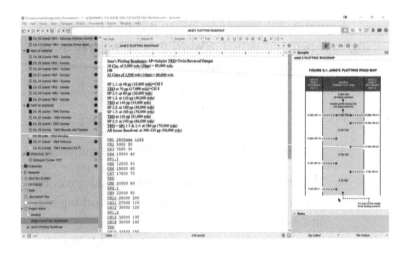

Peters explains, "I use the *Binder* (on the left) to show my chapters, and I have color-coded them, pink for Connie, blue for Leland. Below the chapter listing, there are separate sections for *Characters* and *Research* (where I store documents, photos, links to websites, etc.). On the right is the *Inspector*.

The *Synopsis* section is integrated into the *Inspector*. This is where I place a synopsis of each chapter. Usually, I add an image to help me stay focused, like a photo related to setting. In this case, you'll see *Jane's Plotting Roadmap*, which I use to plot out key twists (TRDs). Below the *Synopsis* section on the *Inspector* is the *Notes* section, where I leave myself reminders about the chapter, words or phrases I want to use or avoid, relevant data, and the like. I do my writing in the middle section, called the *Editor*. You can see here that I've written out notes related to my chapters, including my TRDs. Once I'm done, I'll move this content to the *Notes* section of the *Inspector*." This system works for him, and many other authors, too. The question is, what will work for you as you traverse your writing landscape?

ADAPT ORGANIZATIONAL STRATEGIES USING THE JOURNEY MAPPING CREATIVITY TACTIC

It's helpful to think of your writing career as a journey, not a destination. As international bestselling author Isabel Allende said, "Writing is a process, a journey into memory and the soul." The Journey Mapping creativity tactic helps you navigate your path by ensuring you're organized and ready to write. This tactic is both analytical and proactive. First, you identify your strengths and where you can improve. Second, you experiment with the specific tools, tips, and techniques discussed in this chapter to design an organizational plan that's tailored for your needs. The goal is to find an organizational process that suits your situation, one that frees you up to be your creative best.

Prompt #44: Controlling Clutter

A cluttered physical space often results in feeling overwhelmed and can lead to an inability to focus. Therefore, we need to eliminate clutter. Organizational expert Peter Walsh says, "Clutter is not just the stuff on your floor—it's anything that stands between you and the life you want to be living." Physical clutter means either you lack sufficient storage or you're postponing decisions. Either way, clutter inhibits success. If you can't find things on your desk, consider taking a few minutes a day to sort through the clutter, discarding what you don't need and filing items you want to retain. You'll be amazed at how much clutter you can sort in a minute or two! Keeping your workspace clear of clutter lets you concentrate more fully on your writing. A clear desk is a sign of self-respect—and you're worth it!

Now it's your turn! What do you think? Do you have any ideas on how to control clutter? Complete this sentence: My best tip to control clutter and free up my mind to write is:

_____.

To participate in the *Beat the Bots* TikTok community:

- Record a video of your answer and post it, including the hashtag #beatthebots and tag me at @beatthebotsbook

BEAT THE BOTS

> - You can also tag #authortok and #book-tok to connect with other writer and reader communities!
> - Watch other writers' videos by visiting the TikTok hashtag #beatthebots
>
> Join the conversation!

We've already discussed a variety of tips and techniques to help you become better organized. Here are two more issues for your review and consideration.

1. Select an inspiring and practical workspace.

Getting organized and staying organized can feel overwhelming. Taking control of your workspace enables you to create an environment that promotes your creativity. Remember that as with all aspects of the writing process, there's no right or wrong method. Some authors want mementos in sight. Others prefer only seeing items related to their work. Some prefer small, dark rooms. Others want air and light. Some authors like blaring music. Others want quiet. Some consider their writing space their lair or cave or sanctuary. Others need to get away from home, working most productively at a library or coffee shop. Some authors want their outline, synopsis, or notes available, but out of sight. Others want everything visible. For instance, take a look at bestselling author Jonathan Santlofer's desk.

335

This photo was taken at Yaddo, an artists' retreat located in Saratoga Springs, New York, when he was working on *The Last Mona Lisa*. Here's Jonathan's explanation of the layout:

- The index cards represent/differentiate the past and present scenes. Since the book moves back and forth between past and present when I was laying out the scenes I color-coded them for clarity and to see how often scenes in the past interrupted the contemporary scenes. Having scenes on index cards makes it easy to move them around.
- The Post-it notes attached to index cards track specific things I might want to change or add to that scene.
- I always have two legal pads beside my laptop when I write. One charts all the scenes chronologically, keeps

a timeline, and synopsizes the scene in a line or two. The other pad is for notes and thoughts that come to me, collections of words or a sentence I like that I want to use.

Overall, Santlofer has created an environment that adds structure while cultivating creativity. Here's what I keep on my desk as a constant reminder of what is, to me, the most important imperative:

Identifying what environmental attributes help you write efficiently is a key to organizational—and writing—success.

2. Get good at "guesstimating" how long things take.

If you don't know how long things take, it's impossible to plan properly. In general, people think tasks they enjoy take less time than they do and that tasks they don't enjoy take longer than they do.

"Guesstimating" is my word for the all-important task of estimating when you lack sufficient information to make a fact-based assessment. Guesstimating isn't perfect, but it's better than doing nothing. Whether you're guesstimating or estimating, consider building in extra time. Let's say, for example, that you need to prep dinner before you can write. Based on your knowledge of the recipe, you estimate that you need fifteen minutes. Call it twenty. If it really takes fifteen, yay! You have an extra five minutes to write. If, however, prepping takes twenty minutes, you'll still be on schedule.

AI Weighs In

I asked a bot to recommend the best organizational tool for writers, and it offered twenty-one software options. Twenty-one! Organizational tools should simplify the writing process so you can focus on your craft. Unless you're a tech fan, it seems to me that assessing twenty-one software options does just the opposite: complicating, not simplifying, the process. Instead of overwhelming yourself with options, determine what you need to accomplish, then identify the tools that will support those specific tasks. Here's my solution: I

> operate on a need-to-know basis, learning only what I need to know to do what I want.

The Journey Mapping creativity tactic guides you on your writing journey by focusing on sensible, straightforward tools and techniques to help you organize your work. In the exercise that follows, you'll be able to identify your organizational strengths and areas where you might be able to improve.

Exercise

Journey Mapping

The following self-assessment helps bring the Journey Mapping creativity tactic to life. It's designed to guide you in mastering a customized organizational system—a crucial aspect of the writing process. Ask yourself where your abilities fit using this scale:

- Always = 10
- Almost always = 7 or 8
- Maybe, sometimes, sort of = 4, 5, or 6
- Rarely = 2 or 3
- Never = 0

1. I can quickly and easily find documents and tools I need to write. I know where files are stored. I can put my hands on pen and paper. I track all the aspects of timing that affect my story's foundation.

---

2. I schedule time to write, and I keep to the schedule.

Add those two numbers together:

Here's how to think about your score. If you assessed yourself at or near the top of the scale, anything over a 16, you're saying you can locate what you need to write productively and you adhere to a writing schedule. Congratulations! Without question, you'll be highly productive. If, however, you answered toward the lower end of the scale on either or both of the assessment statements, here are some ideas to help you get back on track.

- If you can't locate the documents or tools you need to write efficiently, review the list below to see how to address your particular issues.
  - Add storage. There's an old saying that sums up the issue: "Everything has a

place and everything in its place." You can't declutter until you have places to put those things you want to keep. This relates to e-materials, too. Add folders to a file cabinet or your computer desktop, or work with a digital writing platform—have a place to store your documents and research materials.

- Declutter. Once you have adequate storage, it's time to make what might be hard choices. Put things away or throw things away. As organizational expert Barbara Hemphill, explains, "Clutter is nothing more than postponed decisions."

- If you're having trouble keeping to a writing schedule, first, confirm your schedule is realistic. Don't set yourself up for failure. Here are tactics for your review and consideration:
  - Consider using a journal to monitor your work output and track any issues you run into. In fact, you might find it inspirational or reassuring to see how much you accomplish. And if you don't accomplish as much as you'd hoped, you can adjust your schedule or your expectations.
  - These insights shared by bestselling authors provide food for thought:

- E. B. White: "A writer who waits for ideal conditions under which to work will die without putting a word on a paper."
- Jodi Picoult: "If you have a limited time to write, you just sit down and do it. You might not write well every day, but you can always edit a bad page. You can't edit a blank page."
- Barbara Kingsolver, regarding balancing writing with child-rearing: "For me, writing time has always been precious, something I wait for and make the best use of. That's probably why I get up so early and have writing time in the quiet dawn hours, when no one needs me...Being a mother has made me a better writer."
- Nathan Englander: "Turn off your cell phone."

How did it go? I'd love to hear about your experience taking this two-question self-assessment. Complete this sentence: I used Jane's Journey Mapping organizational self-assessment and learned:

_____ .

BEAT THE BOTS

To participate in the *Beat the Bots* TikTok community:

- Record a video of your answer and post it, including the hashtag #beatthebots and tag me at @beatthebotsbook
- You can also tag #authortok and #book-tok to connect with other writer and reader communities!
- Watch other writers' videos by visiting the Tik-Tok hashtag #beatthebots

Join the conversation!

In this chapter, we discussed an array of issues related to organization. We also reviewed examples that highlight this fact: the more organized you are, the more productive and creative you can be. In the next chapter, we'll pull together everything we've discussed thus far and talk about creating an action plan customized for you.

Reflection on Creativity

"You can't wait for inspiration. You have to go after it with a club."

—*Jack London*

CHAPTER TWELVE

CREATIVITY TACTIC #12
FAILSAFE: CREATE A CUSTOMIZED ACTION PLAN

"I went for years not finishing anything. Because, of course, when you finish something you can be judged."
Erica Jong

CREATE LASTING CHANGE

To beat the bots, you need to concentrate on elements that promote your uniqueness, your humanity, and your empathy, attributes beyond AI's reach. We've looked at this challenge from a variety of angles. Now it's time to convert theory into practice.

Change requires action, and the foundation of action is commitment. Without commitment, there will be no action; there will be no progress. The first step in creating change is

BEAT THE BOTS

deciding what you want to do differently. Preparing an action plan requires that you bring your knowledge, intuition, judgment, and passion to the task. The Failsafe creativity tactic ensures you ask yourself the hard questions and encourages you to be gentle with yourself when you give honest answers. Since AI can't know the real you, a chatbot can't complete this kind of self-assessment and use the information to develop a meaningful plan—only you can. Once you know where you stand now and identify where you want to end up, you can create an action plan tailored to your individual situation.

FAQ

Q: I'm stuck. I know what I need to do; I just can't seem to muster the gumption to do it.

A: The kind of lethargy you're describing can be debilitating. Worse, the longer it goes on, the more stressed and frustrated you're likely to feel, until taking any action seems all but impossible. One tactic you might try as you work to break the cycle is to revamp your action plan, dividing large tasks into smaller units. Do this by adding specificity. Instead of "Include more about Charlie's emotional state," for instance, which is open-ended and abstract, how about saying, "Show Charlie's emotions growing from irritation to anger by Chapter Three." If I thought it would be helpful, I could divide it even further: "Show Charlie's emotions growing from mild irritation to full-blown annoyance by

---

345

Chapter Two, and from annoyance to anger by Chapter Three." This system can convert what feels overwhelming into something that feels more manageable. As the Chinese philosopher Laozi (also called Lao Tzu), wrote, "The journey of a thousand miles begins with a single step." If you don't begin, you won't get anywhere. But if you take one step, no matter how small, then move to the next step, then a third, and don't stop, eventually, you'll get where you're going. You'll be astonished at how much ground you'll cover, and how quickly you'll reach your writing goals. I know you can do it!

THINK FIRST, THEN PLAN

You might recall this scene from Lewis Carroll's *Alice's Adventures in Wonderland*: "One day Alice came to a fork in the road and saw a Cheshire cat in a tree. 'Which road do I take?' she asked. 'Where do you want to go?' was his response. 'I don't know,' Alice answered. 'Then,' said the cat, 'it doesn't matter.'" So true! If you don't have a specific goal in mind, how will you know when you have achieved it? Your action plan needs to reflect your focused ideas for creating lasting change, the kind of change that shifts the narrative from wishes to plans. Eleanor Roosevelt put it this way, "It takes just as much energy to wish as it does to plan." And let's not forget Benjamin Franklin's words on the topic: "By failing to prepare you are preparing to fail." So let's plan!

BEAT THE BOTS

Prompt #45: How Will an Action Plan Help You?

On a macro level, think about how creating an action plan might positively affect your writing and your writing life. Will you feel more like a professional writer? Will the structure comfort you? Will you become more confident in your writing process? Will the plan give voice to your determination? Will it take what seems amorphous and make it concrete?

Now it's your turn! How might a writing action plan help *you*? Complete this sentence: An action plan will help me:

_____.

To participate in the *Beat the Bots* TikTok community:

- Record a video of your answer and post it, including the hashtag #beatthebots and tag me at @beatthebotsbook
- You can also tag #authortok and #booktok to connect with other writer and reader communities!
- Watch other writers' videos by visiting the TikTok hashtag #beatthebots

Join the conversation!

347

JANE K. CLELAND

THINK ABOUT BOTH CONTENT AND PROCESS

When developing your action plan, you need to consider issues related to both content and process. Content refers to the storytelling itself, the characters, plot, setting, prose, and so on. Process refers to everything you do to complete the story, from developing ideas to revising the story to organizing your workspace.

Let's start with content. One of the best ways to think about what should be included in your action plan, content-wise, is to track what you most admire in other authors' books, then assess whether working on those issues would be helpful. For instance, I love Liane Moriarty's *Big Little Lies*. When I asked myself what, in particular, worked well, I came up with this list.

- Multiple points of view, all clearly delineated
- A clear narrative question, creating a complex through-line plot
- Differentiated characters

Those attributes align with my analyses in Chapters Two, Three, and Five of this book. For my action plan, I would think about what, specifically, Moriarty did that I want to learn how to do. Here's a mini-deconstruction of *Big Little Lies* (also discussed in Chapter Two).

- The book opens with Mrs. Ponder looking out her window. She delivers a monologue to her cat in which she describes what she thinks might be a riot at the nearby elementary school. She's bemused because the school's annual fundraiser (called "Trivia Night") is

348

BEAT THE BOTS

typically quite sedate. The monologue ends with Mrs. Ponder wondering if she should call the police.

- After a small amount of white space, there is a series of quotes from fourteen named characters describing their views of what happened at Trivia Night. At the start, we don't know whom they're talking to.
  - o Gabrielle says it wasn't just the mothers, although "I guess it *started* with the mothers."
  - o Bonnie says, "It was all just a terrible misunderstanding."
  - o Stu blames the mothers because "*Women don't let things go.*"
  - o Carol faults the erotic book club.
  - o Jackie thinks it was a "feminist issue."

And so on. The tenth comment provides the first hint of what was actually going on—the unnamed listener is identified.

  - o Thea says, "You journalists…"
  - o And the last speaker, a detective, states the narrative question: "Let me be clear. This is not a circus. This is a murder investigation."

Boom. We're catapulted into the story—and it's only page six. By recounting witnesses' perceptions of motive and excluding observable facts, Moriarty draws readers into the story. We want to know which perception is true, or whether any of them are. When we see that Chapter Two starts six months earlier, we understand that the rest of the book will lead us to Trivia Night.

With this deconstruction in mind, I might write the following on my action plan:

- Write one- to two-sentence summaries of how all characters involved with my inciting incident perceive it.
- Track how each character's perception differs from the others', and how those perceptions inform their actions.
- Use Jane's Character Transformation Roadmap to ensure the characters' actions line up with their specific motivations.

Prompt #46: Assess Your Storytelling Skills

My storytelling strength is plotting. When it comes to storytelling, I can improve my characterizations. Because I'm better at plotting than characterization, I have to be mindful to align character motivation and incident.

Now it's your turn! What do you think? Complete these two sentences:

My storytelling strengths are:

_____.

When it comes to storytelling, I can improve my:

_____.

To participate in the *Beat the Bots* TikTok community:

BEAT THE BOTS

> - Record a video of your answer and post it, including the hashtag #beatthebots and tag me at @beatthebotsbook
> - You can also tag #authortok and #booktok to connect with other writer and reader communities!
> - Watch other writers' videos by visiting the Tik-Tok hashtag #beatthebots
>
> Join the conversation!

From a process perspective, review the chapters relating to idea development (Chapter One), revising (Chapters Nine and Ten), and organization (Chapter Eleven) and ask yourself, when considering your own writing process and habits, where you think there's room for improvement. I know, for instance, that I echo words. I'm so eager to get the story down, I often fall back on words I habitually use. I've learned to catch these frequently used words and phrases as I'm writing. When I notice one, I list it on a Post-it note. Later, as part of my revision process, I search for each word or phrase and consider alternatives. Yes, I have a system to catch the repetition, but I'd love to avoid making the mistake in the first place.

Pro Tip: Don't Lie to Yourself

Dr. Howard Kingsley, one of my favorite teachers from junior high school, told our class something lo those many decades ago that has stayed with me all this time. I don't remember what inspired him to share this nugget of pure gold advice, but I'm glad he did. Dr. Kingsley said, "There are going to be times in your life when it might make sense for you to lie to your parents, or your siblings, or your boss, or your friend, or someone else. I get it. I'm not recommending it. Lying is bad. All I'm saying is there may be a situation when you need to lie to somebody, but no matter what—don't ever lie to yourself."

Brilliant, right?

When considering your strengths and assessing where you might improve, remember Dr. Kingsley and don't lie to yourself.

My writing goal is: I'd like to get better at writing with unique flair earlier on in the process. That sounds smart, but it's overly general. Here's how I might convert that generic objective to an entry on my action plan:

- If I ever decide to try dual timelines, I'm going to use Jonathan Santlofer's idea. I'll write scenes on color-coded index cards, so when I lay them out, I can easily see the sequence and monitor the pace.

BEAT THE BOTS

- When I run into a word I don't know, I look it up and write the definition on a little piece of paper. I keep the paper-clipped collection on my desk, but I rarely go through them. It just slips my mind. I'm going to read my list of words and definitions once a week so they'll stay with me.

Prompt #47: Assess Your Skills around Process

Years ago, I decided to try a new revising method. Here was how I stated it: *When I finish writing a paragraph, I'll reread it, focusing on the phrasings, aiming to avoid echoing.* Guess what? It didn't work for me at all. Instead of improving my writing, it slowed me down and annoyed the heck out of me. It forced me to put on my editor's hat when all I wanted to do at that point was get the story down on paper. What I discovered was that it made way more sense for me to write first drafts quickly, without judging my work, then take my time revising. Logically, this makes sense, since separating out the creative function from the analytical function enables each part of the brain to work unencumbered by the other.

My experience also demonstrates the value of experimenting. I tried it. It didn't work for me. I moved on. No harm. No foul. That's how you develop a writing process that works for you.

Now it's your turn! What do you think? Complete these two sentences:

353

My writing process strengths are:

_____.

When it comes to process issues, I can improve my:

_____.

To participate in the *Beat the Bots* TikTok community:

- Record a video of your answer and post it, including the hashtag #beatthebots and tag me at @beatthebotsbook
- You can also tag #authortok and #booktok to connect with other writer and reader communities!
- Watch other writers' videos by visiting the TikTok hashtag #beatthebots

Join the conversation!

ASSESS YOUR SKILLS WITH FAILSAFE

The Failsafe creativity tactic is a self-assessment designed to help you create an action plan that results in lasting change. Dictionary.com defines the term "failsafe" as "something designed to work or function automatically to prevent breakdown of a mechanism, system, or the like." That's what this

BEAT THE BOTS

creativity tactic will do for you. It will prevent the breakdown of your writing system.

We don't always think of our writing process as "systems," but it's useful to do so. The Failsafe self-assessment that follows can help you understand your thinking, writing, and revision processes. Once you've identified your strengths and noted where you want to improve, you'll be ready to create your action plan. The following self-assessment is just between you and you, so tell the truth. Remember Dr. Kingsley!

The Failsafe Creativity Tactic Self-Assessment	
Question or Factor to Consider	**Your Honest Answer**
Do ideas simply come to you, or do you use a specific process? If so, in one to two sentences, explain your process. If not, where do you struggle?	
Are you able to develop characters who are distinctive and relatable? If so, in one to two sentences, explain your process. If not, where do you struggle?	

Are you good at identifying the series of incidents that, taken together, form your plot? If so, in one to two sentences, explain your process. If not, where do you struggle?	
Do you write about settings from your characters' points of view? If so, in one to two sentences, explain your process. If not, where do you struggle?	
Are you confident in your point-of-view decisions? If so, in one to two sentences, explain your decision-making process. If not, where do you struggle?	

Do you write with a distinctive voice? If so, in one to two sentences, explain how you developed this unique author's voice. If not, where do you struggle?	
Have you inserted backstory subtly, on an as-needed basis, and without an info dump? If so, in one to two sentences, explain your approach. If not, where do you struggle?	
Does each character speak with an individual voice? If so, in one to two sentences, explain how you developed these distinctive styles. If not, where do you struggle?	

Are you good at writing dialogue that includes subtext, dialogue that does something, not merely says something? If so, in one to two sentences, explain how you decide what subtext to include and how you work it in. If not, where do you struggle?	
Does your story have a theme? If so, did it develop organically or did you choose it in advance? If you don't have one, why not?	

Have you continuously raised the stakes and escalated conflict? If so, in one to two sentences, explain how you determine what incidents to create and where to insert them? If not, where do you struggle?	
Do you thoroughly revise your work, considering both macro and micro issues? If so, in one to two sentences, describe your revision plan. If not, where do you struggle?	
As a writer, are you organized? If so, in one to two sentences, explain your process. If not, where do you struggle?	

That's a lot to think about, isn't it? When writing a novel, there are a lot of moving parts, cogs that need to work together seamlessly to make the wheel turn. If one cog is clunky or off track, the wheel will judder or grind to an unwieldy stop. To keep the gears running smoothly, all the cogs need to be in alignment. And don't forget the role of creativity. It's not enough to write a good book. You need to write a good book that's innovative, one that can't be produced by AI.

Which brings us to your particular situation. Review your answers to the self-assessment questions. Where do you struggle? What new tactics can you try? Review whose chapters to get ideas, then get ready to create your action plan.

Prompt #48: Are You a Planner?

Some people find planning comforting. Others find it inhibiting. How about you? Are you a planner? Do you get excited at the thought of having a roadmap setting out next steps? Complete this sentence: As I think about creating an action plan for myself, I:

_____

BEAT THE BOTS

> To participate in the *Beat the Bots* TikTok community:
>
> - Record a video of your answer and post it, including the hashtag #beatthebots and tag me at @beatthebotsbook
> - You can also tag #authortok and #booktok to connect with other writer and reader communities!
> - Watch other writers' videos by visiting the TikTok hashtag #beatthebots
>
> Join the conversation!

CREATE A FAILSAFE PLAN

In this book, we've discussed ways to develop exciting, fresh content, streamline your writing process, and adopt mental attitudes that propel you forward.

> ### AI Weighs In
>
> I asked a bot what helps writers stick to their writing plan, and the bot replied to *make sure to set SMART goals (specific, measurable, achievable, relevant, time-bound)*. Not to get moored down in semantics, but that's not what George T. Duran wrote in his 1981 article,

"There's a SMART Way to Write Management's Goals and Objectives" (published in the American Management Association's journal, *Management Review*). Once again, AI got it wrong.

Mr. Duran defined "SMART" as "specific, measurable, assignable, realistic, time-related." From the article:

- Specific: target a specific area for improvement
- Measurable: quantify or at least suggest an indicator of progress
- Assignable: specify who will do it
- Realistic: state what results can realistically be achieved, given available resources
- Time-related: specify when the result(s) can be achieved.

Mr. Duran wrote, "It should also be understood that the suggested acronym doesn't mean that every objective written will have all five criteria." Duncan Haughey, writing in *Project Smart*, added. "For example, not everything worth achieving is measurable. And a goal you set for yourself does not need to be agreed-upon."

Whether you use the SMART goal-setting tactic as Mr. Duran originally set it out or as others have adapted it, or whether you tweak it further yourself, the underlying idea is strong. Formulating goals using the acronym as a guide can help you avoid the frustration of flailing around. As Dr. Margaret Chan, former director general of the World Health Organization, put it, "If I can measure it, I can manage it. If I can't measure it, I can't manage it."

BEAT THE BOTS

Now it's time to create an action plan tailored just for you—a failsafe plan, one certain to help you up your writing game.

Exercise

Failsafe: Create a Customized Action Plan

1. From the Failsafe self-assessment, list the areas where you've been struggling.
2. Review the corresponding chapters in this book to consider tactics to address the issues.
3. Write up your SMART goals.

As you set your goals, remember to:

- Avoid vague generalities, like "Write every day." Instead, add specificity, like "Write x number of words every day."
- You might come up with one bullet or five—there's no magic number. It's *your* action plan.

How did it go? I'd love to hear about your experience using the Failsafe creativity tactic to come up with your action plan. Complete this sentence: I used Jane's Failsafe creativity tactic to come up with an action plan and:

_____.

To participate in the *Beat the Bots* TikTok community:

- Record a video of your answer and post it, including the hashtag #beatthebots and tag me at @beatthebotsbook
- You can also tag #authortok and #book-tok to connect with other writer and reader communities!
- Watch other writers' videos by visiting the Tik-Tok hashtag #beatthebots

Join the conversation!

In this chapter, we took the lessons discussed throughout this book and looked at how to apply the principles to your work—to create stories that only you can tell—marrying fresh ideas to masterful storytelling techniques, a strategy certain to set you up for success. In the Afterword, you'll be invited to reflect on three principles that, taken together, are certain to help you beat the bots.

Reflection on Creativity

"An essential element of creativity
is not being afraid to fail."
Edwin Land

AFTERWORD

"Excellence is never an accident. It is always the result of
high intention, sincere effort, and intelligent execution;
it represents the wise choice of many alternatives.
Choice, not chance, determines your destiny."
Aristotle

BE YOURSELF TO BEAT THE BOTS

As you think through the creativity tactics detailed in this
book, you'll notice they share one imperative—it is your
humanity, not a chatbot's algorithms, that will lead to your
writing success. By using the twelve creativity tactics discussed
in this book, you'll be able to move forward with confidence,
knowing your stories are unique, innovative, thematic, complex, and relatable—a captivating combination that ticks all
the boxes.

THREE PRINCIPLES TO BEAT THE BOTS

We writers have to be good at so many different things, from
idea inception to proofreading to everything in between. To
produce your best work, stories that AI can't replicate, you

need more than skills. You need perspectives to help you pull all the lessons, processes, and procedures together. Here are three mindset principles for your consideration:

1. While Being Innovative, Trust Your Gut

In an article in *Science Daily*, researchers at Tel Aviv University's School of Psychological Sciences found that people who relied on gut instinct were right 90 percent of the time. Think about this. If you sense something is wrong in your story, listen to your gut. If you think a plot point or character motivation feels contrived, for example, you may be right. But don't trust your gut blindly—do a gut check. Does your "feeling" reflect reality or does it spring from self-doubt? To sort through the potential options, consider how Matthew Frye-Castillo, who authors literary fiction, handles the situation. He asks his characters for their opinion. "Your characters cannot understand their story without you. When I feel blocked, I remind myself I have an obligation to my characters to treat their stories as real. They require a larger context from which they can eventually understand themselves. Sometimes, my main audience is the characters themselves." How do your characters feel about that scene you feared was contrived? Do their insights help you determine if you can trust your gut?

The lesson here is that trusting your gut requires self-knowledge. Pulitzer Prize winner Michael Cunningham, for instance, knows about his tendency to overwrite. In an interview with Amy Jones, editor-in-chief of *Writer's Digest* magazine, he shared that when he was at the Iowa Writers' Workshop, his much-admired teacher, Hilma Wolitzer, told him, "Here's what I want you to do. I want you, when you've

BEAT THE BOTS

finished with a draft of the story, go through it and grade every line either A or—let's say there's no Cs—the really great ones get As, the perfectly OK ones get Bs. Then I want you to go back and rewrite all the A sentences because those are the ones about your precocity. Those are the ones in which you're doing triple flips in the run-up to the Olympics, and they're not in service to the story." Cunningham added, "So, any novel of mine, any paragraph, most paragraphs, has shed a skin of overwriting that you don't see, that no one sees but me." Cunningham's tactic is terrific, but it will work only if you have a tendency to overwrite (discussed in Chapter Eight). The challenge is to figure out where *you* need to improve.

In the final analysis, it's your intelligence, informed by your experience, that should guide your decisions. If you take a wrong turn, turn back. Writing is a process, and rarely is it linear.

2. Adopt a Principle of Continuous Improvement

The term "continuous improvement" was first introduced in the 1950s in a business context. We can adapt it to writing. The continuous improvement maxim states that even the smallest incremental changes can add up to major improvements. To writers, continuous improvement equates to continuous learning. We need to keep honing our craft by reading analytically, deconstructing books we wish we'd written, and seeing how we can apply those lessons to our own work. The graphic below (and in Appendix Five) shows how the continuous improvement principle applies to the writing process.

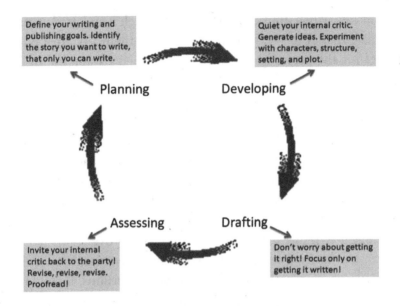

Notice that wherever you start, when you're ready, you move to the next step in the writing process. If you've already written a draft, you can jump in at assessing. If you are currently writing your story, start with drafting. You can add additional steps, say for submitting your work, separate these broad categories into smaller, more specific tasks, or otherwise adapt it to your needs and style. The idea isn't that you follow this rendition of the continuous improvement process exactly; rather, that you adopt the mindset of continuous learning, which invariably leads to continuous improvement.

BEAT THE BOTS

3. Be Bold

Nearly 2400 years ago, the Roman poet Virgil wrote, "Fortune favors the bold."

Be Bold

I'd love to hear about your experience putting these tactics to work. Complete this sentence: After reading Jane Cleland's *Beat the Bots*, my writing is: _____.

To participate in the *Beat the Bots* TikTok community:

- Record a video of your answer and post it, including the hashtag #beatthebots and tag me at @beatthebotsbook
- You can also tag #authortok and #booktok to connect with other writer and reader communities!
- Watch other writers' videos by visiting the TikTok hashtag #beatthebots

Join the conversation!

You have a story to tell. Tell it with verve and vigor and plain truth, emotional truth. Steer to the pain. Write raw.

Here is an unalienable truth: you have the drive to succeed. I know this about you because you're reading this book, which says you're trying to up your game, better your craft, write to your potential. With this attitude, I'm confident you'll beat the bots.

And please remember this: *I believe in you.*

Creativity Reflection

"Always remember, you are braver than you believe, stronger than you seem, smarter than you think, and twice as beautiful as you've ever imagined."
Dr. Seuss

APPENDIX ONE

JANE'S CHARACTER TRANSFORMATION ROADMAP

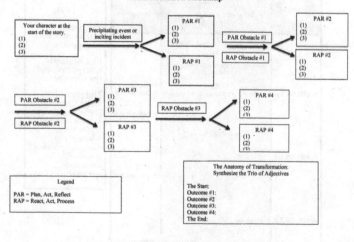

Jane's Characterization
Transformation Roadmap

APPENDIX TWO
JANE'S PLOTTING ROADMAP

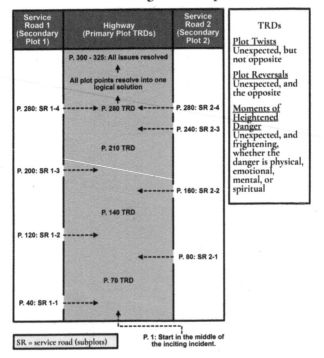

APPENDIX THREE

JANE'S TIMING GRID

Chapter	Pages	Chapter Length	POV	Day/Date	Time
1	1	1	Don	Wed, Jan 15	• 9:14, a.m., stakes out Sue's house • 9:37, a.m., follows Sue
2	2-7	6	Don	Mon, July 15	
3	8-13	6	Don	Mon, July 15	
4	14-18	5	Don	Wed, July 17	
					• Don, 18 consecutive pages
5	19-25	7	Sue	Wed, July 17	
6	26-32	7	Sue	Thurs, July 18	
7	33-37	5	Sue	Thurs, July 18	
					• Sue, 19 consecutive pages
8	38-42	5	Don	Thurs, July 18	
Etc.					

APPENDIX FOUR
SCRIVENER IN USE

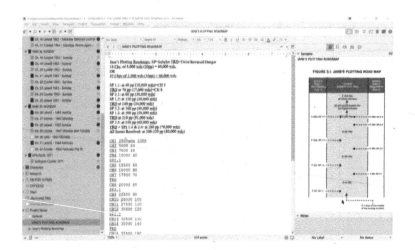

APPENDIX FIVE

THE CONTINUOUS IMPROVEMENT WRITING PROCESS

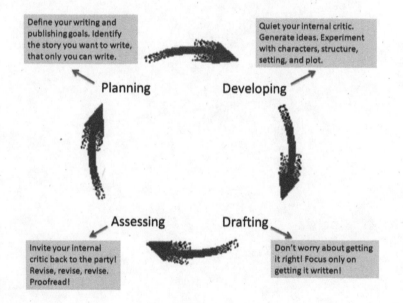

INDEX

A

The Accident (Pavone), 230–231

action planning
artificial intelligence on, 361–362
benefits of, 347
for content, 348–350
failsafe self-assessment method, 354–360, 363
getting unstuck, 345–346
for process, 351–354
storytelling assessment, 350

active verbs, 97, 298–303, 312, 314, 315

active versus passive voice, 303–304, 308

Adegoke, Yomi, 12

adjectives, 34, 98–99, 292–295

adverbs, 195–196, 291–293

Aeon Timeline, 324–325

alignment, in idea assessment. *See* NIA (novelty, impact, and alignment) model

ALL CAPS, for emphasis, 196–197

allegories, 17–18, 26–27, 227–230, 273–278

Alvarez, Julia, 219

Amazing Grace Adams (Littlewood), 309–310

Amend, Allison, 161

American Born Chinese (Yang), 228

Angelou, Maya, 173

Angel's Tip (Burke), 62–63

anger, in dialogue subtext, 189–190

Angoe, Yasmin, 264

animals, point of view of, 134–136. *See also* allegories

Anthony, Meredith, 160

anthropomorphism, 228–230

artificial intelligence
on backstory, 166–167
on character motivation, 45
characters generated by, 30–31
on characters' reaction to settings, 84
dialogue generated by, 203–204
on eliminating "to be" verbs, 312
lack of novelty and, 22–24
limitations of, 3–4, 316–317
on organizational tools, 338–339
plot twist generated by, 76
on point of view, 147
on raising stakes in a novel, 279
on setting, 105–106
on sticking to a writing plan, 361–362
thematic writing example, 233–238
and uniqueness of author's voice, 138–139
Asimov, Isaac, 223

assessment versus judgment, 5
atmosphere. *See* setting
attitude, in mind wandering, 73–74
Austin, Michael, 227
author's voice, 138–143

B
backstory
artificial intelligence on, 166–167
betrayal as, 154–155
devices used to reveal, 163–165
limited revelation of, 151–154, 157
questions to ask regarding, 165
role of, in suspense, 156
sensory connectives, 158–163, 167–173
through-line plot and, 158
Baldacci, David, 153
Bar, Moshe, 72, 74
Baum, L. Frank, 68
Beach Read (Henry), 59
Beanland, Rachel, 12
Beattie, Ann, 83
"Beauty and the Beast" fairy tale, 229–230

"Being Creative Makes You Happier" (Tan et al.), 73–74

betrayal and backstory, 154–155

Big Little Lies (Moriarty), 39, 158, 348–350

Block, Lawrence, 5

Blue Mind (Nichols), 73

boldness principle, 369–370

Boulle, Pierre, 89

Bowen, Rhys, 127

Braithwaite, Oyinkan, 57

breaking the fourth wall, 133

Brown, Brené, 40–41, 221

Brown, Sandra, 261

"Brownies" (Packer), 196–197

building blocks of life, 6–7

Burke, Alafair, 62

Burroughs, Edward Rice, 97

business use, in dialogue, 190–193, 197–198

By a Spider's Thread (Lippman), 101

C

Chan, Margaret, 362

Chandler, Raymond, 77

character transformation across book series, 46–47

details changing with, 46

emotional truth in, 42–45

examples, 32–33

exercise, 49–52

motivation and, 47–49

overcoming discomfort in, 264–269

precipitating events for, 35–39

random access creativity, 240–243, 246, 247

setting and, 93–94

See also stakes, raising the

characters

anthropomorphic, 230

artificial intelligence generated, 30–31

conceptual blending exercise, 107–120

demographics and psychographics of, 39–42

dialogue and individual voices of, 175–183

plot twists and traits of, 68, 76

setting and, 84, 99–101, 103–107

See also backstory; stakes, raising the

chatbots. *See* artificial intelligence

Chatter, The Voice in Our Head, Why It Matters, and How to Harness It (Kross), 72

Chbosky, Stephen, 89

Chessman, Ruth, 295–296

Child, Lee, 47, 151, 156

Christie, Agatha, 8, 324

clarifying quantities, 289–291

clutter control, 334

computer technology, 287–288, 328–333, 338, 374. *See also* artificial intelligence

conceptual blending, 83–84, 107–120

conflict
  dialogue and, 174–175, 185, 205–212
  genre considerations, 21
  narrative question purposes, 55
  setting and, 93–94
  See also stakes, raising the

Conlin, Karen S., 287–288

Consigned to Death (Cleland), 10, 46

content action plan, 348–350

continuous improvement principle, 367–368, 375

controlling clutter, 334

conversation fillers, 175–176

The Corinthian (Heyer), 179–180

cozy mysteries, 20

creative analysis. *See* reenvisioning process; revision

creativity tactics
  action plans, 344–364
  backstory, 151–173
  character transformation, 30–52
  dialogue, 174–212
  idea generation, 3–29
  organization, 318–343
  plot, 53–82
  point of view, 125–150
  raising the stakes, 253–283
  revision, 284–317
  setting, 83–120
  thematic writing, 213–249

Cressey, Donald R., 48

Crichton, Michael, 255

crime fiction, 19–20

cross-connection process, 223, 238–248

cultural issues, as obstacles, 272, 276

Cunningham, Michael, 366–367

D

The Day of the Jackal (Forsyth), 218

daydreaming. *See* mind wandering

Dead End Jobs (Viets), 13

Dead Poets Society (Schulman), 292

deconstructing favorite books, 49–52, 68–69, 348–350

Defending Jacob (Landay), 164

DeLillo, Don, 320

demographics, character, 39–40

description
reader expectations, 89–90, 96, 98
sensory references, 99–101, 158–163, 167–173, 309–310
in support of themes, 230–231

details
adding, during revision, 314
backstory, 152–153

character
transformation, 46
dialogue, 191–192
setting, 87, 98, 103–104
time-tracking, 320, 322, 323, 325

device use, for telling backstory, 163–165

dialogue
artificial intelligence generated, 203–204
avoiding numbers in, 296
backstory in, 153–154
business versus tags, 190–193
character voices, 175–183
emphasis options, 194–199
etymology and, 304–306
exercise, 205–212
punctuation, 199–202
revision, 307–308
setting information in, 101–103
subtext, 185–190
summary versus real-time scene, 183–185

dialogue tags, 101–102, 179–180, 190–193

divergent thinking, 143–147, 149

dominant idea, 216, 219–221

Donoghue, Emma, 89

Dowd, Siobhan, 220

Drowning (Newman), 260–263

Duran, George T., 361–362

E

editing pass, 287–288

Eight Perfect Murders (Swanson), 99

ellipsis use, 197–198

em dash use, 198–199

email account for time tracking, 328

emotional truth
  in backstory, 154–155, 157, 167–168
  in character transformation, 42–45
  concentrating on, 11
  in dialogue, 175
  in the narrative question, 55, 56
  in the reenvisioning process, 254–255, 262
  in setting, 87–88
  in thematic writing, 221
  writing raw and, 267

emphasis, in dialogue, 194–199

The Engagement (Sullivan), 216–217

Englander, Nathan, 342

environment, for mind wandering, 72–73, 74

environmental obstacles, 273, 278

Ephron, Hallie, 153

epigraphs, 215–216, 221–222, 225

etymology, 304–306

Everybody Lies (Stephens-Davidowitz), 44

exclamation point use, 195–196

expectations, reader, 18–22, 89–91

external obstacles and raising the stakes, 270–279, 281

F

fact-based idea sources, 9–12, 15–18

failsafe self-assessment method, 345, 354–360, 363

Falling (Newman), 156

fantasy
  point of view, 132
  world creation, 84–85, 96

Farago, Jason, 316–317

Faro's Daughter (Heyer), 134–136

fillers, conversation, 175–176

first person point of view, 127–128

flashbacks and flashforwards, 161, 165

Florence Adler Swims Forever (Beanland), 12

fly on the wall point of view. *See* third-person objective point of view

Fogarty, Mignon, 287

Forsyth, Frederick, 218

Franchini, Livia, 217

Fraud Triangle, 48–49

Friedman, Thomas, 13

Frye-Castillo, Matthew, 366

G

Gabaldon, Diana, 89

Gaines, Ernest J., 61

Garciá Marquez, Gabriel, 106

Gardner, Rachelle, 141–142

"The General Reading Habits of Americans" (Pew Research Center), 54

genre fiction
  as different from literary fiction, 19
  pace of, 66

point of view in, 126, 127–128, 132

quotation mark use in, 202

reader expectations for, 18–22, 25

settings in, 89–91

TRDs (twists, reversals, danger) in, 68–69

George, Ben, 141

The Giving Tree (Silverstein), 92

goal-setting tactics, 361–362

goals, for mind wandering, 75

The Godfather (Puzo), 216

Grabenstein, Chris, 58

Grafton, Sue, 325

Grammar Girl's Quick and Dirty Tips for Better Writing (Fogarty), 287

groupthink, 143

guesstimating in time planning, 338

Guest, Judith, 91, 187

gut instinct, 366–367

Gutman, Ron, 258–259

H

Hall, Adam, 99, 156

Hamlet (Shakespeare), 218–219, 298–299

happiness and creativity, 73–74

Harris, Nathan, 141

Harris, Rosemary, 12

Hatchet (Paulsen), 93–94

The Haunting of Hill House (Jackson), 91–92

Hello Universe (Kelly), 180–181

Hemingway, Ernest, 52, 188, 258

Henry, Emily, 59

Heyer, Georgette, 134, 136, 179–180

Hierarchy of Needs, Maslow's, 40

high stakes. *See* stakes

Hill, Napoleon, 258

"Hills Like White Elephants" (Hemingway), 188

historical fiction, 89–90, 304–306

Hogan, Chuck, 50

"Home" (Saunders), 181–182

Honoré, Carl, 70

Hosseini, Khaled, 12

I

I Let You Go (Mackintosh), 233

idea generation

assessment model, 22–29

exercise, 15–18

genre expectations and, 18–22

limitations of artificial intelligence for, 3–4

mindset for, 5–8

sources for, 8–13

subconscious creativity and, 4–5

idioms, in dialogue, 177–178

illicit relationships, as obstacles, 272, 277

image-based random access, 244–246

immigrant characters

dialogue of, 177

timeline and, 323–324

impact, in idea assessment. *See* NIA (novelty, impact, and alignment) model

In Praise of Slow (Honoré), 70

In the Time of the Butterflies (Alvarez), 219

incidents

integrating sensory references into, 158–163, 309–310

and the narrative question, 56

raising the stakes with,
271–278, 281

reactions of characters
to, 31, 38–39, 41,
50–51

and TRDs (twists,
reversals, danger), 69

innovation, 223

internal obstacles and raising
the stakes, 270–279, 281

The Island of Dr. Libris
(Grabenstein), 58

italics, for emphasis, 194–
195, 196

J

Jack Reacher series, 47

Jackson, Shirley, 91

James, Henry, 31

Jami, Criss, 212

Jane Austen's Lost Letters
(Cleland), 46–47, 197–
198, 231–232

Jayatissa, Amanda, 268–269

Jeong, You-Jeong, 69

Jobs, Steve, 123

Jong, Erica, 344

Josie Prescott Antiques
Mystery series, 10, 46–47,
157, 231–232

journey mapping, 319, 333,
339–343

Joyce, James, 202

judgment versus assessment
of ideas, 5

Just the Nicest Couple
(Kubica), 66, 90

K

Kelly, Erin Entrada, 180–181

King, Stephen, 105

Kingsley, Howard, 352

Kingsolver, Barbara, 342

The Kite Runner (Hosseini),
12

Koontz, Dean, 284

Koyenikan, Idowu, 29

Kross, Ethan, 72

Kubica, Mary, 66, 90

Kwok, Jean, 319, 323–324,
328

L

Lahiri, Jhumpa, 188

Landay, William, 164

Landrigan, Linda, 152

language. *See* word choices

The Last Picture Show
(McMurtry), 87–88

Lee, Harper, 125, 215–216

Levitin, David J., 70

Lippman, Laura, 101

The List (Adegoke), 12

literary fiction
as different from genre
fiction, 19

omission of quotation marks in, 202

pace of, 66

point of view in, 128, 132

settings in, 91

Littlewood, Fran, 309

Logan, Elizabeth, 230

logistics, in mind wandering, 75–76

Lois, George, 283

London, Jack, 343

The London Eye Mystery (Dowd), 220–221

longing and character motivation, 42–43

lying, by characters, 43–45

M

Mackintosh, Clare, 233

Maslow, Abraham, 40

Maslow's Hierarchy of Needs, 40

McBain, Ed, 326

McCarthy, Cormac, 202

McMurtry, Larry, 87

Melville, Herman, 213

Men We Reaped (Ward), 224

metaphors. *See* allegories; symbolism

middle-grade novels, point of view in, 128

Miller, Arthur, 154

Milne, A. A., 318

mind wandering, 53–54, 59–60, 70–76, 78–81

mindset

for idea fishing, 5–8

for mind wandering, 73–74

for the reenvisioning process, 255–259, 280–282

three principles of, 366–370

Mindwandering (Bar), 72, 74

Moriarty, Liane, 39, 158, 348–349

Morrison, Toni, 227–228

motivation, character. *See* character transformation

multiple points of view, 129, 134–136

Munier, Paula, 163

Murder on the Orient Express (Christie), 324–325

Murdoch, Iris, 224

My Sister the Serial Killer (Braithwaite), 57

My Sister's Keeper (Picoult), 219

mysteries, 19–20, 25, 127

N

Nabokov, Vladimir, 251

narrative question, 54–60, 62–64, 261–262

nature and creativity, 73

naysayers, dealing with, 268

negativity and idea generation, 7–8

Nero Wolfe series, 47

Newman, T. J., 156, 260

NIA (novelty, impact, and alignment) model, 22–29

"nice," use of, 295–296

Nichols, Wallace J., 73

Nicolson, Adam, 130

Nightwork (Shaw), 41–42

Ninth Ward (Rhodes), 224

novel writing software, 330, 332–333, 374

novelty, in idea assessment. *See* NIA (novelty, impact, and alignment) model

Nyren, Neil, 153

O

Oates, Joyce Carol, 3

objectivity and the reenvisioning process, 255, 260–263

obstacles for raising the stakes, 270–279, 281

One Hundred Years of Solitude (Marquez), 106–107

openings, 54–60

opposing forces, as obstacles, 271, 275–276

optimism. *See* positivity

oracular predictions, 273, 277

Ordinary People (Guest), 91, 187

organizational tactics
artificial intelligence on, 338–339

bestselling authors on, 342

clutter control, 334

guesstimating and time planning, 338

journey mapping, 339–343

planning and creativity, 319

tracking progress, 325–327

tracking time, 320–325

working copy and notes, 327–333

workspace, 334, 335–337

The Organized Mind (Levitin), 70

Osman, Richard, 158

The Other Woman (Ryan), 98–99

Outlander (Gabaldon), 89–90

P

pace, 66, 67, 161
Packer, ZZ, 196
Panganiban, Roma, 256, 302
Parker, Dorothy, 82
Paulsen, Gary, 93
Pavone, Chris, 230
Penny, Louise, 10, 160
The Perks of Being a Wallflower (Chbosky), 89
personal issues, as obstacles, 271, 275
personification, 91–92, 229
Peters, G. D., 153, 332–333
Pew Research Center, 54
Phillips, Michelle, 74
Picoult, Jodi, 219, 342
Plan, Act, Reflect (PAR) response, 38, 41, 51
Planet of the Apes (Boulle), 89
plot
    characterization and, 45, 68–69
    mind wandering tactic, 53–54, 70–76, 78–81
    narrative question, 54–60, 62–64
    TRDs (twists, reversals, danger), 61, 65–67, 77
point of view

    divergent thinking regarding, 143–147
    exercise, 148–149
    first person, 127–128
    memory of place and, 130–131
    multiple points of view, 134–136
    questions to ask regarding, 137
    second person, 128
    third-person limited, 129
    third-person objective, 133
    third-person omniscient, 132
    trying different, 140–141
    and the writer's voice, 138–143
"Poor Sherm" (Chessman), 295
Pope, Dan, 253
popular culture and character voice, 179
positivity, 73–74, 255–259
Post, Kate, 194
Practical Optimism (Varma), 257
precision in language, 295–296
Price, Richard, 220

BEAT THE BOTS

Prince of Thieves (Hogan), 50–51

procrastination, 258, 285–288

productivity, tracking, 325–327

proofreading versus revision, 285

Prose, Francine, 174

protagonists. *See* backstory; character transformation; characters; stakes, raising the

psychographics of characters, 39, 40–42

Pushing Up Daisies (Harris), 12

Puzo, Mario, 216

Q

quantities, clarifying, 289–291

query letters, 256

The Quiller Memorandum (Hall), 99, 156

quota system for writing, 326–327

quotation marks, 199–202

quotations. See epigraphs

R

raising the stakes. *See* stakes, raising the

random access, 238–248

React, Act, Process (RAP) response, 38, 41–42, 51

reactions of characters, to incidents, 38–39, 41, 51

reader expectations, 18–22, 89–91

reading analytically, 68–69

reading work aloud, 286–288

reenvisioning process
  as macrorevision, 253–254
  mindset structure for, 255–259, 280–282
  objectivity in, 260–263
  obstacles and character development, 270–279
  raising the stakes on yourself, 264–269
  writing the emotional truth, 254–255

revision
  active versus passive voice, 303–304
  clarifying quantities, 289–291
  creative analysis core question, 288–289
  creative approach to, 284–285

developing a plan, 311–316

eliminating smothered verbs, 307–308

historically accurate language, 304–306

modifiers, 292–295

overcoming procrastination, 285–288

sensory references, 309–310

tips from Dr. Seuss, 296–298

verb choice, 298–303

See also reenvisioning; reenvisioning process

Rhodes, Jewell Parker, 224

Robinson, Ken, 317

romance fiction, 90–91, 106–107

Room: A Novel (Donoghue), 89

Ryan, Hank Phillippi, 98–99, 159, 214–215

S

Saint-Exupéry, Antoine de, 120

Santlofer, Jonathan, 85–86, 326, 335–337, 352

Saunders, George, 181, 297

scheduling writing, 326, 338, 342

Schulman, Tom, 292

science fiction, point of view in, 127–128

Scrivener, 332–333, 374

The Sea, the Sea (Murdoch), 224

second person point of view, 128

self-assessment
of backstory, 169–170
failsafe method, 345, 354–360, 363
journey mapping, 339–342
storytelling, 350
writing process skills, 353–354

Semple, Maria, 164, 325

sensory references, 99–101, 158–163, 167–173, 309–310

sentence structure, 303–304

series books
backstory in, 160
character transformation across, 46–47
point of view in, 129

setting
aligning theme with, 93–94

atmosphere, 87–89,
230–233, 238
authors' immersion in,
95–96
as character, 105–107
characters' observation
of details, 103–104
characters' reaction to,
83–84
conceptual blending,
83–84, 107–120
creating fantasy worlds,
84–85
length of descriptions,
94, 96–99
personification and,
91–92
reader expectations of,
89–91
Santlofer on, 85–86
seamless integration of,
101–103
sensory descriptions of,
99–101
Seuss, Dr., 296–298, 370
Seven Years of Darkness
(Jeong), 69
Shaw, George Bernard, 8,
249
Shaw, Irwin, 41
Shelf Life (Franchini), 217
The Shining (King), 105

showing, not telling, 46, 175,
183–185
Silverstein, Shel, 92
Singer, Isaac Bashevis, 53
SMART goal-setting tactic,
361–362
*Smile: The Astonishing
Powers of a Simple Act*
(Gutman), 258–259
smiling and positivity, 258–
259
"Smiling Can Trick Your
Brain into Happiness—
and Boost Your Health"
(Spector), 258
societal issues, as obstacles,
271, 274–275
software, 328–333, 338, 374
Some Buried Caesar (Stout),
47
sources for ideas. *See* idea
generation
sources for symbolism, 224
speaker identification, in
dialogue, 190–193
specificity and modifiers,
292–295
Spector, Nicole, 258
stakes, raising the
artificial intelligence on,
279
conveying of, in query
letters, 256

mindset structure and, 280–282

obstacles and, 270–279, 281

potential opportunities for raising, 260–263

and the reenvisioning process, 254–255

on yourself, 264–269

See also suspense

Stanko, George F., 48

Stephens-Davidowitz, Seth, 44

storytelling assessment, 350–351

Stout, Rex, 47

Strawser, Jessica, 188

subconscious creativity, 4–5

subplots and pace, 67

subtext in dialogue, 185–190

success, visualizing, 257

Sullivan, J. Courtney, 216

summarizing conversations, 183–185

suspense, 100, 156. *See also* stakes, raising the

Swanson, Peter, 99

The Sweetness of Water (Harris), 141

symbolism, 146, 219, 222–224, 231

T

Tailspin (Brown), 261

Tan, Cher-Yi, 73–74

Tarzan and the Forbidden City (Burroughs), 97–98

Tatar, Maria, 229, 230

technology use, 287–288, 328–333, 338, 374

"A Temporary Matter" (Lahiri), 188

text-based random access, 239–243

Thank You for Being Late (Friedman), 13

Tharp, Twyla, 150

themes

aligning setting with, 93–94

allegory use, 227–230

artificial intelligence generated, 233–237

atmospheric descriptions in support of, 230–233, 238

epigraphs for highlighting, 215–216, 221–222

identification of, 214–215

random access technique for, 238–248

BEAT THE BOTS

symbolism and, 222–224

types of, 216–221

word and phrase choices in support of, 225–226

Thiem, Brian, 46

third-person limited point of view, 129

third-person objective point of view, 133

third-person omniscient point of view, 132, 134–136

thrillers, 19–20, 66, 147

through-line plots
  and the narrative question, 55–56
  on the plotting road map, 65, 66
  reliance of, on backstory, 158
  in thematic writing, 243, 246

The Thursday Murder Club (Osman), 158

time for mind wandering, 72

time tracking, 320–325, 328, 336–337, 338

"to be" verbs, 298–300, 312, 315

To Kill a Mockingbird (Lee), 215–216

Todd, Charles, 101, 138–139

tracking time. *See* time tracking

traditional mysteries, 19–20, 25, 127

TRDs (twists, reversals, danger), 61, 65–69, 77. *See also* mind wandering

trusting your gut, 366–367

Twain, Mark, 292

typographical emphasis, 194–199

U

uncited generalizations and vague terminology (UGVTs), 289–295, 299, 311, 315

unifying principle, 216–219

V

Varma, Sue, 257

verbs, 97, 298–303, 306–308, 311, 312

"very," use of, 292

Viets, Elaine, 13

visualizing success, 257

vocabulary in dialogue. *See* word choices

Vrabel, Beth, 95–96

W

Ward, Jesmyn, 224

weather symbolism, 224
"what if" and "so what"
  questions, 9–10, 12, 13,
  16–17
When Giants Burn (Vrabel),
  95–96
Where'd You Go, Bernadette
  (Semple), 164
White, E. B., 342
White, Kate, 100
Wolitzer, Hilma, 366–367
The Wonderful Wizard of Oz
  (Baum), 68
Woolverton, Linda, 230
word choices
  adjectives, 34, 98–99,
    292–295
  adverbs, 192, 195–196,
    291–293
  for dialogue, 177
  etymology and, 304–
    306
  to support theme, 225–
    226
  verbs, 97, 298–303,
    306–308, 311, 312
workspace, 334–338
world-building, 84–85, 96
writer's block, 10, 366
writer's voice, 138–143
writing raw, 264–269
writing software, 330, 332–
  333, 374

Y

Yang, Gene Luen, 228
young-adult novels, point of
  view in, 128

Z

Zafarris, Jess, 304
Zayas, David, 30

ACKNOWLEDGMENTS

Thanks to the hundreds of aspiring and professional writers who attend my monthly webinars and the scores of student authors who have participated in my small group Mystery Mastermind virtual workshops. Your thoughtful questions and insightful comments led to this book. Thanks also go to Jon Stone, technical whiz and master webinar facilitator.

Special thanks to my literary agent, Adam Chromy, of Movable Type Management, for his astute guidance in developing this project. A supersized thank-you goes to all the authors, agents, editors, and other industry professionals who generously shared their knowledge and experience in this book.

Thanks also to the entire Regalo Press team who worked so hard to bring this book to life, publisher Gretchen Young, editor Caitlyn Limbaugh, copy editor Kate Post, managing editor Aleigha Koss, production manager Alana Mills, and cover designer Cody Corcoran.

I'm grateful to work with a publisher committed to uniting philanthropy with the business of book publishing. A portion of Regalo Press's profits will be donated to Reef Renewal Foundation International. Coral reefs are essential to human survival, and the foundation, which supports a global network of coral restoration programs, does remarkable work. Their global partners develop innovative techniques to restore coral reefs and share their work with scientists worldwide. https://www.reefrenewal.org/